On Economic Inequality

On Economic Inequality

Amartya Sen

Enlarged edition with a substantial annexe
'*On Economic Inequality* after a Quarter Century'

James Foster and Amartya Sen

CLARENDON PRESS · OXFORD

OXFORD
UNIVERSITY PRESS

Great Clarendon Street, Oxford OX2 6DP

Oxford University Press is a department of the University of Oxford.
It furthers the University's objective of excellence in research, scholarship,
and education by publishing worldwide in

Oxford New York

Athens Auckland Bangkok Bogotá Buenos Aires Calcutta
Cape Town Chennai Dar es Salaam Delhi Florence Hong Kong Istanbul
Karachi Kuala Lumpur Madrid Melbourne Mexico City Mumbai
Nairobi Paris São Paulo Singapore Taipei Tokyo Toronto Warsaw

with associated companies in Berlin Ibadan

Published in the United States
by Oxford University Press Inc., New York

First edition © Oxford University Press, 1973
Annexe © Amartya Sen and James Foster, 1997

First edition published in cloth and paperback 1973
Expanded edition published 1997

British Library Cataloguing in Publication Data
Data available

Library of Congress Cataloging in Publication Data
Data available

ISBN 0-19-829297-X (Hbk)
ISBN 0-19-828193-5 (Pbk)

3 5 7 9 10 8 6 4 2

Printed in Great Britain
on acid-free paper by
Biddles Ltd.,
Guildford and King's Lynn

1001733203

Dedication to the first edition

To Antara and Nandana

*with the hope that when they grow up
they will find less of it no matter
how they decide to measure it*

Preface to the First Edition

The idea of inequality is both very simple and very complex. At one level it is the simplest of all ideas and has moved people with an immediate appeal hardly matched by any other concept. At another level, however, it is an exceedingly complex notion which makes statements on inequality highly problematic,[1] and it has been, therefore, the subject of much research by philosophers, statisticians, political theorists, sociologists and economists. While this book is concerned with economic inequality only, the presentation reflects this duality. I have had to employ a fair number of technical concepts and use some mathematical operations, but the concepts have also been explained in non-technical terms and the mathematical results have been given intuitive explanation. It is hoped that the non-technical reader will not be put off by the formalities. The importance of the formal results lies ultimately in their relevance to normal communication and to things that people argue about and fight for.

While the technical and non-technical sections have not been put into separate compartments, it should be possible for someone not interested in technicalities to skip (or skim through) the formal sections and to go directly from the intuitive presentation of the axioms to the intuitive explanation of the results. The section headings used throughout the book should help the reader in this sorting out.

In many ways this book is a development of some ideas I studied in my *Collective Choice and Social Welfare*.[2] The framework of thought presented there I have tried to apply here to the specific field of economic inequality. The approaches to social evaluation that I rejected then, I reject more strongly now, and what I defended in that work, I have tried to develop

---

[1] See Bernard Williams, 'The Idea of Equality', in P. Laslett and W. G. Runciman, *Philosophy, Politics and Society*, Second Series, Blackwell, Oxford.

[2] Holden-Day, San Francisco, 1970, and Oliver & Boyd, Edinburgh, 1971, Mathematical Economics Texts, No. 5.

more fully in this one in the particular context of inequality. No apologies for that, but I ought to put my cards on the table.

I owe debts to many. While preparing the Radcliffe Lectures, I was working with Partha Dasgupta and David Starrett on a joint paper on the measurement of economic inequality.[3] I am grateful to them not only because I have incorporated into the lectures some results from our joint paper (in particular, Theorems 3.1 and 3.2), but also because I have learnt a great deal from them and I have used that knowledge quite freely.

The Radcliffe Lectures, which were delivered last May, were informally presented, and in the discussions that followed I have gained much. I should particularly mention the searching questions raised by David Epstein, John Muellbauer, Graham Pyatt and John Williamson. In revising the lectures for this book, I have expanded some sections, incorporating not merely those things that I could not put into the lectures because of shortage of time or because of stylistic limitations (footnotes sound nasty in a lecture), but also some additional bits which are essentially responses to the queries raised. I have also benefited from discussions following my lectures on related topics at Essex University (Economics Department Seminar, January 1972), Columbia University (Joint Seminar of Economics and Philosophy Departments, March 1972), Harvard University (Political Economy Lecture, March 1972), the Delhi School of Economics (Special Lectures, August 1972), and the Indian Statistical Institute (Research Seminars, August 1972). I am grateful to Tony Atkinson, Pranab Bardhan, Nikhiles Bhattacharya, Sanjit Bose, Terence Gorman, Peter Hammond, and Richard Layard, for helpful comments and criticisms. This is a long list, and there must have been others.

For astonishingly skilful typing against the heavy odds of my impossible writing, I am very grateful to Celia Turner and Luba Mumford.

[3] 'Notes on the Measurement of Inequality', *Journal of Economic Theory*, Vol. 3 (1973).

Finally I am most grateful to the University of Warwick, and in particular to Professor Graham Pyatt, for the honour of an invitation to deliver the Radcliffe Lectures for this year.

London School of Economics   A.K.S.
November, 1972

Preface to the Enlarged Edition

The first edition of this book was based on my Radcliffe Lectures at the University of Warwick, given nearly a quarter century ago, in 1972. It was meant as a contribution to the newly developing technical literature on economic inequality, while also attempting to integrate that literature with substantive issues that make inequality a matter of great practical interest. Even though a large part of the book was devoted to analytical and mathematical reasoning, the axioms used as well as the results presented were interpreted in intuitive terms. The work was based on the belief that 'the importance of the formal results lies ultimately in their relevance to normal communication and to things that people argue about and fight for' (p. vii).

In this enlarged edition, with a substantial annexe (as large as the original book), the motivational commitments remain much the same. Over the last quarter of a century, issues of inequality have become even more central (and also more contentious) in public debates and arguments. At the same time, an enormous—and often formidable—technical literature has grown and flourished in the pure theory of the measurement and evaluation of economic inequality. Some of the analytical issues partially examined in the original edition of this book have become much more fully explored, and some results presented there have been consolidated or substantially extended. And many new issues have been identified and successfully investigated.

The Annexe is largely an attempt to examine and assess the present state of the analytical literature on the measurement of inequality and poverty. I have worked on it jointly with James Foster, who has co-authored it. Foster has been an ideal collaborator, not only because of his superb skills and congenial temperament, but also because of his mastery of the relevant literature. Indeed, Foster has himself made several of the major contributions in the recent theoretical developments in the measurement and evaluation of inequality and poverty.

In writing this annexe, James Foster and I have had to weigh the intellectual interest in, and the practical importance of, the diverse investigations and results that have been presented in the monumental literature that has developed over the last quarter of a century on this subject. Our focus has been on the 'substance' of the analytical results, rather than on technical details. For those interested in pursuing a more fiercely technical course, we have tried to provide reasonably comprehensive references to the formal literature, with identification of the issues addressed and the general nature of the results obtained. We have also tried to clarify, in accessible terms, the main technical issues underlying the formal literature.

The 1972 Radcliffe Lectures were much influenced by lines of formal reasoning developed in social choice theory, pioneered by Kenneth Arrow.[1] I was then—as I still am—greatly involved in this field. The analyses in the first edition of this book used a distinctly 'social choice perspective'.[2] The 1973 edition of *On Economic Inequality* had, among other things, included proposals for making social choice theory more directly relevant to policy judgements as well as to public debates and social criticism. As it happens, the literature on social choice theory has also dramatically expanded since the early 1970s (to a great extent in the direction hoped for in the 1973 edition).[3] The Annexe takes note, *inter alia*, of these

---

[1] K. J. Arrow, *Social Choice and Individual Values* (Wiley, New York, 1951). From a different direction, A. B. Atkinson's works on inequality measurement much influenced the 1972 Radcliffe Lectures, as did the exploration of social justice by John Harsanyi, Serge Kolm, John Rawls, and Patrick Suppes.

[2] *On Economic Inequality* was, in many ways, a follow-up of my earlier book, *Collective Choice and Social Welfare* (Holden-Day, San Francisco, 1970; republished, North-Holland, Amsterdam, 1979).

[3] For an account and critical assessment of the technical literature in social choice theory until about the middle 1980s, see my 'Social Choice Theory' in K. J. Arrow and M. Intriligator (eds.), *Handbook of Mathematical Economics* (North-Holland, Amsterdam, 1986); see also K. Suzumura, *Rational Choice, Collective Decisions and Social Welfare* (Cambridge University Press, Cambridge, 1983).

explorations and results, and examines their bearing on the evaluation and measurement of inequality and poverty.

Earlier versions of the Annexe were read by Sudhir Anand, Tony Atkinson, and Tony Shorrocks, and their comments and suggestions have been particularly helpful in revising it. Over the years, we have also benefited from interactions with Kenneth Arrow, Fabrizio Barca, Kaushik Basu, Charles Blackorby, Andrea Brandolini, Satya Chakravarty, Frank Cowell, G. A. Cohen, Partha Dasgupta, Angus Deaton, David Donaldson, Jean Drèze, Bhaskar Dutta, Ronald Dworkin, Gary Fields, Peter Hammond, Wulf Gaertner, Nanak Kakwani, Ravi Kanbur, Peter Lambert, John Muellbauer, Robert Nozick, Martha Nussbaum, Siddiq Osmani, Prasanta Pattanaik, Derek Parfit, Douglas Rae, Martin Ravallion, John Rawls, V. K. Ramachandran, John Roemer, Thomas Scanlon, David Starrett, Nicholas Stern, Kotaro Suzumura, Larry Temkin, Philippe Van Parijs, John Weymark, Peyton Young, and Stefano Zamagni, among others, and both James Foster and I would like to take this opportunity of thanking them all for their help. James Foster would also like to express his deep appreciation to Irene Raj Foster for her help and support, and I join James warmly in this. We have received research assistance of the highest quality from Arun Abraham, and we are grateful to him.

Acknowledgement is also due to the MacArthur Foundation for supporting the research on which the Annexe has drawn. I am, furthermore, indebted to STICERD, at the London School of Economics, and to the Bank of Italy, for giving me research facilities when I respectively visited them.

The material included in the first edition of this book has been left quite unchanged in this enlarged edition. Even the old page numbers have been retained as far as possible (to facilitate reference). The new Annexe ('*On Economic Inequality* after a Quarter Century'), by James Foster and myself, follows those pages, and takes the story from there on.

Cambridge, Massachusetts   A.K.S.
September, 1996

Contents

1

Welfare Economics, Utilitarianism, and Equity

'Of all human sciences the most useful and most imperfect appears to me to be that of mankind: and I will venture to say the single inscription on the Temple of Delphi[1] contained a precept more important and more difficult than is to be found in all the huge volumes that moralists have ever written.' Thus wrote Jean-Jacques Rousseau in the Preface to his *A Dissertation on the Origin and Foundation of the Inequality of Mankind*, dedicated to the Republic of Geneva on the 12th of June 1754. While the essay, alas, failed to qualify for the prize of the Dijon Academy for which it was considered (and which his less rebellious earlier piece on 'arts and sciences' had received in 1750), the ideas contained in it did help to crystalize the demands that gripped the revolution of 1789.

The relation between inequality and rebellion is indeed a close one, and it runs both ways. That a perceived sense of inequity is a common ingredient of rebellion in societies is clear enough, but it is also important to recognize that the perception of inequity, and indeed the content of that elusive concept, depend substantially on possibilities of actual rebellion. The Athenian intellectuals discussing equality did not find it particularly obnoxious to leave out the slaves from the orbit of discourse, and one reason why they could do it was because they could get away with it. The concepts of equity and justice have changed remarkably over history, and as the intolerance of stratification and differentiation has grown, the

---

[1] The Delphic injunction, it may be recalled, was the somewhat severe advice: 'Know thyself!'

2   WELFARE ECONOMICS

very concept of inequality has gone through radical transformation.

In these lectures I am concerned with *economic* inequality
only, and that again in a specific context,[2] but I should argue
that the historical nature of the notion of inequality is worth
bearing in mind before going into an analysis of economic
inequality as it is viewed by economists today. Ultimately the
relevance of our ideas on this subject must be judged by their
ability to relate to the economic and political preoccupations
of our times.

Objective and normative features

The main focus of these lectures will be on the problem of the
measurement of inequality of income distribution in aggregative terms, though I shall try to go into some of the policy
issues, especially in the context of the socialist economy. On
the question of the measurement of inequality, we might begin
with a methodological point. The measures of inequality that
have been proposed in the economic literature fall broadly into
two categories. On the one hand there are measures that try
to catch the extent of inequality in some *objective* sense, usually employing some statistical measure of relative variation
of income,[3] and on the other there are indices that try to
measure inequality in terms of some *normative* notion of social
welfare so that a higher degree of inequality corresponds to a
lower level of social welfare for a given total of income.[4] It is
possible to argue that there are some advantages in taking the
former approach, so that one can distinguish between (a)
'seeing' more or less inequality, and (b) 'valuing' it more or
less in ethical terms. In the second approach inequality ceases
to be an objective notion and the problem of measurement is
enmeshed with that of ethical evaluation.

[2] In particular I shall be concerned primarily with the distribution of
income and not directly with *wealth*.
[3] The usual measures include the variance, the coefficient of variation, the
Gini coefficient of the Lorenz curve, and other formulae, which will be discussed in Chapter 2.
[4] For examples of the normative approach to the measurement of income
distribution, see Dalton (1920), Champernowne (1952), Aigner and Heins
(1967), Atkinson (1970a), Tinbergen (1970), and Bentzel (1970).

This methodological point essentially reflects the dual nature of our conception of inequality. There is, obviously, an objective element in this notion; a fifty-fifty division of a cake between two persons is clearly more equal in some straightforward sense than giving all to one and none to the other. On the other hand, in some complex problems of comparing alternative income distributions among a large number of people, it becomes very difficult to speak of inequality in a purely objective way, and the measurement of the inequality level could be intractable without bringing in some ethical concepts.

Which of the two approaches it would be correct to pursue is not an easy question to answer, and the two approaches in terms of their practical use would not be all that different from each other. Even if we take inequality as an objective notion, our interest in its measurement must relate to our normative concern with it, and in judging the relative merits of different objective measures of inequality, it would indeed be relevant to introduce normative considerations. At the same time, even if we take a normative view of the measures of income inequality, this is not necessarily meant to catch the totality of our ethical evaluation. It would presumably aim to express one particular aspect of the normative comparison, and which particular aspect will depend on the objective features of the inequality problem. To say that 'x involves less inequality than y', even if meant to be a normative statement, will not imply an unqualified recommendation to choose x rather than y, but would presumably be combined with other considerations (e.g., those involving total income and such features) to arrive at an overall judgement.[5] In one way or another, usable measures of inequality must combine factual features with normative ones.

Types of measurement

A second methodological issue concerns the type of measurement that is being sought. Various degrees of measurement

[5] In terms of the classification of value judgements used in Sen (1967b), inequality judgements are *non-compulsive evaluative* judgements.

are conceivable. The strictest type of measure is a ratio-scale like weight or height, in which it makes sense to say that one object weighs twice as much as another (and it does not matter whether we measure it in kilogrammes or pounds). A somewhat looser measure is that of an interval-scale, in which ratios make no sense but the ratios of differences do. The gap between 100° Centigrade and 90° Centigrade is recorded as twice that between 90°C and 85°C no matter whether we express these temperatures in Centigrade or in Fahrenheit (in which they correspond respectively to 212°F, 194°F and 185°F), but the ratio of the temperatures themselves will vary according to the scale chosen.

This interval-scale measure is usually referred to in utility theory as 'cardinal', and if a set of numbers x represents the utilities of different objects, a positive linear transformation of these numbers such as $y = a + bx$, with $b > 0$, can also be used.[6] A looser measure than this corresponds to what is called an 'ordinal' scale in utility theory, where any positive monotonic transformation will do as well, e.g., a set of numbers 1, 2, 3, 4 can be replaced by 100, 101, 179, 999, respectively, since the ranking of the numbers is all that matters.

A closely related measure to the 'ordinal' scale does not involve any numerical representation whatsoever, and just an ordering of all the alternatives is presented, e.g., a set of four alternatives, x_1, x_2, x_3 and x_4, may be ranked as x_3 highest, x_2 and x_1 next together and x_4 last. This kind of an ordering involves a ranking with two specific properties, viz., completeness and transitivity. Completeness requires that if we take any pair of alternatives then in terms of the ranking relation R, either xRy holds or yRx holds, or both. Interpreting R as the relation 'at least as good as', if xRy holds but not yRx then we can say that x is strictly better than y and indicate this as xPy; the case of yPx is exactly the opposite of this. If both xRy and yRx hold, we can declare x and y as 'indifferent' and refer to this as xIy. The property of transitivity demands that if we take any three alternatives x, y, z, and xRy and yRz both hold,

[6] For example, if F is the temperature in the Fahrenheit scale and C that in the Centigrade scale, we have: $F = 32 + 1.8C$.

then so does xRz. It might appear that an ordering can be easily converted into an 'ordinal' numerical measure, and this is indeed so for a finite set of alternatives, but is not invariably possible for an infinite set.[7] In fact, an ordering is a weaker requirement than the existence of an ordinal numerical representation.

Quasi-orderings and inequality judgements

A still weaker measure would be a case where the ranking relation R is not necessarily complete, i.e., not all pairs are rankable vis-à-vis each other. If a relation like this is transitive but not necessarily complete, it is called a quasi-ordering. Another case also weaker than an ordering is one where the ranking relation is complete but not necessarily transitive, of which a special case is one where the strict preference is transitive but indifference is not so.[8]

Most statistical measures of the inequality level assume a high degree of measurement, usually a ratio-scale or at least an interval-scale. This is true not only of the so-called objective measures, but also of normative evaluation (see Chapter 2). It is, however, possible to argue that the implicit notion of inequality that we carry in our mind is, in fact, much less precise and may correspond to an incomplete quasi-ordering. We may not indeed be able to decide whether one distribution x is more or less unequal than another, but we may be able to compare some other pairs perfectly well. The notion of inequality has many aspects, and a coincidence of them may permit a clear ranking, but when these different aspects conflict an incomplete ranking may emerge. There are reasons to believe that our idea of inequality as a ranking relation may indeed be inherently incomplete. If so, to find a measure of inequality that involves a complete ordering may produce artificial problems, because a measure can hardly be more precise than the

---

7 The problem arises from not necessarily having a sufficient stock of real numbers to give each alternative an appropriate number in special cases such as lexicographic orderings over a many-dimensional real space. On this see Debreu (1959), Chapter 4.

8 See Fishburn (1970), Sen (1970a), and Pattanaik (1971).

concept it represents. It will be argued in Chapter 3 that this might well account for some of the difficulties with the standard measures of inequality.

In this context it is perhaps worth saying that the historical connection between the notion of inequality and discontent—and more so rebellion—suggests that the need is for a measure that comes into its own with sharp contrasts, even though it may not provide a scale sensitive enough to order finely distinguished distributions. The unfortunate fact is that in putting up a scale of measurement or ranking, the economist's and the statistician's inclination is to look for an ordering complete in all respects, so that the translation of the notion of inequality from the sphere of political debate, which gives the notion its importance, to the sphere of well-defined economic representation may tend to confuse the mathematical properties of the underlying concept. Indeed inequality measurement is by no means the only field of economic analysis in which the predisposition towards a complete ordering has proved to be a major liability.

Non-conflict economics and Pareto optimality

How much guidance—it is reasonable to ask—can we expect to get from modern welfare economics in analysing problems of inequality? The answer, alas, is: not a great deal. Much of modern welfare economies is concerned with precisely that set of questions which avoid judgements on income distribution altogether. The concentration seems to be on issues that involve no conflict between different individuals (or groups, or classes), and for someone interested in inequality this can hardly make the air electric with expectations.

The so-called 'basic' theorem of welfare economics is concerned with the relation between competitive equilibria and Pareto optimality.[9] The concept of Pareto optimality was evolved precisely to cut out the need for distributional judgements. A change implies a Pareto-improvement if it makes no

[9] For the relevant theorems with proofs see Debreu (1959) and Arrow and Hahn (1972), and for an illuminating informal discussion see Koopmans (1957).

one worse off and someone better off. A situation is Pareto optimal if there exists no other attainable situation such that a move to it would be a Pareto-improvement. That is, Pareto optimality only guarantees that no change is possible such that someone would become better off without making anyone worse off. If the lot of the poor cannot be made any better without cutting into the affluence of the rich, the situation would be Pareto optimal despite the disparity between the rich and the poor.

Suppose we are considering the division of a cake. Assuming that each person prefers to have more of the cake rather than less of it, every possible distribution will be Pareto optimal, because any change that makes someone better off is going to make someone else worse off. Since the only issue in this problem is that of distribution, Pareto optimality has no cutting power at all. The almost single-minded concern of modern welfare economics with Pareto optimality does not make that engaging branch of study particularly suitable for investigating problems of inequality.

Social welfare functions

At a more general level, however, there has been quite a bit of discussion in recent years on distributional judgements going beyond Pareto optimality, and indeed the famous Bergson–Samuelson social welfare function was partly motivated by the recognition that policy decisions in economics would require the economist to go beyond Pareto optimality. In its most general form the Bergson–Samuelson social welfare function is any ordering of the set of alternative social states. If X is the set of social states, then a Bergson–Samuelson social welfare function is an ordering R defined over the entire X. In numerical terms it was conceived of as a functional relation W that specifies a welfare value $W(x)$ for each social state x belonging to the set X. The measure of W has been usually taken to be 'ordinal'.

While this is the most general conception of the social welfare function, something more has to be said about the nature of the function $W(x)$ to get some results of practical importance out of this concept. A favourite assumption has been that the social welfare function is 'individualistic' in the sense of making social welfare W a function of individual utilities, i.e., $W(x) = F(U_1(x), \ldots, U_n(x))$, where U_i stands for the utility function of individual i, for $i = 1, \ldots, n$.[10] Further, assuming that W increases with any U_i given the set of utilities of all other individuals, Pareto optimality can be built into the exercise of maximizing W. But the main object of the social welfare function is to take us *beyond* this limited concept by ranking all the Pareto optimal states vis-à-vis each other. The distributional judgements would then depend on the precise social welfare function chosen.

While the conception of a function such as F permits the use of cardinal utilities of individuals as well as of interpersonal comparisons, orthodox welfare economics has been somewhat neurotic about avoiding both these activities. Much of the concentration has, therefore, been on arriving at social welfare, or at any rate at an ordering R of the set of social states X, based exclusively on the set of individual orderings of X. Representing the ordering of individual i as R_i, this line of thinking leads to the search for a functional relation $R = f(R_1, \ldots, R_n)$.

A natural question to ask in this context is whether certain general conditions can be imposed on the relation between the set of individual preferences and the social ordering. In a justly celebrated theorem, Arrow (1951) has shown that a set of extremely mild-looking restrictions eliminate the possibility of having any such functional relation f whatsoever. I do not intend here to go into Arrow's 'impossibility theorem', which

---

[10] See, for example, Bergson (1938), Lange (1942) and Samuelson (1947). Lange, however, seems to have thought that even if social welfare were based '*directly* [on] the distribution of commodities or incomes between the individuals, without reference to the individuals' utilities', social welfare could still 'be expressed in the form of a *scaler function of the vector u*, i.e., W(u)' (p. 30). While it is true that for any distribution of commodities or incomes there would be one and only one vector u and one and only one W, we could still have two distributions leading to the same vector u but to two different values of W, so that in this case W could not really be viewed as a function of u.

has produced much awe, some belligerence, and an astounding amount of specialized energy devoted to finding an escape route from the dilemma. Instead I wish to present a theorem which does not rule out all functional relations f but only those that express any distributional judgements whatsoever, thereby ruling out any meaningful discussion of inequality within the logical framework of this model. The object of presenting and discussing this result is to clarify a basic weakness of the approach in handling problems of distribution and inequality.

A result concerning distributional judgements

Given Arrow's 'impossibility' result, it is clear that the system needs some give. This we provide by relaxing the requirement that social preference R be an ordering, in particular the requirement that R be 'transitive' (i.e., that xRy and yRz should imply xRz). Instead we demand only that the strict preference relation P be transitive (without indifference being necessarily transitive). We continue to require that R should be 'complete', i.e., either x is regarded as at least as good as y, or y regarded as at least as good as x (or both, in which case indifference holds), and of course that R should be 'reflexive', which is the entirely reasonable demand that x be regarded as at least as good as itself. Altogether we impose five conditions on the relation f between individual preference orderings and social preference relation R.

Condition Q (Quasi-transitive Social Preference): The social preference R must be reflexive, complete and quasi-transitive, i.e., the range of f must be confined to preference relations R that are reflexive and complete and which involve a transitive strict preference relation P.

Condition U (Unrestricted Domain): Any logically possible combination of individual preference orderings can be admitted.

Condition I (Independence of Irrelevant Alternatives): Social preference R over any pair x, y depends only on individual preferences over x, y.

Condition P (Pareto Rule): For any pair x, y if all individuals find x to be at least as good as y and some individual finds x

to be strictly better than y, then x is socially strictly preferred to y; and if all individuals are indifferent between x and y, then so is society.

Condition A (Anonymity): A permutation of individual orderings over the individuals keeps the social preference unchanged.

The first condition permits systematic social choice. The second permits individuals to have any preference pattern. The third establishes a relation between individual and social preferences that can be viewed pair by pair. The fourth is simply the familiar Pareto rule. The last condition—originally introduced by May (1952) in the context of the simple majority rule—requires that no special importance should be attached to who in particular holds which preference, all that matters being the combination of preferences that are held (no matter who holds what). These conditions may look reasonable enough, but together they rule out distributional judgements *in toto*.[11]

Theorem 1.1

The only functional relation f satisfying Conditions Q, U, I, P, and A must make all Pareto-incomparable states socially indifferent.

There are various alternative ways of proving this theorem, and I give here the sketch of a proof which I have spelt out elsewhere.[12] Define a person k as 'semidecisive'[13] if his preferring any x to any y implies that socially x is regarded as at least as good as y. He is 'almost semidecisive' if xRy holds whenever he prefers x to y and furthermore everybody else prefers y to x. By using Conditions Q, U, P, and I, it can be shown that if a person is almost semidecisive over some or-

---

[11] This theorem was presented in a slightly different version in Sen (1970a) as Theorem 5*3.

[12] Sen (1970a), pp. 75–7.

[13] This is a weakening of Arrow's (1963) definition of a set of individuals being 'decisive'.

dered pair (x, y) then he must be semidecisive over every ordered pair. I shall not spell out the entire argument here, but only demonstrate how the argument works. Assume that everyone other than k prefers y to x and also y to z, and let person k prefer x to y and y to z. By the Pareto rule, yPz. If we now assume that zPx, by quasi-transitivity (Condition Q) we would end up getting yPx; but since k is almost semidecisive over (x, y), clearly xRy. So zPx is false, and since R must be complete, xRz holds. By Condition I this must depend on individual preferences only over (x, z). Since only k's preference over (x, z) has been specified, k must be semidecisive over (x, z). Proceeding this way it can be shown that k would be semidecisive over every ordered pair in the set of social alternatives S.[14]

Next, a set V of individuals is 'almost decisive' over a pair (x, y) if as a result of everyone in V preferring x to y, and everyone not in V preferring y to x, the social ranking is xPy. The group of all individuals is, of course, an almost decisive set by virtue of the Pareto principle. Let the smallest almost decisive set for any pair in S be V^*, and let V^* be almost decisive over (x, y). Partition V^* into V_1^*, consisting of one person, and V_2^* the rest. The rest of the people not in V^* form set N. Let everyone in V_1^* prefer x to y and y to z, everyone in V_2^* prefer z to x and x to y, and everyone in N prefer y to z and z to x. Since V^* is almost decisive, clearly xPy. If we take zPy, this would make V_2^* an almost decisive set, which is impossible since V^* was the *smallest* almost decisive set. Hence yRz. If we now take zPx, then by quasi-transitivity we would get zPy and end up in a contradiction. Hence xRz. But then the solitary man in V_1^* is almost semidecisive over (x, z), and therefore must be semidecisive over every ordered pair of alternatives.

So far Condition A (anonymity) has not been used at all. Using that we see that *everyone* must be semidecisive over *every* ordered pair. But then for x to be socially preferred to y, it is necessary that no one regards y to be better than x. That is, we need then that everyone regards y as being at least as

[14] See the proof of Lemma 5*f in Sen (1970a).

good as x, which means that either (i) everyone is indifferent between x and y, or (ii) someone prefers x to y and everyone regards x to be at least as good as y. By Condition P, (i) implies that x and y are socially indifferent and (ii) implies that x is socially preferred to y. So x is socially preferred to y if and only if x is Pareto-superior to y. This means that if x is not Pareto-superior to y, then y is socially at least as good as x. And if x and y are Pareto-incomparable, then each is socially as good as the other and they must be socially indifferent.

Interpretation of Theorem 1.1

Theorem 1.1 makes Pareto comparisons the only basis of social choice. Since Pareto optimal points by definition are either Pareto-indifferent or Pareto-incomparable, they must all be declared socially indifferent. Even if one person prefers one state to another—however mildly—and all others have the opposite preference, the two states must still be declared to be *equally* good from the social point of view given the axioms of Theorem 1.1. We are back to a situation where judgements on inequality are not permitted and Pareto optimality is both necessary *and* sufficient for overall social optimality. Anyone wishing to make distributional judgements must reject something or other in the framework of Theorem 1.1.

Which of the five conditions is guilty? I would argue that the real trouble lies in the very conception of a social welfare function, which makes social preference dependent on individual orderings only, using neither valuations of intensities of preference, nor interpersonal comparisons of welfare. Avoiding interpersonal comparisons has been the dominant tradition in economics since the depression of the nineteen-thirties, for reasons that must have been—I suspect—unconnected with the depression itself, since the celebrated lambasting of interpersonal comparisons by Robbins (1932), (1988), and others, which started it all, could have hardly been inspired by the sight of obvious human misery. Be that as it may, the attempt to handle social choice without using interpersonal comparability or cardinality had the natural consequence of the social welfare function being defined on the set of individual orderings. And this is precisely what makes this framework so remarkably unsuited to the analysis of distributional questions. The conditions used in Theorem 1.1 simply precipitate this fundamental weakness.

The point can be illustrated in terms of the exercise of dividing a cake of volume 100 between two persons 1 and 2, with $y_1 + y_2 = 100$, assuming that each prefers more to less. Armed only with individual orderings we know that person 1 prefers a 50–50 division to a 0–100 division, while person 2 prefers the latter. Now comparing the 50–50 division with a 49–51 division, we still have exactly the same ranking on the part of both individuals. We cannot say that the preferences were much sharper in the first case than in the second, since cardinality of individual utilities is not admitted; and this, combined with the ruling out of interpersonal comparisons, kills twice over any prospect of being able to make a statement of the kind that the gain of person 1 in going from 0 to 50 may be larger than the loss of person 2 in coming down from 100 to 50, or even from 51 to 50. The ruling out of interpersonal comparisons even eliminates the possibility of our being able to say that person 2 is better off than person 1 under a 0–100 division. In fact all the characteristics of individual welfare levels in the distribution problem are precisely left out of account in this framework, and it is no wonder that a set of fine-looking conditions can complete the kill and eliminate distributional judgements altogether. Thus Theorem 1.1.

Interpersonal comparisons

The crucial question really concerns interpersonal comparability, since cardinality alone—it is easy to check—will not help us much. With cardinality we can compare each person's gains and losses with alternative values of his own gains and losses, but distributional judgements would seem to demand some ideas of the relative gains and losses of different persons and also of their relative levels of welfare. Indeed Arrow's 'impossibility theorem', which I referred to earlier, remains virtually intact even when cardinality is introduced in the absence of interpersonal comparability, as has been shown.[15] Theorem 1.1 has the same characteristic.

It seems reasonable, therefore, to argue that if the approach of social welfare functions is to give us any substantial help in measuring inequality, or in evaluating alternative measures of inequality, then the framework must be broadened to include interpersonal comparisons of welfare. The question will be asked at this stage whether such comparisons are at all legitimate, and if so in what sense. Despite the widespread allergy to interpersonal comparisons among professional economists, it is I think fair to say that such comparisons can be given a precisely defined meaning. In fact, various alternative frameworks are possible.[16] One in particular will be pursued here.[17]

If I say 'I would prefer to be person A rather than person B in this situation', I am indulging in an interpersonal comparison. While we do not really have the opportunity (or perhaps the misfortune, as the case may be) of in fact becoming A or B, we can think quite systematically about such a choice, and indeed we seem to make such comparisons frequently.

Representing (x, i) as being individual i (with his tastes and mental qualities as well) in social state x, a preference relation $\tilde{R}$ defined over all such pairs provides an 'ordinal' structure of interpersonal comparisons.[18] To obtain interpersonally comparable cardinal welfare levels, one would have to go beyond such a ranking $\tilde{R}$ and introduce additional features for the sake of cardinalization.[19] The numerical representation of $\tilde{R}$ will be unique only up to an increasing monotonic transfor-

[15] Theorem 8*2 in Sen (1970a).

[16] See Vickrey (1945), Fleming (1952), and Harsanyi (1956). On the philosophical side, see in particular Kant (1788), Sidgwick (1874), Hare (1952), Rawls (1958), (1971), and Suppes (1966).

[17] Cf. Sen (1970a) and Pattanaik (1971).

[18] Formally, $\tilde{R}$ is a ranking of the Cartesian product of X (the set of social states) and J (the set of individuals).

[19] For a discussion of the axiomatic approach to cardinalization, see Fishburn (1970).

mation if the measure is ordinal, and unique up to a positive linear transformation if it is cardinal. For any individual welfare function chosen $U(x, i)$ will stand for the welfare level of being person i in state x. While bearing in mind this general framework for interpersonal comparisons, we shall, however, represent this as $U_i(x)$ and think of this as our view of the welfare function of individual i. If the framework of complete interpersonal comparability is used, we must also specify that if any particular transformation of U_i is done for any individual i, then a corresponding transformation would have to be done to everyone else's welfare function as well. For example, given an accepted configuration of welfare functions of the different individuals, if one person's welfare function is doubled, then so should be the welfare function of everyone else as well. While the precise set of welfare functions chosen remains arbitrary, which is unavoidable given the fact that welfare has no natural 'unit' or 'origin', arbitrary *relative* variations are not permitted in the framework of 'full comparability'.[20]

Utilitarianism

Once the information content of individual preferences has been broadened to include interpersonally comparable cardinal welfare functions, many methods of social judgement become available. The most widely used approach is that of utilitarianism in which the sum of the individual utilities is taken as the measure of social welfare, and alternative social states are ordered in terms of the value of the sum of individual utilities. Pioneered by Bentham (1789), this approach has been widely used in economics for social judgements, notably by Marshall (1890), Pigou (1920), and Robertson (1952). In the context of the measurement of inequality of income distribution, and in that of judging alternative distributions of income, it has been used by Dalton (1920), Lange (1938),

[20] The logical and intuitive bases of alternative frameworks of interpersonal comparisons of individual welfare are discussed in some detail in Sen (1970a), Chapter 7, 7*, 9 and 9*.

Lerner (1944), Aigner and Heins (1967), and Tinbergen (1970), among others.[21]

The trouble with this approach is that maximizing the sum of individual utilities is supremely unconcerned with the interpersonal distribution of that sum. This should make it a particularly unsuitable approach to use for measuring or judging inequality. Interestingly enough, however, not only has utilitarianism been fairly widely used for distributional judgements, it has—somewhat amazingly—even developed the reputation of being an egalitarian criterion. This seems to have come about through a peculiar dialectical process whereby such adherents of utilitarianism as Marshall and Pigou were attacked by Robbins and others for their supposedly egalitarian use of the utilitarian framework. This gave utilitarianism a ready-made reputation for being equality-conscious.

The whole thing arises from a very special coincidence under some extremely simple assumptions. The maximization of the sum of individual utilities through the distribution of a given total of income between different persons requires equating the marginal utilities from income of different persons, and if the special assumption is made that everyone has the same utility function, then equating marginal utilities amounts to equating total utilities as well. Marshall and others noted this particular aspect of utilitarianism, though they were in no particular hurry to draw any radical distributive policy prescription out of this. But when the attack on utilitarianism came, this particular aspect of it was singled out for an especially stern rebuke.

While this dialectical process gave utilitarianism its ill-deserved egalitarian reputation, the true character of that approach can be seen quite easily by considering a case where one person A derives exactly twice as much utility as person

---

[21] There is the question as to whether it is correct to identify individual 'welfare levels' with individual 'utilities' as the classical utilitarians saw these concepts. On this see Little (1950), Robertson (1952), and Sen (1970a). In this work, I shall treat the two as identical following the traditional practice in economics.

B from any given level of income, say, because *B* has some handicap, e.g., being a cripple. In the framework of inter-personal comparisons outlined earlier, this simply means that the person making the judgement regards *A*'s position as being twice as good as *B*'s position for any given level of income. In this case the rule of maximizing the sum-total of utility of the two would require that person *A* be given a higher income than *B*. It may be noted that, even if income were equally divided, under the assumptions made *A* would have received more utility than *B*; and instead of reducing this inequality, the utilitarian rule of distribution compounds it by giving more income to *A*, who is already better off.

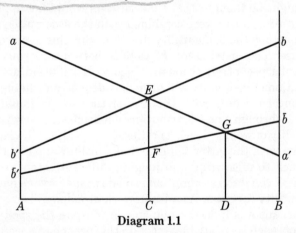

Diagram 1.1

Diagram 1.1 illustrates the problem. The total amount of income to be divided between the two is *AB*. The share of *A* is measured in the direction *AB* and that of *B* in the direction *BA* and any point such as *C* or *D* reflects a particular division of total income between the two. The marginal utility of *A* is measured by *aa′* and that of *B* by *bb′*, and as drawn they are exact mirror-images of each other. The maximum total of utility is secured by dividing income equally as given by point *C* with *AC* = *BC*. So far so good. Assume now that *B*'s marginal utility schedule is exactly half that of *A*, so that his marginal utility is no longer given by *bb′* but by *b̄b̄′*. If the income distribution is left unchanged, A's total utility will be $AaEC$ and B's only $BbFC$, and B will be much worse off. To compensate this an egalitarian criterion will now shift income from A to B. Would utilitarianism recommend this? It would recommend precisely the opposite, viz., a transfer of income from poor B to rich A! The new optimal point will be D with A enjoying a total utility of $AaGD$ and B merely $BbGD$.

It seems fairly clear that fundamentally utilitarianism is very far from an egalitarian approach. It is, therefore, odd that virtually all attempts at measuring inequality from a welfare point of view, or exercises in deriving optimal distributional rules, have concentrated on the utilitarian approach.

It might be thought that this criticism would not apply at all if utilitarianism were combined with the assumption that everyone has the same utility function. But this is not quite the case. The distribution of welfare between persons is a relevant aspect of any problem of income distribution, and our evaluation of inequality will obviously depend on whether we are concerned only with the loss of the *sum* of individual utilities through a bad distribution of income, or also with the inequality of welfare levels of different individuals. Its lack of concern with the latter tends to make utilitarianism a blunt approach to measuring and judging different extents of inequality even if the assumption is made that everyone has the same utility function. As a framework of judging inequality, utilitarianism is indeed a non-starter, despite the spell that this approach seems to have cast on this branch of normative economics.

The Weak Equity Axiom

To bring in egalitarian considerations into the form of the social welfare judgements, we might propose various alternative axioms, of which the following is an interesting case.

The Weak Equity Axiom: Let person i have a lower level of welfare than person j for each level of individual income. Then in distributing a given total of income among n individuals including i and j, the optimal solution must give i a higher level of income than j.

This Axiom, which we shall call WEA, puts a restriction on the class of group welfare functions that can be considered. Note that the requirement does not specify how much more is to be given to the deprived person but merely that he should receive more income as a compensation, possibly partial, and even a minute extra amount would satisfy WEA. In this sense the requirement is rather mild.

Three qualifications should be specified here. First, the normative appeal of WEA would very likely depend on the precise interpretation of interpersonal comparisons. The framework in terms of which WEA seems to me to make a great deal of sense is the one that is being used in this work, viz., considering the possibility of being in different persons' positions and then choosing among them. Thus interpreted WEA amounts to saying that if I feel that for any given level of income I would prefer to be in the position of person A (with his tastes and his other non-income characteristics) than in that of person B, then I should recommend that B should get a higher income level than A.

Second, the more equity-conscious one is and the less concerned with the 'aggregate', the more should WEA appeal. It might be argued that if a unit of income gives much more marginal utility to A than to B despite A being in general better off than B, perhaps one should give the additional unit of income to A rather than to B. This type of 'marginalist' comparison is in the spirit of utilitarianism, whereas the philosophy behind WEA lies in a completely different direction. Part of the difference is purely normative, but there are technical problems of measurability and interpersonal comparability that have a bearing on this and which will be discussed in Chapter 2.

Third, it is possible to give person B so much more income that, despite having a lower welfare function, he may end up being much better off than person A. Such possibilities are not ruled out by WEA. It just indicates a *direction* of adjustment, but if the adjustment is quantitatively excessive the inequality may well finish up in the opposite direction. Other conditions have to be introduced to rule out such an occurrence. WEA is a pretty mild force towards equity, and it is at best a necessary but not a sufficient condition for achieving that objective.

It is clear from our earlier discussion that: utilitarianism will violate WEA in many cases. Indeed the example portrayed in Diagram 1.1 shows this quite convincingly. To keep track of the more significant analytical results we elevate this piece of rustic wisdom into a theorem.

Theorem 1.2

There exist social choice situations such that the utilitarian rule of choice would violate the Weak Equity Axiom.

The proof is straightforward; look again at Diagram 1.1.[22]

WEA and concavity

The utilitarian rule is to maximize simply the sum of individual utilities:

$$W = \Sigma_{i=1}^{n} U_i(x) \qquad (1.1)$$

To bring in a built-in bias towards equality, the functional relation between social welfare W and individual utilities may be assumed to be strictly concave. That is if U^1 and U^2 are two n-tuples of individual utilities, then for any t with $0 < t < 1$, we may require that:

$$[tW(U^1) + (1 - t)W(U^2)] < W(tU^1 + (1 - t)U^2) \qquad (1.2)$$

This would imply that any 'averaging' of utilities, thereby reducing disparity, would tend to raise social welfare, which does of course push us in the egalitarian direction.

It is interesting to enquire into the relation between the Weak Equity Axiom and strict concavity, since both have egalitarian aspects. It should be clear, however, that the two conditions are in fact independent of each other. WEA is a condition of *optimal* choice in a restricted class of choice situations, and there is no real hope of being able to get the fulfilment of strict concavity (or even weaker conditions like

---

[22] Utilitarianism can satisfy WEA only if the ranking of total utilities is the opposite of that of marginal utilities at equal levels of income.

concavity or quasi-concavity) everywhere in the W-function on the basis of these restricted choice results.[23]

What about the converse? This does not follow either. WEA would require that the inequality-increasing result of the utilitarian case in the situation portrayed in Diagram 1.1 would have to be completely knocked out and instead the inequality-decreasing result brought in. And a W-function that is strictly concave in a mild way and is very close to the linear W of the utilitarian case would not be able to do this.

If not convinced by this reasoning, consider the following example. Take two utility functions identical except for a proportional displacement:

$$U_2(y) = mU_1(y), \text{ for all income level } y, \text{ with } m < 1 \quad (1.3)$$

Assuming that $U_1(y)$ is strictly positive for all positive values of y, person 2 is worse off than person 1 for all y. The group welfare function W is of the following form:

$$W = \frac{1}{\alpha}[(U_1)^\alpha + (U_2)^\alpha] \quad (1.4)$$

For strict concavity we need $\alpha < 1$. If the problem is to maximize W subject to:

$$y_1 + y_2 \leq Y, \quad (1.5)$$

the optimal distribution would have the property:

$$[U(y_1)^{\alpha-1} U'(y_1) - [U(y_2)]^{\alpha-1} U'(y_2)m^\alpha = 0, \quad (1.6)$$

putting $U(y) = U_1(y)$. This implies:

$$U'(y_1)/U'(y_2) = m^\alpha[U(y_1)/U(y_2)]^{1-\alpha} \quad (1.7)$$

Note that if $\alpha > 0$, then $m^\alpha < 1$, and if $\alpha < 0$, then $m^\alpha > 1$. Since U increases and U' decreases with income y, it is clear that this condition will fulfil $y_1 < y_2$ if and only if $\alpha < 0$.[24] Since

---

[23] Note also that in some cases (see footnote 22) it is possible for WEA to be satisfied *by* utilitarianism, which must always violate strict concavity.

[24] In this case social welfare W is bounded from above. There is an analogy here with Ramsey's (1928) social welfare picture with a level of 'bliss'.

strict concavity only requires $\alpha < 1$, and WEA, in this case, would be fulfilled only if $\alpha < 0$, obviously WEA does not follow from strict concavity.[25]

Equity and welfare economics

WEA and the requirement of strict concavity have the common property of being in conflict with utilitarianism for essentially egalitarian reasons. But they do differ from each other in the way they bring in egalitarian values. Strict concavity does it by putting in a preference for the averaging process everywhere in the social welfare valuation, but the preference could be quite mild. In contrast WEA demands a sharper preference for equality in optimal choices but only for a specific class of situations. The two conditions are similar in spirit, but one is weak and widespread and the other is somewhat stronger but more confined in its scope.

It is worth mentioning in this context that in rejecting utilitarianism we have made use here of very mild conditions. Much stronger egalitarian criteria have been proposed before, e.g., Rawls's (1958), (1971) 'maximin' rule, whereby the social objective is to maximize the welfare level of the worst-off individual. In a 2-person world, WEA is a much weaker requirement than that of Rawls. If one person has a uniformly lower welfare function than another, and if the first person can be made better off by transferring income from the second, then the Rawls criterion would require that the person with the lower welfare function should have *that much* more income which would make his actual level of utility equal with that of the other.[26] In contrast, WEA merely requires that the unfor-

[25] If $\alpha > 0$, then $y_1 > y_2$, and if $\alpha = 0$, which is the borderline logarithmic case, $y_1 = y_2$.

[26] This requirement cannot, of course, be satisfied if the person with the lower welfare function remains worse off than the other despite having all the income, in which case he *should* have all the income according to the Rawls criterion. This is not a very interesting case for obvious reasons. In fact, it can be argued that the pure model of distribution involving costless transfers is, in general, not very relevant for practical policy making and how egalitarian the Rawls criterion would, in fact, be would depend upon the dependence of the total income on its distribution. Problems of incentives and related matters are discussed in Chapter 4.

tunate person should get a bit more—how much more is not specified. The fact that utilitarianism cannot even clear such a small hurdle seems to make it inappropriate as a theory for evaluating inequality.[27]

To conclude, we do not seem to get very much help in studying inequality from the main schools of welfare economics—old and new. The literature on Pareto optimality (including the famous 'basic theorem' of 'new' welfare economics) avoids distributional judgements altogether. The standard approach of 'social welfare functions' because of its concentration on individual orderings only (without any use of interpersonal comparisons of levels and intensities) fails to provide a framework for distributional discussions. This is brought out rather dramatically by Theorem 1.1. Finally, utilitarianism, the dominant faith of 'old' welfare economics, is much too hooked on the welfare *sum* to be concerned with the problem of distribution, and it is, in fact, capable of producing strongly anti-egalitarian results. As an approach to the measurement and evaluation of inequality it cannot take us very far. For the problem of inequality evaluation, the royal roads of welfare economics do look a trifle bleak.

[27] Note that the conflict with utilitarianism would have arisen even if WEA had demanded only that the person with the uniformly lower welfare function should get *no less* income than the other.

2

Measures of Inequality

In this chapter I shall discuss a number of measures of inequality that have been proposed in the literature. As mentioned in the last chapter, these measures fall into two classes, viz., positive measures which make no explicit use of any concept of social welfare, and normative measures which are based on an explicit formulation of social welfare and the loss incurred from unequal distribution. While I did argue that the line between these two types of measures is not a firm one, it is clear that there is a distinction, and it may be useful to discuss the two types of measures in turn. I shall begin with positive measures.

The range

Consider distributions of income over n persons, $i = 1, \ldots, n$, and let y_i be the income of person i. Let the average level of income be μ, so that:

$$\Sigma_{i=1}^{n} y_i = n\mu \tag{2.1}$$

The relative share of income going to person i is x_i. That is:

$$y_i = n\mu x_i \tag{2.2}$$

Perhaps the simplest measure is based on comparing the extreme values of the distribution, i.e., the highest and the lowest income levels. The range can be defined as the gap between these two levels as a ratio of mean income. Thus defined the range E is given by:

$$E = (\text{Max}_i \, y_i - \text{Min}_i \, y_i)/\mu \tag{2.3}$$

If income is divided absolutely equally, then clearly $E = 0$. At the other extreme if one person receives all the income, then $E = n$. And E lies in general between 0 and n.

The difficulty with the range as a measure is obvious enough. It ignores the distribution in between the extremes.

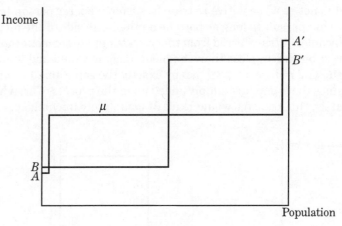

Diagram 2.1

The distribution AA' has a wider range E than BB', but most people under AA' enjoy the mean income μ with only a few aberrations. On the other hand BB' involves a division of the population into two distinct classes of the rich and the poor. By concentrating on the extreme values only, the range misses important features of the contrast.

The relative mean deviation

One way of looking at the entire distribution and not merely at the extreme values is to compare the income level of each with the mean income, to sum the absolute values of all the differences, and then to look at that sum as a proportion of total income. This yields the so-called relative mean deviation M:

$$M = \Sigma_{i=1}^{n} |\mu - y_i| / n\mu \qquad (2.4)$$

With perfect equality $M = 0$, and with all income going to one person only, $M = 2(n-1)/n$. But unlike E, M takes note of the entire distribution. For example, in Diagram 2.1 the value of M is much higher for BB' than for AA', which corresponds well to our intuitive notion of inequality.

The main trouble with the relative mean deviation is that it is not at all sensitive to transfers from a poorer person to a richer person as long as both lie on the same side of the mean income. £1 transferred from the poorest man to someone more rich but having less than the mean income would add to one gap and reduce another gap by exactly the same amount, and since these gaps are simply added up in the process of arriving at M, this transfer would leave M completely unchanged.

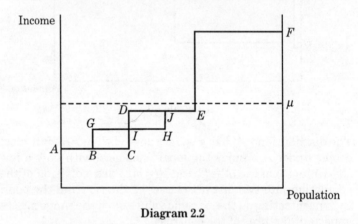

Diagram 2.2

In Diagram 2.2 the distribution $ABCDEF$ is transformed into $ABGHJEF$ by transferring income to some of the poorest from a richer class. But the value of M remains unchanged since the diminution of the gap by $BGIC$ is exactly compensated by the increase of the gap by $DIHJ$, since—as drawn— BC and DJ are equal and so are BG and JH. As a measure M seems to take no notice of income transfers whatsoever unless they cross the dividing line of μ on the way. It is, therefore, rather arbitrary—a bit like some criminal laws in the United States which come into operation only if some state boundary is crossed in the process of the crime. As a measure M fails to catch the commonly accepted ideas on inequality, which would tend to regard $ABCDEF$ as more unequal than $ABGHJEF$.

The variance and the coefficient of variation

Rather than simply adding the absolute values of the gaps, if we square them and then add, this would have the result of accentuating differences further away from the mean, so that a transfer like the one shown in Diagram 2.2 would reduce the inequality measure. Variance, the common statistical measure of variation, does have this property.

$$V = \Sigma_{i=1}^{n} (\mu - y_i)^2/n \qquad (2.5)$$

In Diagram 2.2, $ABCDEF$ has a higher variance than $ABGHJEF$ since in the process of squaring, BG has a stronger impact than JH. Any transfer from a poorer person to a richer person, other things remaining the same, always increases the variance, and this would appear to be an attractive property for an inequality measure. In fact as early as 1920, Hugh Dalton had argued that any measure of inequality must have this minimal property[1] and since in this Dalton was following a lead of Pigou,[2] whom he quoted in this context, we shall call this the Pigou–Dalton condition.

However, the variance depends on the mean income level, and one distribution may show much greater *relative* variation than another and still end up having a lower variance if the mean income level around which the variations take place is smaller than with the other distribution. A measure that does not have this deficiency and concentrates on relative variation is the coefficient of variation, which is simply the square root of the variance divided by the mean income level:

$$C = V^{1/2}/\mu \qquad (2.6)$$

While the coefficient of variation captures the property of being sensitive to income transfers for all income levels and,

[1] Dalton (1920), p. 351.
[2] Pigou (1912), p. 24.

unlike the variance, is independent of the mean income level, the procedure of squaring the differences is a very particular one. And the question may be asked: Why choose this particular formula? It is easily checked that C does have the characteristic of attaching equal weights to transfers of income at different income levels, i.e., the impact of a small transfer from a person with income y to one with income $(y - d)$ is the same, irrespective of the value of y.[3] Is this neutrality a desirable property? It is possible to argue that the impact should be greater if the transfer takes place at a lower income level, and a transfer from a person with an income level of £1,000 to one with £900 should be greater than a similar transfer from a man with £1,000,100 to one with £1,000,000. However, by now we are dealing with areas in which our intuitive ideas of inequality are relatively vague and checking the measures in terms of some commonly accepted notions of inequality is no longer altogether easy. But the question remains: Why use the squaring procedure rather than some other operation which would also make the inequality measure sensitive to transfers from the rich to the poor (in line with the Pigou–Dalton condition)?

There is another methodological issue. Is it best to measure the difference of each income level from the mean only, or should the comparison be carried out between every pair of incomes? The latter will capture everyone's income difference from everyone else, and not merely from the mean, which might not be anybody's income whatsoever.

The standard deviation of logarithms
If one wishes to attach greater importance to income transfers at the lower end, a reasonable way of going about it is to take some transformation of incomes that staggers the income levels, and of course the logarithm recommends itself. One other advantage of the logarithm, in contrast with taking the variance or the standard deviation of *actual* values, is that it eliminates the arbitrariness of the units and therefore of abso-

3 Atkinson (1970a), p. 255.

lute levels, since a change of units, which takes the form of a multiplication of the absolute values, comes out in the logarithmic form as an addition of a constant, and therefore goes out in the wash when pairwise differences are being taken. It is, therefore, no wonder that the standard deviation of the logarithm has frequently cropped up as a suggested measure of inequality. As used in the standard statistical literature, the deviation is taken from the geometric mean rather than from the arithmetic mean, but in the income distribution literature using the arithmetic mean seems more common (see Atkinson 1970a, Stark 1972).

$$H = [\Sigma_{i=1}^{n} (\log \mu - \log y_i)^2/n]^{1/2} \qquad (2.7)$$

The fact that a logarithmic transformation staggers the income levels tends to soften the blow in reflecting inequality since it reduces the deviation, but on the other hand it has the property—as noted before—of highlighting differences at the lower end of the scale. But since income levels, as they get higher and higher, suffer increasingly severe contraction, this makes $-H$ as a measure of welfare not concave at all at high income levels. If one wants social welfare to be a concave function of individual incomes, then H as a measure of inequality can cause problems, despite attractive features in other respects.

Furthermore, H does depend on the arbitrary squaring formula—albeit after a logarithmic transformation—and it shares with V and C the limitation of taking differences only from the mean.

The Gini coefficient and the relative mean difference

A measure that has been very widely used to represent the extent of inequality is the Gini coefficient attributed to Gini (1912) and much analysed by Ricci (1916) and later by Dalton (1920), Yntema (1938), Atkinson (1970a), Newbery (1970), Sheshinski (1972), and others. One way of viewing it is in terms of the Lorenz curve due—not surprisingly—to Lorenz (1905), whereby the percentages of the population arranged from the poorest to the richest are represented on the

horizontal axis and the percentages of income enjoyed by the
bottom x% of the population is shown on the vertical axis.

Obviously 0% of the population enjoys 0% of the income and
100% of the population enjoy all the income. So a Lorenz curve
runs from one corner of the unit square to the diametrically
opposite corner. If everyone has the same income the Lorenz
curve will be simply the diagonal, but in the absence of perfect
equality the bottom income groups will enjoy a proportion-
ately lower share of income. It is obvious, therefore, that any
Lorenz curve must lie below the diagonal (except the one of

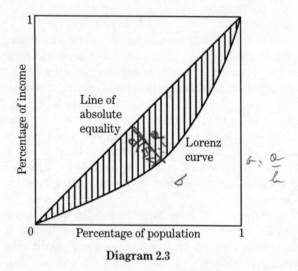

Diagram 2.3

complete equality which would be the diagonal), and its slope
will increasingly rise—at any rate not fall—as we move to
richer and richer sections of the population.

The Gini coefficient is the ratio of the difference between
the line of absolute equality (the diagonal) and the Lorenz
curve—represented in Diagram 2.3 as the shaded area—to the
triangular region underneath the diagonal. There are various
ways of defining the Gini coefficient, and a bit of manipula-
tion—tedious as it is—reveals that it is exactly one-half of the

relative mean difference, which is defined as the arithmetic average of the absolute values of differences between all pairs of incomes.

$$G = (1/2n^2\mu)\Sigma_{i=1}^{n}\Sigma_{j=1}^{n} \, |y_i - y_j| \qquad (2.8.1)$$

$$= 1 - (1/n^2\mu)\Sigma_{i=1}^{n}\Sigma_{j=1}^{n}\mathrm{Min}(y_i, y_j) \qquad (2.8.2)$$

$$= 1 + (1/n) - (2/n^2\mu)[y_1 + 2y_2 + \ldots + ny_n] \qquad (2.8.3)$$

for $y_1 \geq y_2 \geq \ldots \geq y_n$.

In taking differences over all pairs of incomes, the Gini coefficient or the absolute mean difference avoids the total concentration on differences vis-à-vis the mean which C, V, or H has. In avoiding the arbitrary squaring procedure of C, V, or H, it may seem to be a more direct approach as well, without sacrificing the quality of being sensitive to transfers from the rich to the poor at every level. Undoubtedly one appeal of the Gini coefficient, or of the relative mean difference, lies in the fact that it is a very direct measure of income difference, taking note of differences between *every* pair of incomes.

Welfare interpretations of the alternative measures

In comparing these measures it is obvious that the range E and the relative mean deviation M are, more or less, non-starters.[4] The real competition would be between such measures as the coefficient of variation C, the standard deviation of logarithms H and the Gini coefficient G. In comparing the relative usefulness of these measures it is necessary to examine the precise properties.

First, as far as the Pigou–Dalton condition is concerned, both the coefficient of variation and the Gini coefficient, pass the test, i.e., a transfer from a richer man to a poorer person always reduces the value of both C and G. The same is,

[4] Measures of 'skewness' of income distributions have also been used as measures of inequality. But this is essentially a confusion of 'equality' with 'symmetry'. An un-skewed symmetric distribution need not be an equal one. Cf. Stark (1972), pp. 139–40.

however, not true of the standard deviation of logarithms H, and it is possible for H to rise even when there are rich-to-poor transfers. Although this can happen only at very high levels of income, the fact remains that H can violate the Pigou–Dalton condition.[5]

Second, as far as relative sensitivity is concerned, we have already noted that the coefficient of variation C is equally sensitive at all levels, whereas the standard deviation of logarithms H is more sensitive for transfers in the lower income brackets. As noted earlier, if the welfare impact of a tiny transfer from a man with £1,000 to one with £900 is thought to be more important than that from a man with £100,100 to one with £100,000, the coefficient of variation faces some problems. The standard deviation of logarithms shows precisely the required type of sensitivity, but it becomes so insensitive to transfers *among* the rich, that it may end up by violating even the Pigou–Dalton condition as well. It would have been nice if the sensitivity direction could be preserved (unlike with C) without violating the Pigou–Dalton condition (unlike with H). Would the Gini coefficient meet this gap?

The answer is: No, it will not. For the sensitivity of the Gini coefficient depends not on the size of the income levels but on the number of people in between them. As is clear from the expression (2.8.3), the Gini coefficient implies a welfare function which is just a weighted sum of different people's income levels with the weights being determined by the rank-order position of the person in the ranking by income level. Thus the rate of substitution between the person with the i-th highest income and the one with the j-th highest income is simply j/i. For example £3 to the second richest person is given the same weight as £2 to the third richest man. So the actual weights would depend upon precisely how the population is distributed over income sizes. If A has an income of £2,000 and B of £1,900, and if A is the 1,000th richest man while B is the 1,100th richest man, then £1.00 to B is taken to be equivalent to £1.10 to A. But if some other people turn up inside the

---

[5] See Dasgupta, Sen and Starrett (1972), and also Chapter 3 below.

income gap, e.g., if an additional 100 people get incomes between £1,900 and £2,000, then the Gini coefficient would attach the same weight to £1.00 income to B as to £1.20 to A. The income levels of A and B have remained the same, but the relative weighting between them is now completely altered because some other people have shown up inside the income range defined by A's and B's income levels.[6]

The Gini coefficient can be interpreted in a number of different ways. The visual picture given by Diagram 2.3 is itself quite expressive. The expression (2.8.3), on which we have been commenting, shows that the implicit welfare function underlying the Gini coefficient is a rank-order-weighted sum of different persons' income shares. On the other hand, expression (2.8.2) throws a somewhat different light on the Gini coefficient. Suppose the welfare level of any pair of individuals is equated to the welfare level of the worse-off person of the two.[7] Then if the total welfare of the group is identified with the sum of the welfare levels of all pairs, we get the welfare function underlying the Gini coefficient.

Finally, expression (2.8.1) suggests yet another interpretation. In any pair-wise comparison the man with the lower income can be thought to be suffering from some depression on finding his income to be lower. Let this depression be proportional to the difference in income. The sum total of all such depressions in all possible pair-wise comparisons takes us to the Gini coefficient.

One characteristic of the Gini coefficient is that it does not imply a strictly concave group welfare function.[8] This is obvious from (2.8.3), since G is a linear function of income levels.

[6] There is an obvious analogy here with the violation of Arrow's (1951) 'independence of irrelevant alternatives', which we have used in Chapter 1. The similarity is not a pure coincidence. A rank-order-based system typically does make choices sensitive to 'irrelevant' alternatives, and this is as true of the 'rank-order method' of voting, which violates Arrow's condition, as of the Gini coefficient, which has the property described in the text.

[7] There is an analogy here with Rawls's (1971) 'maximin' criterion of justice but applied pair-wise.

[8] Note that the welfare function must be thought to be $-G$, since a higher value of G shows *greater* inequality, which corresponds to *less* welfare. It is $-G$ that is concave but not strictly concave.

This property has come under attack recently,[9] but it is not at all clear how serious an objection it really is. The implied group welfare function may not be strictly concave, but it is concave all right, and furthermore any transfer from the poor to the rich *or* vice versa is strictly recorded in the Gini measure in the appropriate direction.[10] The fact that the standard deviation of logarithms does not even satisfy this condition of response may appear to be, in some sense, much more clearly objectionable.[11]

Theil's entropy measure

An interesting measure of inequality, proposed by Theil (1967), derives from the notion of entropy in information theory, and it is, in terms of motivation, rather different from the class of measures we have been looking at. When x is the probability that a certain event will occur, the information content $h(x)$ of noticing that the event has in fact occurred must be a decreasing function of x—the more unlikely an event, the more interesting it is to know that that thing has really happened.

[9] See Atkinson (1970a), Newbery (1970), Dasgupta, Sen and Starrett (1970). Newbery (1970) shows that the Gini coefficient cannot order distributions in the same way as any *additive* group welfare function given strictly concave and differentiable individual utility functions. Sheshinski (1972) questions additivity and gives an example of a non-additive group welfare function that would reflect the Gini ranking. Dasgupta, Sen and Starrett (1972) and Rothschild and Stiglitz (1973) demonstrate that the Gini ranking cannot be reflected by any group welfare function (additive or not) if it is strictly quasi-concave on individual incomes. (Sheshinski's example is not only non-additive, but it is also non-strictly-quasi-concave on incomes.)

[10] The Gini coefficient is strictly S-concave though not strictly concave, or strictly quasi-concave. On this see Dasgupta, Sen and Starrett (1972), and Chapter 3 below.

[11] Measures like the variance and the coefficient of variation are strictly concave throughout. But the use of the mean-variance analysis in an additive framework would imply a very specific class of individual utility functions, viz., the quadratic class:

$$U(y) = k_1 + K_2 y + K_3 y^2, \text{ with } K_3 < 0 \qquad (2.9)$$

The coefficient of variation is, however, mean-independent, though it too would fall in a relatively narrow category in terms of implicit welfare functions.

One formula that satisfies this property—among others—is the logarithm of the reciprocal of x.

$$h(x) = \log \frac{1}{x} \qquad (2.10)$$

When there are n possible events $1, \ldots, n$, we take the respective probabilities $x_1, \ldots, x_n$, such that $x_i \geq 0$ and $\Sigma_{i=1}^{n} x_i = 1$. The entropy or the expected information content of the situation can be viewed as the sum of the information content of each event weighted by the respective probabilities.

$$H(x) = \Sigma_{i=1}^{n} x_i h(x_i)$$

$$= \Sigma_{i=1}^{n} x_i \log \left(\frac{1}{x_i} \right) \qquad (2.11)$$

It is clear that the closer the n probabilities x_i are to $(1/n)$, the greater is the entropy. While in thermodynamics entropy is taken to measure disorder,[12] if x_i is interpreted as the share of income going to person i, $H(x)$ looks like a measure of equality. When each x_i equals $(1/n)$, $H(x)$ attains its maximum value of $\log n$. If we subtract the entropy $H(x)$ of an income distribution from its maximum value of $\log n$, we get an index of inequality. This is Theil's measure.

$$T = \log n - H(x)$$

$$= \Sigma_{i=1}^{n} x_i \log n x_i. \qquad (2.12)$$

Given the association of doom with entropy in the context of thermodynamics, it may take a little time to get used to entropy as a good thing ('How grand, entropy is on the increase!'), but it is clear that Theil's ingenious measure has much to be commended. A shift from a richer to a poorer person lowers T, i.e., it satisfies the Pigou–Dalton condition, and it can be aggregated in a simple manner over groups.[13]

---

[12] The second law of thermodynamics warns that there is an inherent tendency for disorder to increase.
[13] Theil (1967), pp. 94–6.

But the fact remains that it is an arbitrary formula, and the average of the logarithms of the reciprocals of income shares weighted by income shares is not a measure that is exactly overflowing with intuitive sense.[14] It is, however, interesting that the concept of entropy used in the natural sciences can provide a measure of inequality that is not immediately dismissable, however arbitrary it may be.

Different mean incomes

It is important to note that all these measures with the exception of the case of the variance have the property of being invariant if everyone's income is raised in the same proportion. This is true of the relative mean deviation, the coefficient of variation, the standard deviation of the logarithms, the relative mean difference, the Gini coefficient, and Theil's entropy measure. Is this a property we want? Can it be asserted that our judgement of the extent of inequality will not vary according to whether the people involved are generally poor or generally rich? Some have taken the view that our concern with inequality increases as a society gets prosperous since the society can 'afford' to be inequality-conscious. Others have asserted that the poorer an economy, the more 'disastrous' the consequences of inequality, so that inequality measures should be sharper for low average income.

This is a fairly complex question and is bedevilled by a mixture of positive and normative considerations. The view that for poorer economies inequality measures must be themselves sharper can be contrasted with the view that greater *importance* must be attached to any given inequality measure if the economy is poorer. The former incorporates the value in question into the measure of inequality itself, while the latter brings it in through the evaluation of the relative importance of a given measure at different levels of average income. In a fundamental sense it does not really matter

---

[14] If for some reason the individual welfare functions are proportional to $x_i \log(1/x_i)$, then Theil's measure will be particularly attractive within the utilitarian framework, but I can't think of a good reason why individual welfare functions should take such a form.

whether these values are brought in through the measure itself or through the evaluation of the measure, but it is important to be clear about precisely what one is doing.

Dalton's measure

It is time now to move from the positive measures to normative ones. In a classic contribution, Dalton (1920) argued that any measure of economic inequality must be concerned with economic welfare to be of relevance. The particular measure that he chose followed directly from the utilitarian framework, and he based it on a comparison between actual levels of aggregate utility and the level of total utility that would obtain if income were equally divided. Since he took a strictly concave utility function, i.e., with diminishing marginal utility of income, and the same function for all, the maximization of aggregate welfare required an equal division. Dalton took the ratio of actual social welfare to the maximal social welfare as his measure of equality, taking the utility levels to be all positive.[15]

$$D = [\Sigma_{i=1}^{n} U(y_i)]/nU(\mu). \qquad (2.13)$$

Atkinson (1970a) has pointed out that this measure suffers from the difficulty that it is not invariant with respect to positive linear transformations of the utility function; cardinal utility implies that any positive linear transformation would do just as well and Dalton's measure takes arbitrary values depending on which particular transformation is chosen. I must confess that I am not entirely persuaded that this argument is a very strong one, since the ordering of Dalton's measure would not be affected by taking positive linear transformations, and what is really significant with these measures is the ordering property. However, it is possible to redefine the measure in such a way that the actual numbers used in measuring would be invariant with respect to permitted transformations of the welfare numbers, and this is what Atkinson does in his own approach.

[15] See Wedgwood (1939) for an application of Dalton's measure. See Bentzel (1970) for a critical evaluation of this approach.

Atkinson's measure

Atkinson defines what he calls 'the equally distributed equivalent income' of a given distribution of a total income, and this is defined as that level of *per capita* income which if enjoyed by everybody would make total welfare exactly equal to the total welfare generated by the actual income distribution.[16] Putting y_e as 'the equally distributed equivalent income', we see that:

$$y_e = y \mid [nU(y) = \Sigma_{i=1}^{n} U(y_i)] \qquad (2.14)$$

The sum of the actual welfare levels of all equals the welfare sum that would emerge if everyone had y_e income. Since each $U(y)$ is taken to be concave, i.e., with non-increasing marginal utility, y_e cannot be larger than the mean income μ. Further, it can be shown that the more equal the distribution the closer will y_e be to μ. Atkinson's measure of inequality is:

$$A = 1 - (y_e/\mu) \qquad (2.15)$$

Obviously if income is equally distributed then y_e is equal to μ, and the value of Atkinson's measure will be 0. For any distribution the value of A must lie between 0 and 1.

There are some difficulties with Atkinson's measure which relate to the problems that we discussed in the last chapter. To begin with, a relatively simple problem. Atkinson requires that the function $U(y)$ be concave but not necessarily strictly concave, i.e., $U' > 0$ and $U'' \le 0$.[17] Consider two distributions between two persons with a given total amount of income, say, (0, 10) and (5, 5). If we choose a $U(y)$ function such that it is proportional to y, both will have precisely the same Atkinson measure of inequality. However, it would seem to be rather absurd to describe the two as being equally unequal.

We are confronting two distinct problems here. First, being

[16] For an earlier use of the approach of 'equally distributed equivalent income', see Champernowne (1952), one of whose measures was 'the proportion of total income that is absorbed in compensating for the loss of aggregate satisfaction due to inequality' (p. 610).
[17] Atkinson (1970a), pp. 245–6.

based exclusively on a normative formulation, the measure of inequality has ceased to have the descriptive content that is associated with it in normal usage, and the idea of inequality has become totally dependent on the form of the welfare function. Since under the assumptions both distributions produce the same level of social welfare, they appear to have the same measure of inequality. But, of course, in the sense in which the word inequality is used in normal communication, it has a straightforward descriptive content as well. And it would be odd to describe (0, 10) and (5, 5) as having the same degree of inequality. The second problem concerns the use of the utilitarian framework whereby the values of U of each person are simply added to arrive at the aggregate social welfare. If, instead of that, social welfare were taken to be a strictly concave function of individual utilities—in the line suggested in the last chapter—then these two distributions would not have had the same measure of inequality and indeed (0, 10) would have been more unequal than (5, 5).

Of course, Atkinson himself is careful not to call his $U(y)$ a utility function. Perhaps we can even think of it as some kind of a strictly concave transform of individual utilities, i.e., the component of social welfare corresponding to person i, being itself a strictly concave function of individual utilities. What one would have to do then is to require strict concavity of the $U(y)$ function.

Axioms for additive separability

However, while this takes care of the problem of strong concavity, it is still fairly restrictive to think of social welfare as a sum of individual welfare components. There are in fact two separate issues in utilitarianism, viz., the question of simply adding the individual utilities and the question of additive separability; the former implies the latter but not the other way around.[18] If we take each U as a strictly concave function of individual utilities we are avoiding the simple additive formula of utilitarianism, but we are still sticking to the notion

[18] The group welfare function given by equation (1.4) in Chapter 1 is additively separable, but not utilitarian except for the special case of $\alpha = 1$.

of additive separability. Individual components of social welfare continue to be judged without reference to the welfare components of others, and the social welfare components corresponding to different persons are eventually added up to arrive at an aggregate value of social welfare.

There are various ways of axiomatizing additive separability in the context of income distributional judgements.[19] An interesting version of this is presented by Hamada (1973) in an illuminating paper in which he proceeds in terms of an analogy with behaviour under risk. Though Hamada's model is rather complex, it is worth examining carefully because the requirements of additive separability are brought out sharply by his axiom set.

Consider incomes (taken for convenience to be integers) ranging from 1 to m, which is the maximum possible income. Let r_i be the percentage of population receiving income i, for $i = 1, \ldots, m$. So any income distribution can be represented by $(r_1, \ldots, r_n)$, which will be called vector r. Hamada calls this 'the income distribution vector', but this may cause confusion in our context since r is not a vector of income but of percentages of population. I shall call r a Hamada-vector. Obviously the sum of the components equals 1, i.e., $\Sigma_i r_i = 1$. Consider two Hamada-vectors r and s. Split each into two vectors r^1 and r^2 and s^1 and s^2, respectively, i.e., $r^1 + r^2 = r$, and $s^1 + s^2 = s$. Assume that $\Sigma r^1_i = \Sigma s^1_i$, and therefore $\Sigma_i r^2_i = \Sigma_i s^2_i$. Multiply each of these vectors r^1 and s^1 by a suitable number such that the resultant vectors $\hat{r}^1$ and $\hat{s}^1$ are Hamada-vectors, i.e., $\Sigma_i \hat{r}^1_i = \Sigma_i \hat{s}^1_i = 1$. Do the same to r^2 and s^2 to get Hamada-vectors $\hat{r}^2$ and $\hat{s}^2$. The crucial axiom that Hamada uses (his Assumption 2) requires that if we regard $\hat{r}^1$ to be at least as good as $\hat{s}^1$ and $\hat{r}^2$ at least as good as $\hat{s}^2$, then we must regard r to be at least as good as s. Moreover, if we strictly prefer $\hat{r}^1$ to $\hat{s}^1$ and regard $\hat{r}^2$ to be at least as good as $\hat{s}^2$, then we must strictly prefer r to s.

Is this a reasonable axiom for income distribution? Consider

[19] On the general question of additive separability, see Debreu (1960), Gorman (1968b), Fishburn (1970), and Hammond (1972). See also the controversies between Strotz (1958), (1961), and Fisher and Rothenberg (1961), (1962), and between Harsanyi (1955) and Diamond (1967), on related issues.

two Hamada-vectors $(0, 100, 0, 0)$ and $(50, 0, 0, 50)$. The former, which we shall call $\hat{r}^1$, has absolute equality at income 2 for each, while $\hat{s}^1$ is a two-class society with the 'haves' getting income 4 each while the 'have-nots' make do with only income 1 each. Despite the higher total income of the latter, it is possible that someone impressed by the vision of total equality in $\hat{r}^1$ will swear by Babeuf that it is superior to $\hat{s}^1$. Next, this man is given a choice between $(39, 22, 0, 39)$ and $(40, 20, 0, 40)$, which we shall call respectively r and s. All that vision of equality is now gone, and in this rather mundane choice it is possible that the same man may not really be able to say that he prefers r to s. While r is a bit more of an equal distribution, s does have a bit more of total income, and in going from s to r one person each is taken out from income groups 1 and 4 respectively to be put into income group 2, but that still leaves 39 others at the two poles. Our hero may not, thus, be too impressed with r and may not prefer r to s. But then he has had it with Hamada. We can split r into $(0, 2, 0, 0)$, and $(39, 20, 0, 39)$, which we call r^1 and r^2 respectively, and s into $(1, 0, 0, 1)$ and $(39, 20, 0, 39)$, which—as our hero would have by now guessed—we are going to call s^1 and s^2 respectively. Normalized into Hamada-vectors r^1 and s^1 reveal themselves to be $\hat{r}^1$ and $\hat{s}^1$, and we know that our hero prefers $\hat{r}^1$ to $\hat{s}^1$. He must be indifferent between $\hat{r}^2$ and $\hat{s}^2$, since they are the same. So he must prefer r to s by Hamada's axiom, but no, he doesn't. Our little hero gets into difficulty with additive separability because he is taking an *interdependent* view of income distribution.

In general, if one feels that the social valuation of the welfare of individuals should depend crucially on the levels of welfare (or incomes) of others,[20] this property of the independence of each person's welfare component from the position of others has to be sacrificed. And this requires the use of a less narrow class of social welfare functions. Hamada's axiom system precipitates this independence property in a clear form, but these axioms are both sufficient *and* necessary for additive separability, and the difficulty is in fact quite pervasive.

[20] Cf. Runciman (1966) on 'relative deprivation'.

An alternative measure

Consider social welfare W to be an increasing function of individual income levels:

$$W = W(y_1, \ldots, y_n).$$

A more general normative measure of inequality is the following. Define y_f (the generalized equally distributed equivalent income) as that level of *per capita* income which if shared by all would produce the same W as the value of W generated by the actual distribution of income.

$$y_f = y \mid [W(y, \ldots, y) = W(y_1, \ldots, y_n)] \qquad (2.16)$$

Assuming W to be symmetric and quasi-concave, y_f would be less than or equal to μ for every distribution of income. In this more general form, W need not even be a function of individual utilities, i.e., it need not even be 'individualistic'.

The measure of inequality that we can use with this more general approach will now be given by:

$$N = 1 - (y_f/\mu) \qquad (2.17)$$

It is quite clear that A and N given by (2.15) and (2.17) will be completely equivalent if the welfare function to be used is of the utilitarian form:

$$W = \Sigma_{i=1}^n U(y_i)$$

Positive and normative measures

If we choose a general formula like N for measuring inequality of income distribution we have considerable freedom about specifying the social welfare function. We can then choose whatever we think are the appropriate assumptions about the valuation of the welfare implications of inequality. Any use of N will of course require a specification of the W function. While N avoids the problem of additive separability, it is a totally normative measure—a characteristic that it shares with Dalton's and Atkinson's measures. But, as argued in the last chapter, inequality measures do have positive elements which are difficult to disassociate from the welfare picture.

In some ways the positive measures of inequality discussed earlier can also be viewed as normative measures with specific assumptions about social welfare evaluation. For example, Theil's entropy measure is almost strictly in the form of a utilitarian social welfare function which makes the individual welfare components equal to $x_i \log (1/x_i)$, where x_i is the share of income going to person i. This is a rather peculiar welfare function, and the other measures could be justified in normative terms also with rather special representations of social welfare. I do not intend to go through each of these measures one by one to see what they translate into; some of the welfare aspects of measures like V, C, H and G were discussed earlier. There is no great analytical difficulty in putting all the measures within the same framework and then differentiating between them in terms of their normative assumptions. But this is not a fair thing to do as far as the positive measures are concerned, since the motivation underlying these measures is quite different.

Assumptions of measurability and comparability

The rationale for using a general measure like N is its independence from the narrow framework of additively separable individualistic group welfare functions. The utilitarian welfare function corresponds to the most common example of this narrow framework and, given utilitarianism, A and N would coincide, and D would also generate the same ordering. The relevance of utilitarianism to the problem of normative evaluation of income distributions is, therefore, of significance. While evaluating the merits of utilitarianism in Chapter 1, I made the assumption of cardinal measurability and full interpersonal comparability of individual welfares. It is worth investigating whether a defence of utilitarianism can rest on some other specific measurability and comparability assumptions.

The lack of equity considerations in the utilitarian framework (combined with the case for strict concavity of social welfare on individual welfare levels) was spelt out in Chapter

1. The Weak Equity Axiom was chosen as an illustration of an equity-conscious requirement. There are others one can suggest. But all these requirements—and indeed the very idea of equity—would seem to need comparisons of levels of welfare in addition to comparisons of differences. If one assumed a framework whereby gains and losses of welfare of different individuals could be compared but absolute levels could not be, it would be possible to use the utilitarian approach without being able to apply WEA or other equity considerations of that type. This is because the utilitarian formula declares x to be socially preferred to y if and only if the welfare differences for all the individuals between x and y summed together turn out to be positive, and in defining differences the question of the 'origin' of the utility function is irrelevant. If, for example, a certain constant is added to one person's utility level but not to that of another, it will not affect the utilitarian rule of choice at all. But it can affect the ordering of different persons' welfare levels, thereby rendering the WEA and other equity conditions unusable.

Measurability \ Comparability	Non-comparability	Only units comparable	Only levels comparable	Units and levels both comparable
Ordinal	W_U and W_E both unusable	✕	W_E usable, not W_U	✕
Cardinal	W_U and W_E both unusable	W_U usable, not W_E	W_E usable, not W_U	W_U and W_E both usable

W_U = any 'utilitarian' group welfare function

W_E = any 'equity based' group welfare function (e.g., satisfying WEA)

Table 2.1

Let W_U stand for any 'utilitarian' group welfare function and W_E any group welfare function satisfying WEA or some similar equity condition involving comparisons of relative well-being of different people. In Table 2.1 the consequences of different measurability and comparability assumptions are presented.

It is clear that, should we assume ordinality of individual welfare, there would be no possibility whatsoever of using utilitarianism, while equity conditions like WEA could still be used if ordinal interpersonal comparability were permitted. On the other hand, if we take cardinality of individual welfare and assume that welfare differences are comparable, but not levels, then utilitarianism can be used, but equity conditions like WEA cannot be.

The real conflict comes when both levels and differences are comparable and the assumption of cardinality with full comparability puts utilitarianism in potential conflict with WEA and other equity-conscious rules, since both are usable and they can be mutually inconsistent. The arguments used in the last chapter concentrated on this case and I shall not repeat them. It seems to me clear that a concern for equity must militate against the use of utilitarianism.

Inequality judgements and comparability

In defending utilitarianism, therefore, one's best bet would be in making the rather peculiar assumption that utility differences are comparable but levels are not.[21] In this context it is important to bear in mind the meaning of interpersonal comparisons of utility which was discussed in the last chapter. As we argued there, to judge that $U_i(x) > U_j(y)$ is the same thing as preferring to be individual i in state x rather than individual j in state y. These *as if* comparisons are an essential part of thinking about the normative aspects of the problem of income distribution. It is, of course, certainly the case that these comparisons are subjective, but they are, I would submit, a particularly relevant way of understanding problems of

---

21 Cf. Harsanyi (1955), Diamond (1967), and Sen (1970a), pp. 143–6.

equity. And in so far as putting oneself in the position of another includes the exercise of having his tastes and mental make-up as well, the exercise may indeed be quite complex. But in understanding the interpersonal aspects of social choice involving human well-being, one is inevitably put in the position of having to make these comparisons, though very often this is done implicitly. The advantage of making the comparisons explicitly is to crystalize one's values on the subject, and this is a significant part of any normative recommendation in a situation of conflict between the interests of different individuals or groups.

Formally, if we think of the ordering $\tilde{R}$ over elements like (x, i), i.e., being person i in state x, we can think of interpersonal welfare comparisons as simply numerical reflections of such an ordering $\tilde{R}$. As discussed in Chapter 1:

$$U_i(x) \geq U_i(y) \text{ if and only if}$$

$$(x, i) \, \tilde{R} \, (y, j) \tag{2.18}$$

If the problem is viewed in this way it should be clear that comparisons of levels are *prior* to comparisons of differences. Indeed, the utility functions will have to be first defined in terms of the ranking $\tilde{R}$, which immediately introduces comparability of *levels*, and only if, on top of that, some additional characteristics (like 'independence') are satisfied, would differences be also comparable in an interpersonally usable cardinal scale. It would thus seem that there is rather little scope for defending utilitarianism by making the assumption of comparability of differences of utility with levels being non-comparable.

3

Inequality as a Quasi-Ordering

It can be argued that part of the difficulty in using the measures of inequality presented in the last chapter arises from the fact that they are all 'complete' measures in the sense that every pair of distributions can be compared under each of these measures. If we take any two distributions x and y—each being a vector of incomes—then according to any of these criteria either x will be more unequal than y, or vice versa, or both will be equally unequal. The possibility of non-comparability is not at all entertained. In fact, to each distribution x there is attached—under any of these measures—a real number $I(x)$ which is supposed to represent the degree of inequality of x. While various ways of arriving at $I(x)$ have been presented (e.g., using specific 'positive' measures such as the coefficient of variation, or the standard deviation of logarithms, or the Gini coefficient, or using particular measures of welfare loss such as $(1-D)$, A, or N, after specifying the relevant welfare functions), each way leads to the conversion of the set of distributions x, y, z, etc., into a set of corresponding inequality numbers $I(x)$, $I(y)$, $I(z)$, and so on. And since any two numbers are comparable, i.e., either $I(x) > I(y)$, or $I(x) < I(y)$, or $I(x) = I(y)$, there is never any gap in the picture of comparative inequality.

It is, however, possible to argue that this approach is inherently defective since inequality as a notion does not have any innate property of 'completeness'. In a trivial sense it is, of course, the case that one can define 'inequality' precisely as one likes, and as long as one is explicit and consistent one may think that one is above criticism. But the force of the expression 'inequality', and indeed our interest in the concept, derive from the meaning that is associated with the term, and we are not really free to define it purely arbitrarily. And—as it happens—the concept of inequality has different facets which may point in different directions, and sometimes a total ranking can not be expected to emerge. However, each of the standard measures does yield a complete chain, and arbitrariness is bound to slip into the process of stretching a partial ranking into a complete ordering. It is arguable that each of these measures leads to some rather absurd results precisely because each of them aims at giving a complete-ordering representation to a concept that is essentially one of partial ranking.

Lorenz partial ordering and Atkinson's results

One measure of inequality that does not aim at 'completeness' is the relation of the Lorenz curve of one distribution being strictly inside that of another. In Diagram 3.1 the Lorenz curve x lies wholly inside curve z, and so does curve y as well.

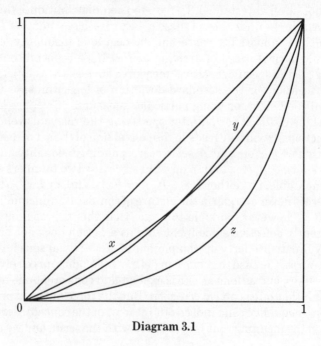

Diagram 3.1

But the curves x and y intersect, so that neither can be said to be more unequal than the other in terms of the Lorenz-curve ranking. Treating L as the relation of being strictly inside,[1] we can say xLz and yLz, but neither xLy, nor yLx.

Are there reasons to believe that the Lorenz-curve ranking catches the essence of the concept of inequality, including its partial nature? Up to a point the answer probably is 'yes', and I propose now to discuss the nature of the Lorenz ranking L in some detail. Later on, however, it will be shown that it does miss some essential features of the concept of inequality.

A remarkable theorem on the Lorenz ranking was proved by Atkinson (1970a), using the normative approach. Suppose that social welfare is the sum of individual U functions which are themselves strictly concave functions of income y_i, i.e., have strictly diminishing marginal utility.

$$W(y) = \Sigma_{i=1}^{n} U(y_i) \qquad (3.1)$$

Let the Lorenz curve of distribution x lie strictly inside that of y, i.e., xLy. The total income is the same for both distributions. Then even without knowing which precise U function is used, we can say that $W(x)$ is greater than $W(y)$, where $W(x)$ and $W(y)$ are the social welfare levels from x and y respectively. Furthermore, the converse is also true, i.e., if we can say that $W(x) > W(y)$ irrespective of which individual U function is chosen (as long as it is strictly concave), then xLy. Thus xLy implies $W(x) > W(y)$ irrespective of the precise concave utility function chosen, and if for all strictly concave utility functions $W(x) > W(y)$, then xLy.

Non-additive formulation

The great attraction of Atkinson's result is that it permits us to rank the inequality levels of distributions in terms of the social welfare levels even without knowing the precise utility function to be chosen. However, since social welfare is taken to be of the utilitarian additive kind, the result may be thought

---

[1] This is taken to mean that xLy if the Lorenz curve of x lies nowhere outside that of y and at some place (at least) it lies strictly inside the latter.

to be somewhat limited. This is not merely because simply adding individual utilities is a very dubious procedure for arriving at social welfare, but also because even the relatively less demanding assumption of additive separability is quite restrictive, as discussed in the preceding chapters.

What will happen if the class of social welfare functions is extended to include non-additive ones as well? We can define social welfare W simply as a symmetric and concave function of individual welfare levels while the individual welfare functions are strictly concave.

$$W = G(U(y_1), \ldots, U(y_n)). \tag{3.2}$$

It stands to reason that Atkinson's results can be extended to this case as well. After all, if xLy leads to $W(x) > W(y)$, even when we are simply adding individual utilities, that tendency must be strengthened if we make W a concave function of individual welfare levels (preserving symmetry), with diminishing relative importance of individual welfare as we consider richer and richer men. This could only *reinforce* the tendency towards $W(x) > W(y)$. Having a concave social welfare function defined on individual welfare levels gives a further egalitarian bias, and this adds to the egalitarian tendencies arising from concave individual welfare functions. It would thus appear that Atkinson's results must be generalizable in terms of a wider class of social welfare functions, of which his additive function will be a special case.

Non-individualistic welfare functions

There is another respect in which it may be useful to view the problem in more general terms than Atkinson has done. It is possible to view social welfare in non-individualistic terms, i.e., not relating social welfare to individual utilities as such. For example, social welfare may be defined directly on the distribution of incomes without going through the intermediary of individual utilities. The distinction has been discussed earlier in Chapter 1. Thus defined we can think of social welfare being given by a function of the following type:

$$W = F(y_1, \ldots, y_n). \tag{3.3}$$

It is clear that, given the individual utility function U, the individualistic form of the function as given by G in the earlier formulation is really a special case of this. That is, even when using a function like F, we can go, if we like, through the intermediary of individual utilities, but we are not obliged to do so.

There are at least two different reasons for preferring a more general function of the kind of F. First, the planner, or the social critic, or the political leader, or whoever is making the distributional judgement, may under certain circumstances feel inclined to bypass individual preferences. There is, perhaps, a 'paternalistic' element in this, but such a thing is frequently present in policy discussions. The argument may relate to considerations of individual 'irrationality', 'short-sightedness', and similar matters, and how seriously we entertain these possibilities remains an open question. Second, sometimes the person making the distributional judgement might simply not have detailed information on individual utility functions. Under these circumstances, even though one might prefer to go via individual utilities, it might not be practically possible to do so. It may be then necessary to deal with the function of the type of F dispensing with the unworkable intermediary.

How convincing these arguments are, I do not wish to debate. The question is not crucial for our purpose, since we lose nothing in our exercises by operating on functions like F rather than G in view of the fact that G is a special case of F. In what follows, therefore, I shall stick to the more general form.

Weakening of concavity

A third respect in which the Atkinson picture can be extended concerns the restrictions to be imposed on the concavity of the welfare functions. It may be recalled that, since social welfare is defined in the Atkinson framework as a sum of strictly concave individual U functions (the same function for all), translated into the F-form the social welfare function F will be strictly concave. However, for incorporating the egalitarian bias for distributional judgements, it is sufficient to consider strict quasi-concavity.[2]

The distinction between concavity and quasi-concavity is a technical one, but is worth commenting on. A concave welfare function E requires that the weighted average of social welfare levels from two income distributions x and y must be less than or equal to the social welfare of the weighted average of the two distributions, using the same weights.

$$tF(x) + (1 - t)F(y) \leq F(tx + (1 - t)y),$$

$$\text{for any } t, 0 < t < 1. \tag{3.4}$$

On the other hand quasi-concavity requires that the *minimum* of the two social welfare levels from x and y respectively should be less than or equal to the social welfare of the weighted average of the two distributions.

$$\text{Min}[F(x), F(y)] \leq F(tx + (1 - t)y),$$

$$\text{for any } t, 0 < t < 1. \tag{3.5}$$

For *strict* quasi-concavity the weak inequality $\leq$ is to be replaced by $<$, so that the social welfare from the weighted average must be strictly larger than the minimum of the two welfare levels from x and y respectively.

Essentially strict quasi-concavity simply requires that the social indifference curves (for more than two persons, social indifference surfaces) must be themselves concave outwards, i.e., be shaped like curved dishes. That this follows immediately from the definition is clear from Diagram 3.2, where the two axes y_1 and y_2 represent the income levels of the two persons. Since x and y lie on the same indifference curve they must have the same level of social welfare, and therefore the minimum social welfare of the two must be the social welfare from either. z is a weighted average of the two distributions x and y, and strict quasi-concavity requires that social welfare

---

[2] In fact, a bit of further weakening is possible, viz., requiring only S-concavity (on this, see Berge, 1963), used in the extension of the Atkinson theorem presented in Dasgupta, Sen and Starrett (1972).

from z be strictly larger than social welfare from x or y. That is, the social indifference curve through z must be higher than the one through x and y. This is guaranteed if and only if the social indifference curves are shaped concave outwards. Strict quasi-concavity means that, as we increase the income level

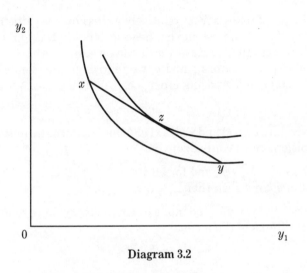

Diagram 3.2

of one given the income levels of the others, less and less relative importance is attached to the income level of the person whose income is going up. This is a strictly egalitarian feature, which is all we need for building equality-consciousness into our social welfare function.

A general result
Considering, therefore, the social welfare function F defined over individual incomes, implying neither the necessity to go through the intermediary of individual utilities, nor the use of the utilitarian additive framework, nor even the necessity of strict concavity, let F be simply any function that is symmetric and strictly quasi-concave. The following theorem is true.

Theorem 3.1

Taking F to be symmetric and strictly quasi-concave, if for two different distributions x and y with the same total of income, yLx, then $F(y) > F(x)$, and if *not* yLx, then for some F, $F(y) \leq F(x)$.

The proof follows from relatively well-known results in the theory of inequalities[3] and has been spelt out in Dasgupta, Sen and Starret (1972).[4] However, it can be easily outlined.

Taking two vectors x and y, we rearrange the elements of each vector in increasing order, i.e.,

$$x_1 \leq \ldots \leq x_n, \text{ and } y_1 \leq \ldots \leq y_n.$$

Hardy, Littlewood and Polya (1984) have shown the following conditions to be equivalent.

(1) $\Sigma_{i=1}^{n} x_i = \Sigma_{i=1}^{n} y_i$, and for all $k \leq n$, $\Sigma_{i=1}^{k} x_i \leq \Sigma_{i=1}^{k} y_i$, with at least one $k < n$ such that $\Sigma_{i=1}^{k} x_i < \Sigma_{i=1}^{k} y_i$.   (3.6)

(2) x can be transformed into y by a non-empty finite sequence of operations of the form:

$$x_i^{\alpha+1} = x_i^{\alpha} + e^{\alpha} \leq x_j^{\alpha},$$

$$x_j^{\alpha+1} = x_j^{\alpha} - e^{\alpha} \geq x_j^{\alpha},$$

$$\text{for } i < j \text{ and } e^{\alpha} > 0, \text{ with } x_k^{\alpha+1} = x_k^{\alpha} \text{ if } k \neq i, j \qquad (3.7)$$

(3) For any strictly concave real-valued function U,

$$\Sigma_{i=1}^{n} U(x_i) < \Sigma_{i=1}^{n} U(y_i). \qquad (3.8)$$

(4) While y is not x, nor a permutation of x, there is a bistochastic matrix Q, such that:

$$y = Qx \qquad (3.9)$$

---

[3] See Hardy, Littlewood and Polya (1934). Through an interesting linguistic coincidence their book is called *Inequalities*, which refers of course to < and ≥ and not to the slums and Marie Antoinette.

[4] In fact in that paper only strict S-concavity is assumed of which a special case is strict quasi-concavity, for a symmetric function. See also Kolm (1969), and Rothschild and Stiglitz (1973).

These standard results in the theory of inequalities are exceedingly handy for Theorem 3.1 as well as for understanding the general properties of Lorenz partial orderings. It can be readily recognized that condition (1) is simply the statement that the Lorenz curve of y lies strictly inside the Lorenz curve of x. Since the Lorenz curve is computed by taking the percentage of income going to the bottom m per cent of the population, and since the total income is the same in the two cases, the set of inequalities simply shows that for some bottom m per cent of the population a lower share of income is yielded by x than by y, and for *all* bottom m per cent of the population, x yields no higher a share of income than y.

This condition of Lorenz-curve ranking is equivalent to condition (2), which can be readily seen as a finite sequence of transformations transferring income from the rich to the poor, taking us from x to y. (This is so *after* interpersonal permutations since the i-th man in x need not be the same as the i-th man in y.) With a quasi-concave and symmetric social welfare function it is not surprising that this sequence of shifts from the rich to the poor must imply that the social welfare from y would be larger than from x.

Condition (3) takes us back to the Atkinson framework and shows that if y has a higher Lorenz curve than x, then any additive social welfare function with the same strictly concave U function for all individuals must yield a higher total social welfare in y than in x. Furthermore, since condition (3) is not only implied by condition (1) but also implies condition (1), it also follows that *not* (1) implies *not* (3). Therefore, Theorem 3.1 must obviously be true, viz., that if not yLx, then for some strictly concave U function, $\Sigma_i U(y_i) \leq \Sigma_i U(x_i)$. This Atkinson case being a special case of a strictly quasi-concave and symmetric F function, it is clear that if not yLx, then for some admissible F, $F(y) \leq F(x)$. So only the first part of the theorem remains to be proved.

Condition (4) is the only one with some technical content. A bistochastic matrix is a square matrix, all of the entries of which are non-negative and each of the rows and columns of which adds up to one. Multiplying a vector x by a bistochastic matrix Q converts it into another vector y, which also has the same sum of its elements taken together. A special case of a bistochastic matrix is a permutation matrix which simply re-orders the elements of a vector, i.e., permutes them. It is well known that any bistochastic matrix of order n is some convex combination of the set of permutation matrices of order n.[5] With P^s being any permutation matrix we can obtain Q from the set of such permutation matrices thus:

$$Q = \Sigma_s a_s P^s, \ \Sigma_s a_s = 1, \text{ and each } a_s \geq 0. \qquad (3.10)$$

Therefore, y lies inside the convex hull of the permutations of x, i.e., in the convex hull of the set $(P^s x)$ for all s. But y is not an extreme point of this convex hull. So y can be obtained as a convex combination of the set of permutations of x, which themselves are socially indifferent to each other, by virtue of symmetry. It follows immediately that for any strictly quasi-concave F satisfying symmetry:[6]

$$F(y) > F(x). \qquad (3.11)$$

Intuitive explanation

The last result indicates that if y has a higher Lorenz curve than x, then it must yield a higher social welfare than x for all symmetric, strictly quasi-concave group welfare functions. The last part of the proof, which is the only technical bit, may, however, be understood intuitively quite easily by considering the three person case. Diagram 3.3 presents such a picture with the three axes representing the income of the three individuals. Viewing the picture as a three-dimensional one (some exercise of imagination is certainly called for here), the shaded triangle ABC can be seen to be a portion of a plane caught between the three axes and lying slanted in this three-

---

[5] See Berge (1963), p. 182, on the 'Theorem of Birkhoff and von Neumann'.

[6] Strict S-concavity is defined in the following way: F is strictly S-concave if and only if for all bistochastic matrices Q, $F(Qx) > F(x)$, if Qx is not x, nor a permutation of it. (3.11) follows directly from (3.9) given strict S-concavity and strict quasi-concavity is not really necessary. Cf. Dasgupta, Sen and Starrett (1972). Note, however, that Qx can be a permutation of x without Q being a permutation matrix.

dimensional diagram with the characteristic that for any point on it the sum of its coordinates equals unity (i.e., it is the so-called 'unit simplex').

Consider, now, this triangle ABC on its own (Diagram 3.4). The distribution x will be a point on this triangle, assuming that the total income to be distributed is unity, which is just

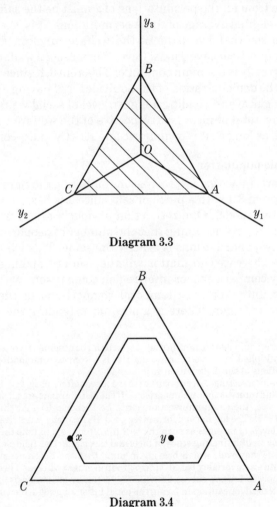

Diagram 3.3

Diagram 3.4

a matter of choosing units. It is clear that in the three-dimensional case there are six distributions of income which are exact interpersonal permutations of the distribution x, and they are represented as the six corner points of the hexagon drawn through x. The point y will lie inside this hexagon.[7] Thanks to the assumption of symmetry, social welfare from all the permutations of x must be the same, and y is a weighted average of these permutations. It is, therefore, easy to see that by virtue of the welfare function F being strictly quasi-concave y must have a higher social welfare than x. This really is the main content of Theorem 3.1, since it completes the demonstration of the equivalence of having a higher Lorenz curve and yielding a higher level of social welfare, for the same total of income, irrespective of the welfare function chosen, as long as it is symmetric and strictly quasi-concave.[8]

Variable population

There are, however, several reasons for taking the significance of Theorem 3.1 with a pinch of salt, since it is based on a very restrictive model. One restriction obviously arises from the fact that we are assuming that the number of people involved in the two distributions is exactly the same. This will hardly ever be the case, no matter whether we are making inter-country comparisons, or inter-region comparisons within the same country, or inter-temporal comparisons in the same country or region. There is a need for extending the results

[7] This is equivalent to noting that y, which can be obtained from x through being multiplied by a bistochastic matrix, is a convex combination of the permutations of the distribution x.

[8] Non-intersecting Lorenz curves have been often observed in inter-country and inter-temporal comparisons. If the distributions are all of the log-normal type, then non-intersection must be the case (see Aitchison and Brown, 1957). The log-normal form gives good fits for many countries, though for high levels of incomes as such the best fits often seem to take the Pareto-form. (For an illuminating study of facts and theories in this field, see Lydall, 1966.) It is, however, worth bearing in mind that the Lorenz curves from actual data are invariably based on size-group averages whereas Theorem 3.1 would apply to Lorenz curves drawn on a person-by-person basis. There is, therefore, need for caution in facing the usual Lorenz curves armed only with Theorem 3.1.

presented in Theorem 3.1 to the case of variable population. This, as it happens, is not a very difficult thing to do *provided* we accept a relatively unobjectionable assumption.

Consider two countries with exactly identical populations and income distributions. Obviously they both must have the same level of social welfare and the same *per capita* welfare. If we now consider the two countries together rather than separately it stands to reason that they must continue to have the same *per capita* welfare, since nothing has changed except that the two are now considered together rather than separately. Generalizing this reasoning, we can put forward an axiom in the following form, denoting the social welfare function for a community with n people as:

$$W = F^n(y_1, \ldots, y_n). \qquad (3.12)$$

The Symmetry Axiom for Population (SAP): For any income distribution $(y_1, \ldots, y_n)$, consider the distribution x over nr people such that $x_i = x_{2i} = \ldots = x_{ri} = y_i$ for $1 \le i \le n$, with r any integer. Then

$$F^{nr}(x) = rF^n(y). \qquad (3.13)$$

What this axiom demands is simply that if r countries with the same population and identical income distributions are considered together, then the mean welfare of the whole must be equal to the mean welfare of each part. This would seem to be an undemanding axiom.

Given this axiom, however, the Lorenz-curve result can be extended to the case of variable population.[9]

Theorem 3.2

Let y^1 and y^2 be two income distributions with the same mean income over population sizes n^1 and n^2 respectively and let $y^1 L y^2$. Each F^n is symmetric and strictly quasi-concave and satisfies SAP. Then $(F^{n^1}/n^1) > (F^{n^2}/n^2)$. And if *not* $y^1 L y^2$, then for some symmetric and strictly quasi-concave welfare functions satisfying SAP, $(F^{n^1}/n^1) \le (F^{n^2}/n^2)$.

[9] Strict quasi-concavity can be replaced by strict S-concavity; see Dasgupta, Sen and Starrett (1972).

The proof of this theorem is not difficult to devise. Consider a country with a population size of n^1n^2. Let it have an income distribution exactly like y^1 with each member in that distribution being replicated n^2 times. Consider a second hypothetical country with n^1n^2 population size with an identical distribution to that of y^2, each member of the latter being replicated n^1 times. Obviously hypothetical country 1 and hypothetical country 2 both have exactly the same Lorenz curves as y^1 and y^2 respectively,[10] and if y^1Ly^2, then hypothetical country 1 also has a higher Lorenz curve than hypothetical country 2. Both the hypothetical countries have, of course, the same population and the same total income. Therefore, by Theorem 3.1 the social welfare of hypothetical country 1 would be larger than the social welfare of hypothetical country 2. Now, we know from the symmetry axiom that the mean welfare of hypothetical country 1 must be the same as the mean welfare of actual country 1 and the mean welfare of the hypothetical country 2 must equal the mean welfare of actual country 2. Thus country 1 must have a higher mean welfare than country 2, which proves the first part of the theorem. The second part of the theorem follows from a similar construction, again using Theorem 3.1.

Mean income variations

This extension takes care of the problem of variable population. Lorenz-curve rankings seem to make good sense in comparisons of mean welfare even when the population size is a variable. However, the problem of variable mean income still remains. It would, of course, be possible to tackle the problem in a similar way to that of variable population by making a corresponding axiom. However, while SAP is, I think, quite defendable, the corresponding symmetry axiom for income will not be, since welfare may not be homogeneous with respect to the size of income. It is obvious that any possibility of making distributional judgements independently of the size

[10] There is, in fact, some ambiguity as to how we define Lorenz curves in the discrete case. For our purpose we can plot the Lorenz points for each discrete number of people and connect them by straight lines.

of income will make sense only if the relative ordering of welfare levels of distributions were strictly neutral to the operation of multiplying everybody's income by a given number. We might not, however, wish to make this assumption, since our judgement about social welfare may not be scale-independent in this sense. Thus, the problem of extending the Lorenz partial ordering to cases of variable mean income is quite a serious one, and this—naturally enough—restricts severely the usefulness of this approach.

Since the art of practical economics often involves compromises it may be necessary sometimes to make Lorenz-curve comparisons for countries with different mean income, but it must be borne in mind that in reading welfare implications in such comparisons in the light of Theorems 3.1 and 3.2, one would have to bring in some symmetry axiom for income, which may not be particularly justifiable.

Non-compulsive judgements

This question relates generally to the case for viewing the usual income-distributional comparisons as 'non-compulsive judgements'. A non-compulsive judgement indicates the belief that there is a reason for acting in a certain way and that there is a *prima facie* case for that action. But it is not a compelling recommendation, and contrary reasons could be produced.[11] The fact that one distribution has a higher Lorenz curve than another can be taken to constitute a *prima facie* case that it is a better distribution from the welfare point of view. Of course, contrary arguments may exist, and variation of mean income may well be one such. But it seems reasonable to demand that someone rejecting the Lorenz results on these grounds must specify *how* he expects the differences in mean income to affect the distributional judgements from the welfare point of view. While the Lorenz ranking is not in itself compelling, the onus of demonstration may well be thought to lie on the person wishing to reject this ranking on other grounds.

[11] The distinction between 'compulsive' and 'non-compulsive' judgements is presented and analysed in Sen (1967b).

Descriptive content

It should also be said in defence of the Lorenz judgements that the purely descriptive content of the Lorenz partial ordering is also not negligible. First of all, for the simple case of the same population size and the same total income, it may be recalled that the equivalence of conditions (1) and (2) outlined earlier means that y's having a higher Lorenz curve than x implies that one can transform x into y by shifting income from the rich to the poor. This is an unambiguous sense in which income distribution must be thought to be more equal in y than in x. Even without bringing in anything about welfare, a transfer from the rich to the poor must mean descriptively that the level of inequality has gone down, and thus a higher Lorenz curve must mean less inequality even in the purely descriptive sense.

The same picture is brought out also by Diagram 3.4 where y can be seen to be lying strictly *inside* the symmetric hexagon on which x lies. This is a purely descriptive feature, and while it has normative implications, the statement that y is less unequal than x can also be viewed as a factual one in terms of definitions corresponding closely to the normal usage of the term inequality.

The same feature survives the case of variable population as well, since everything can be done in terms of percentages of population, and once again the statement that y is less unequal than x would seem to be meaningful and acceptable. Stretching this picture to the case of variable mean income may not be too objectionable from the positive, as opposed to the normative, point of view. The triangle in Diagram 3.4 takes the total income as 1, and if two communities with different mean income are compared, we can still think of y being a less unequal distribution than x in *relative* terms. The fact that our welfare judgements may crucially depend on the size of income per head does not affect this picture since here we are concerned not with the normative features but with purely descriptive ones in relative terms. We could, of course, still say that while y represents a more equal relative distribution than

x from a descriptive point of view, the relative impact on welfare of the inequality level, low as it is, of y may still be larger than the consequence of the relatively higher level of inequality of x, because of differences of mean income. We would then be dissociating the measure of inequality from the judgement of its welfare implications.

As I have tried to outline earlier, income-distributional measures have these two distinct but interlinked features. Even in normal communication both the normative and positive aspects can be observed in the use of the concept of inequality. While the Lorenz relation catches both aspects, it seems to take a firmer grip of the descriptive aspect than it does of the normative, especially when the mean income level varies.

Inequality quasi-orderings

The Lorenz dominance relation yields a partial strict ordering. I had begun this chapter by arguing that there is a good general case for expressing our judgements on inequality in the form of quasi-orderings. What is the precise difference between a partial strict ordering and a quasi-ordering? The answer is: Not very much, but a quasi-ordering is 'reflexive', which a strict partial ordering is not, and the latter is 'asymmetric', which a quasi-ordering is not. Stripped of the technicalities this means roughly that a quasi-ordering is a relation like 'at least as unequal as', whereas a strict partial ordering is one like 'more unequal than'.[12] It is, of course, obvious that a slight extension will permit us to get a quasi-ordering out of the Lorenz partial ordering. What is perhaps more interesting is the fact that in the process the conditions imposed on the form of the group welfare function can also be relaxed further.

Being concerned with the weak inequality relation 'at least as unequal as', we look now for the welfare ranking 'being at

[12] Note that the former is 'reflexive' in the sense that any distribution x is, of course, 'at least as unequal' as itself, and not 'asymmetric' in the sense that x being 'at least as unequal' as y does not preclude the possibility that y may also be 'at least as unequal' as x, since the two distributions may be judged to be equally unequal. For 'more unequal than', the opposite holds.

least as great as' and not for the relation 'greater than', i.e., we are interested in conditions that yield $F(y) \geq F(x)$ and not also $F(y) > F(x)$. This permits an immediate extension of the permitted class of group welfare functions from strictly quasi-concave ones to those simply quasi-concave (irrespective of whether they are strictly so or not).

Let yRx stand for either yLx, i.e., y being Lorenz-superior to x, or x and y being identical distributions. The latter we include to permit reflexivity of R, but we do not of course rule out the possibility that two distributions may be judged to be 'equally unequal' despite not being identical distributions.

Theorem 3.3

R is a quasi-ordering and furthermore yRx implies that:

for all symmetric and quasi-concave F: $F(y) > F(x)$.

It is obvious that R is reflexive and transitive. The rest of the proof follows from the weak set of equivalent inequalities corresponding to (1)–(4) used in proving Theorem 3.1 above,[13] and it need not be spelt out here.[14]

The judgement that R provides on inequality seems to be very broad-based indeed. From the purely descriptive point of view if yRx then y can be obtained from x either by permuting incomes between the individuals, or by a combination of that with a sequence of transfers of income from the richer to the poorer. Its normative justification is also based on very mild assumptions. Quasi-concavity will be satisfied if a transfer from the richer to the poorer *does not worsen* the welfare level (whether or not it improves it). This follows from the *absence* of positively anti-egalitarian values. And, of course, the other attractive features of Theorems 3.1 and 3.2 are retained, viz., there is no need to assume the additive framework of utilitarianism, or even additive separability, or for that matter an 'individualistic' group welfare function.

[13] In fact, the original versions used in Hardy, Littlewood and Polya (1984) were the weak ones.
[14] Note also that Theorem 3.3 can be extended to the case of S-concavity instead of requiring quasi-concavity. Further, *strict* S-concavity is no longer needed. S-concavity is defined as $F(Qx) \geq F(x)$ for all bistochastic matrices Q.

But there are gaps in this picture of normative solidarity. First, the idea that social welfare is a function of money incomes only is itself a very restrictive one. Consider the same distribution of money incomes, with a change in prices. Even if the price index, defined as some kind of a weighted average, remains the same, still the effective distribution of purchasing power can now be different, since price changes have a different impact on different people in view of the variation (i) in the tastes and (ii) in the money income levels of different persons. The former is obvious enough, but the latter is also easily seen. Even when everyone has the same tastes, if the price of food goes up a poorer person's welfare level goes down relatively more, since food represents a bigger part of his budget.

Second, variations of income may effectively limit the applicability of Theorems 3.1–3.3, for reasons that have already been spelt out. How should comparisons be made when the mean income level varies?

Finally, there is the question of the appropriateness of the symmetry property of the group welfare function and the assumption of equal needs. In Chapter 1 the relaxation of this assumption was shown to have crucial effects, but in the theorems covered in this chapter we have stuck to this axiom like a leech. I shall postpone further discussion of this last problem until the next chapter, when the concepts of deserts and needs will both be reviewed. But I intend to go into the first two problems now.

Price variations and inequality

The complexity caused by price variations may be taken up first. This is undoubtedly an important question, but we must try to avoid being mesmerized by its nihilistic pretensions. Indeed, the possibility of price variations, which is virtually always present in any comparison of two different situations, has frequently been used to rule out welfare judgements altogether and has thus been an effective means of terrorizing the egalitarian. But the analytical picture is, in fact, by no means so clear.

Consider an observed situation with the vector of money incomes y and the vector of prices p. Each pair (y_i, p) gives us the money income of person i as well as the prices at which he has spent that income. Evidently his welfare can be thought to be given by a utility function based on (y_i, p), in the absence of externalities, and more generally by a function of (y, p) even when person i is affected by the well-being and consumption of others. Social welfare can be defined over (y, p) either directly or through the intermediary of individual welfare levels.[15]

More generally, social welfare judgements can take the form of a ranking relation B defined over the set of pairs of (y, p). If (y, p^1) is regarded as at least as good as (x, p^2), we can write:

$$(y, p^1) B (x, p^2). \tag{3.14}$$

The relation B can be expected to be reflexive and transitive, i.e., to be a quasi-ordering. If B is also complete then the social welfare ranking would be an ordering. Given that, and with some additional assumptions,[16] we can define social welfare W as a real-valued function $E(y, p)$.

$$W = E(y, p). \tag{3.15}$$

If welfare judgements are not easy to make given the complexity of price comparisons, B may not be complete. It is one thing to say that we *can* make social welfare judgements based on y and p; it is quite another to say that we shall find it easy to formulate such judgements. Frequently they will be particularly difficult to make.[17] In some cases the contrast may

---

[15] Formally, each (y, p) is an element of the Cartesian product of the set of n-vectors of money incomes and the set of k-vectors of prices, when there are n people and k commodities.

[16] Cf. Chapter 1, footnote 7.

[17] For a penetrating analysis of the general question of distributional judgements in a many-commodity world, see Fisher (1956) and Kenen and Fisher (1957). Note that the Fisher–Kenen analysis proceeds on the basis of $k \times n$ distribution matrices in which there are k goods and n people (with no direct use of information on prices), whereas the system used here relates such judgements to the money income n-vector and the price k-vector (without information on the interpersonal distribution of the physical commodities).

be so glaring that the ranking may be extremely easy, but this may not be so in other cases. It may be, therefore, advisable to take B to be a quasi-ordering rather than assume it to be an ordering.

A very serious difficulty lies in the fact that frequently welfare judgements may have to be made without any clear knowledge of the relevant price vectors. Typically, distributional judgements are made with only a modicum of knowledge about the prices that are ruling. Would it be correct to assume that such judgements made in the absence of precise information on prices must be completely arbitrary? This need not be the case at all. Often we may have a reasonably clear idea of the range within which the vector of prices may lie even though we may not know the exact price vector, and we may commit ourselves only to those judgements which would hold for *all* price vectors within that range.

Formally, let Δ be the set of possible price vectors and define the binary relation J as:

$$yJx \text{ if and only if}$$
$$[\text{For all } p^1, p^2 \text{ in } \Delta: (y, p^1) \, B \, (x, p^2)] \qquad (3.16)$$

The following result is of some interest.

Theorem 3.4

If B is transitive, then so is J. If B is an ordering, then Δ being a unit set is sufficient but not necessary for J to be an ordering.

The result is quite straightforward. If for all p^1, p^2, p^3, p^4 in Δ, $(y, p^1)B(x, p^2)$ and $(z, p^3)B(y, p^4)$, then obviously for all p^1, p^2, in Δ, $(z, p^1)B(x, p^2)$, given the transitivity of B. So J is also transitive. If Δ is a unit set, then J must also be reflexive. Further, since B is complete if it is an ordering, clearly with only one p in Δ, J must be complete too. On the other hand, let there be only there alternatives (x, y, z), and say $(y, p^1)B(x, p^2)$ and $(z, p^3)B(y, p^4)$, for all p^1, p^2, p^3, p^4 in Δ. Thus, (z, y, x) is a J-ordering despite Δ not being necessarily a unit set.

Note that J is not necessarily reflexive and therefore may not be a quasi-ordering. Two identical money-income distributions may indeed not be socially as good as each other if prices differ. In fact, two identical distributions of money income would typically be ranked differently depending on the prices ruling in each case, and we may not be able to say much without knowing the prices. On the other hand, if one distribution involves a much higher extent of concentration than another, it may be possible to be sure that its welfare value would be less than that of the other within a fairly wide range of price variations.

The transitivity of J is an interesting property. If we define B to be asymmetric, as we well might, then J would be a 'strict partial ordering'. How extensive J would be would, of course, depend on the range defined by the set Δ of possible price vectors as well as on the relation B. The more complete the price information and the more extensive B is, the more extensive would J tend to be. What is most important to recognize is that the choice is not of all-or-none type, and some systematic welfare judgements on money-income distributions with incomplete price information may be still possible.

The real trouble lies with defining the *same* level of real income, separating out the problem of distribution from that of the size of the total income. This is an old problem and has been much discussed in the literature of welfare economics.[18] If one considers distributions of the same level of *money* income with different prices, it is tempting to distinguish between two elements in the welfare variation, viz., (i) that due to differences in the aggregate real income, and (ii) that due to differences in the distribution of that income. There is, however, no uniquely appropriate method of doing the split up, and the arbitrariness of the pure distribution problem is just the 'dual' of the much-studied arbitrariness of real-income comparisons.

Nevertheless, for any *given* definition of real income, we can apply distributional judgements within that framework. If x and y are two money-income distributions that are judged to

---

[18] See Samuelson (1950b).

have the same total real income, then yBx can be identified as reflecting that y is a better distribution than x. If we are uncertain of the price vector, we can relate distributional judgements to the strict partial ordering J.[19] Any such judgement would be conditional on a particular method of real-income comparison, but it can scarcely be otherwise. The problem of distribution of a 'given' real income clearly must depend on the definition of real income.

Variations of mean income

I turn now to the problem of the variation of mean income. The usual descriptive measures of inequality—such as the range E, the relative mean deviation M, the coefficient of variation C, the Gini coefficient G, or the standard deviation of logarithms H—all concentrate on *relative* variations of income. Among the descriptive measures studied in Chapter 2 only the variance V was not mean-independent. However, the normative measures presented in that chapter all operated on the *same* mean income, and measures D, A, and N, were all cast in this narrow framework. Can these measures be made mean-independent? And should we wish to do this?

Because of its dependence on the convention of utility scaling, Dalton's measure D may be thought to be inferior to Atkinson's A. The measure N is, however, more general, since it is not based on the restrictive assumption of additive separability. But, for the same reason, its general properties are more difficult to specify than those of A. In fact, the condition that the measure N be independent of mean income and be dependent only on the *relative* distribution of income does not yield any very obvious pattern, whereas the same condition when imposed on the additive structure of Atkinson's measure A with identical individual U functions immediately

---

[19] It might be wondered whether there is not a contradiction in assuming that prices are known for determining whether the real income is the same but not for using welfare judgements B. But the prices relevant for the two exercises are not the same, and real-income comparisons are partly a matter of pure convention whereas welfare judgements require very specific price information for each year.

yields a straightforward pattern for the welfare function. It is easily checked that A will be independent of the level of mean income if and only if the individual utility function U takes the following form:[20]

$$U(y_i) = k_1 + (k_2/\alpha)(y_i)^\alpha, \qquad (3.17)$$

where k_1 and k_2 are two constants, and the elasticity α must be less than or equal to 1 for the concavity of the U function. This constant elasticity form is obligatory if social welfare takes the utilitarian shape of being additive on identical U functions. While the case is rather restrictive, as Atkinson (1970a) notes, the group welfare function is still capable of varying from the one extreme of being linear on individual incomes, thereby ranking distributions solely according to total income (for $\alpha = 1$), to the other extreme of ranking distributions solely according to the minimum income level $\min_i\{y_i\}$ and ignoring the other incomes (for $\alpha = -\infty$).[21]

Despite this pleasing robustness, the fact remains that (3.17) is a highly restrictive form. It also corresponds to the very limited case of the additive group welfare function, the weakness of which I have tried to discuss earlier. What is really restrictive, however, is the condition itself, viz., the requirement that the inequality measure should be independent of the mean income level. One can argue that for low income levels the inequality measures should take much sharper note of the same degree of *relative* variation on the ground that inequality pinches most when people are closer to starvation. On the other side, I have heard it argued that equality is a 'luxury' that only a rich economy can 'afford', and while I cannot pretend to understand fully this point of view, I am impressed by the number of people who seem to be prepared to advocate such a position. Though the considerations run in opposite directions, that in itself is no justification for making

[20] See Atkinson (1970a), p. 261. This result is, as Atkinson notes, essentially a reinterpretation of a result derived by Pratt (1964) and Arrow (1965) for the theory of risk bearing. For the case of $\alpha = 0$, we have $U(y_i) = \log_e(y_i)$.

[21] The latter corresponds to the criterion of justice proposed by Rawls (1971).

the inequality measure *independent* of the level of mean income.

We are caught in a bit of a dilemma here. Making inequality measures independent of the mean income seems objectionable, but no alternative general assumption about the relationship of the mean income to these measures seems to be acceptable to all. Also, quantitative specification of the extent of the dependence on the mean income would bring in division even within a camp that may be united on the *direction* of the dependence and *only* on the direction.

Description and non-compulsive judgements

As discussed earlier, a possible alternative is to use mean-independent measures as *prima facie* but tentative measures of inequality, but to supplement them with other considerations that relate systematically to the level of mean income. This supplementation can be done in one of two ways. First, it may be possible to argue that while distribution x is more unequal than y according to some mean-independent measure, since y involves a lower mean income than x, maybe y represents more 'real' inequality. A second alternative is to be unambitious from the normative point of view as far as the measure itself is concerned, and to confine oneself to mean-independent inequality measures with a frank recognition that such measures may not have a high normative content. One can then argue that x may be more equal than y in the only sense in which the measurement is being made, but the relative welfare *impact* of inequality could be greater for y than for x since y corresponds to a lower mean income. The difference between this position and the first lies precisely in the extent to which inequality measures are themselves expected to reflect the relevant normative values rather than being positive measures in terms of which normative judgements may be conveniently expressed. I have discussed this distinction earlier.

Of course, even in this limited form a measure of relative inequality derived from some welfare considerations (though being independent of mean income) would, naturally, have a normative content. This would reflect a 'non-compulsive' judgement implying *prima facie* evaluation of welfare which should be interpreted as entailing a recommendation unless other arguments can be summoned against such a recommendation. In having this qualified normative aspect combined with descriptive features, such a measure seems also to be reasonably close to the non-technical concept of inequality as employed in normal communication.

Intersection quasi-orderings

Turning now to the descriptive side, it is significant to note that the alternative indicators tend to involve some conflicts and some corroboration of each other. We can sort out the picture of partial correspondence by taking the intersection of the set of chosen measures. When there are k criteria, C^j for $j = 1, \ldots, k$, each yielding a complete ordering, we can define their intersection Q as:

$$yQx \text{ if and only if}$$
$$[\text{For all } j = 1, \ldots, k: yC^jx]. \qquad (3.18)$$

Theorem 3.5

Q is a quasi-ordering.

This is readily checked, since the reflexivity of Q is not in doubt given the reflexivity of each C^j, and transitivity of Q follows from the fact that if zC^jy and yC^jx for all j, then zC^jx for all j, given the transitivity property of each C^j.

Such an intersection quasi-ordering has the advantage of avoiding exclusive reliance on any particular measure and on the complete ordering generated by it which reflects its arbitrary features. On the other hand, Q might be rather severely incomplete and precisely how incomplete would depend on the extent to which the various C^j measures conflict. Some comparisons would yield definite results while others would not. The point may be illustrated by the quasi-ordering of income distributions in five countries, viz., the U.K., the U.S.A., Mexico, Ceylon, and India shown in Diagram 3.5, based on three measures, viz., the Gini coefficient, the coefficient of variation, and the standard deviation of logarithms.[22]

---

[22] The data are taken from Table 1 in Atkinson (1970a).

The U.K., the U.S.A., Ceylon and Mexico can be put on a simple ordering in terms of Q, but India brings out the incompleteness in being non-comparable with the U.S.A. and Ceylon, though it has a more unequal distribution than the U.K. and a less unequal one than Mexico. In particular, India seems to have a lower Gini coefficient and a lower standard deviation

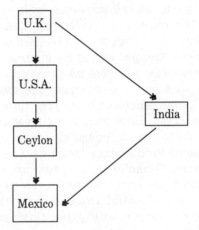

Quasi-ordering based on C, G, and H

Diagram 3.5

of logarithms than Ceylon but a higher coefficient of variation, and similarly it has a higher Gini coefficient and a higher coefficient of variation than the U.S.A. but a lower standard deviation of logarithms.

Would Q be more extensive than the Lorenz relation L or the weak version of it, R? Or less so? Either is possible. Obviously the three criteria C, G, and H together cannot guarantee that the Lorenz relation will go the same way. This is obvious since the Lorenz relation requires that n inequalities be satisfied when n is the population size.[23] The three rankings C, G and H will yield only three inequalities, and that can hardly cover it.

On the other hand, the Lorenz relation cannot subsume the

[23] See inequalities (3.6) in the proof of Theorem 3.1.

set of three descriptive criteria, since they do not all have the required concavity properties. The coefficient of variation C is concave, but the Gini coefficient G is not strictly quasi-concave, but just quasi-concave. G does not, however, conflict with the Lorenz relation, but the standard deviation of logarithms H does, as can be readily checked.[24] Q based on the intersection of C, G, and H thus neither subsumes the Lorenz relation, nor is it subsumed by it.

Obviously Q has a strong element of arbitrariness, since the choice of the set of C^j to be used would reflect some kind of rule of thumb, but as an approach that of an intersection quasi-ordering opens up a new set of possibilities. In eschewing exclusive reliance on any one measure and on the complete ordering generated by it, Q restrains the arbitrariness of such measures. Since each of the measures chosen for deriving Q has some merit though also some deficiencies which are not shared by the other measures (see Chapter 2), their intersection Q combines many relevant features and helps to sort out the relatively less controversial rankings from those that are more doubtful. In fact even the three measures mentioned yield a quasi-ordering that turns out to have quite a bit of cutting power; it is a matter of some empirical interest—though not of any great analytical significance—that the Q generated by the intersection of these three criteria for the twelve countries for which Atkinson (1970a) presents data remains *completely unchanged* when the set of C^j is expanded to include Atkinson's three normative measures ('equally distributed equivalent') as well.[25]

[24] The welfare function corresponding to H is not strictly S-concave, which is the necessary and sufficient condition for the Lorenz ranking to be a sub-relation of H. On the other hand, G *is* strictly S-concave.

[25] However, the quasi-ordering Q generated by the three normative measures shrinks when Q is made to take note of the three descriptive measures as well. That is, the intersection of the descriptive measures is a sub-relation of the intersection of Atkinson's three normative measures, but not vice versa. Note, however, that the three normative measures the values of which are given by Atkinson are all of the particular form of (3.17) and differ only in values of α. If a wider class of normative measures are considered, their intersection would tend to be smaller.

A less uptight framework

I have tried to argue in favour of weakening the inequality measures in more than one sense. First of all, the mixture of partly descriptive and partly normative considerations weakens the purity of an inequality index. A purely descriptive measure lacks motivation, while a purely normative measure seems to miss important features of the concept of inequality. Some alternative ways of combining normative and descriptive considerations have been considered.

Second, even as normative indicators the inequality measures are best viewed as 'non-compulsive' judgements recommending something but not with absolutely compelling force. This has implications in terms of the treatment of inequality rankings as *prima facie* arguments and permitting situation-specific considerations to be brought into the evaluation if such supplementation is needed.

Third, a number of reasons for taking inequality rankings as quasi-orderings rather than as complete orderings have been suggested. One reason is the uncertainty about the welfare function to be used in the normative approach. Another is uncertainty about prices and real income, as well as the general difficulties of forming distributional judgements in a multi-commodity world. If we wish to incorporate dependence on the mean income into the measure itself (this is not, of course, the only way of handling the problem), then that too would push us in the direction of incompleteness, requiring abstention from ranking inequalities when the mean income differences are large and significant.

Even the descriptive measures, each of which yields a complete ordering, point collectively towards incomplete quasi-orderings. The intersection of these rankings tends to separate out relatively simpler comparisons from the more complex ones.

The very notion of inequality seems to have this quasi-ordering framework. The concept is not geared to making fine distinctions and comes into its own with sharper contrasts. This is also suggested by the relation—discussed earlier—

between the idea of inequality and the inclination to protest and rebel.

Treating inequality as a quasi-ordering has much to be commended from the normative as well as the descriptive point of view. I would suspect that the empirical work in this field would gain in meaningfulness if the all-or-none approach of traditional theory were abandoned and the arbitrariness of the usual complete orderings avoided. The glib man who can make inequality comparisons perfectly between every pair of distributions and the wise guy who finds all such comparisons 'arbitrary' both seem to miss essential aspects of the concept of inequality.

4

Work, Needs, and Inequality

In this last chapter I should like to go into some rather broader issues concerning economic inequality. Inequality is sometimes viewed in relative terms, viz., as a departure from some notion of appropriate distribution. There are essentially two rival notions of the 'right' distribution of income, based respectively on needs and desert. It is easy to recognize the contrast between arguments of the kind: 'A should get more income than B since his needs are greater', and those of the type: 'A should get more income than B since he has done more work and deserves a higher reward'. Inequality can, therefore, be viewed not merely as a measure of dispersion but also as a measure of the difference between the actual distribution of income on the one hand and *either* (i) distribution according to needs, *or* (ii) that according to some concept of desert. I shall discuss each of the two approaches in turn.

Needs and welfare
The concept of relative needs is, of course, closely connected with the pattern of individual welfare functions and *the* type of interpersonal considerations that were discussed in Chapter 1. However, there are some pitfalls in doing the translation from needs to welfare. It might, for example, appear that a more needy man should get more out of a given income and, therefore, his welfare from a given level of income y should be *higher* than that of a person with less needs. But a little reflection should make clear that the inequality should point the other way. Clearly one would prefer to be a person with income y and less needs (e.g., normal health) than a person with in-

come y and more needs (e.g., a malfunctioning kidney); and in terms of the framework of interpersonal comparisons outlined in Chapter 1 (viz., in terms of $\bar{R}$), this means that the first person would have a higher level of welfare than the second.

The Weak Equity Axiom and other equity considerations discussed in Chapter 1 would recommend a higher share of total income going to a person with a uniformly lower welfare function, i.e., to a person with greater needs. It might be considered how such needs could be determined and whether, in practice, greater needs could really serve as a basis for receiving a higher share of income. Can one really identify greater needs in any convincing way?

The problem of assessing relative needs is indeed a very serious one, and there can be hard problems of decidability. There is, however, the danger of falling prey to a kind of nihilism that characterizes much of normative economics and which we have been battling against in other contexts in the earlier chapters. This takes the form of noting, quite legitimately, a difficulty of some sort, and then constructing from it a picture of total disaster. Sure enough, greater needs are hard to identify sometimes, but they are quite clear at other times. For anyone making the judgement, the test is to ask oneself: Would you prefer to be person A with income y or person B with income y? An illustration may make the point clearer.

National Health service versus medical insurances

The rationale of medical facilities as a public service has been the subject of some debate in economics. The failure of the market to provide insurance against medical uncertainties has been illuminatingly analysed by Arrow (1963), but as Arrow himself points out, if the insurance markets were perfectly competitive, 'those in groups of higher incidences of illness should pay higher premiums'.[1] This means that those with a higher incidence of illness would end up with less income *net* of insurance premiums. This is, of course, precisely

[1] Arrow (1963), p. 205.

what a national health service run independently of market profitability can avoid. But what is the rationale of avoiding it? Precisely the needs principle which we have been examining. An ill person has identifiably greater needs, and by spending more money on him the society would give him a greater effective income, which is precisely in line with the Weak Equity Axiom discussed in Chapter 1.

While this is perhaps not the occasion to comment on the relative merits of giving ill people cash subsidies against those of providing them with free medical services, I would nevertheless comment briefly on an aspect of the problem which seems to me to touch on the question of decidability of relative needs. I do not wish to go into the organizational advantages of providing medical services through a national health network and the possible economies of large scale involved in this, but it is pertinent to note that the provision of cash subsidies opens up greater possibilities of abuse through pretensions of greater needs, thereby bedevilling the problem of decidability. When medical services are provided in kind, the link-up with needs is more direct and the practical problem of identifying needs is to that extent reduced. The national health service has a built-in system of attempting to match payments to needs, and this is of obvious relevance to any comparison of the merits of the two systems of compensation.

Non-income determinants of welfare

In taking a group welfare function of the form $F(y_1, \ldots, y_n)$, non-income considerations of relevance to social welfare (e.g., sweat of work) can be brought into the picture only through the shape of the function F. Taking the individualistic case, in which social welfare is a function of individual welfare levels, $W(U_1, \ldots, U_n)$, if it is further specified that each U_i is a function of income only, $U_i(y_i)$, or more generally $U_i(y_1, \ldots, y_n)$, once again there will, of course, be no way of bringing considerations like variable sweat except through the form of the functions U_i. This functional variation would, formally, reflect variable 'needs' for income of the persons given by their non-income characteristics.

For example, consider two income distributions x and y, with identical totals, over a collection of n people who are symmetrical in all respects except that person 1 works in a nasty coal mine and has tougher working conditions than persons 3 to n, while person 2 works under more pleasant working conditions than these other persons. Let x be a completely equal distribution, whereas y gives more income to person 1 and less to person 2 than the rest. We might conceivably decide to prefer y to x on the grounds that for the same level of income person 1's welfare would be less, and person 2's greater, than the welfare of everybody else. The Weak Equity Axiom would recommend choosing some y (not necessarily *every* arbitrarily picked y) satisfying these inequalities, and if y is preferred to x on that ground, the way of characterizing it would be in terms of person 1 having greater need for income given his tough work conditions and person 2 having less need given his favourable non-income situation.[2] In terms of our model of interpersonal comparisons, preferring to be person 2 than person 1 at the same level of income, is equivalent to asserting that 2 has greater welfare than 1 at the same level of income, and that in its turn is taken to be equivalent to the first person having greater needs than the second.[3]

The assumption of symmetry in the *evaluation* of income distributions may, therefore, have to be rejected not merely on grounds of inherent differences in needs (e.g., some people being chronically ill or crippled), but also because of differences in non-income characteristics (e.g., particular working conditions). In a system geared to ranking distributions of income as such, considerations of this type must come under

[2] An alternative way of handling this particular problem is to look at the distribution not merely of income but of utilities defined as functions of income and work efforts. See, for example, Kolm's 'leisurely equivalent income' (Kolm, 1969, pp. 181–2). But, of course, there would also be other differences of relevance to the distribution problem, e.g., location characteristics, cultural propensities, etc. Kolm (1969) provides an interesting discussion of the distribution problem in a highly general setting.

[3] Note that the same would hold if person 2 had greater wealth than person 1, i.e., it would be judged that he had less 'need' for income, other things given.

the broad hat of variations of needs, and would take the form of differences in welfare functions defined on the income levels.

Variations of unidentifiable characteristics

The historic controversy on the difficulty of interpersonal comparisons of welfare, and therefore of needs, took place not in the context of these identifiable differences of need characteristics (such as being a cripple or having terrible working conditions), but in that of alleged interpersonal differences which were not necessarily identifiable in objective terms. In his classic article on interpersonal comparisons Robbins (1988) made use of a story attributed to Sir Henry Maine in which a Brahmin, confronted with a Benthamite, kept insisting: 'I am ten times as capable of happiness as that untouchable over there.' Reflections on this argument led Robbins to the conclusion: 'I could not escape the conviction that, if I chose to regard men as equally capable of satisfaction and he to regard them as differing according to a hierarchical schedule, the difference between us was not one which could be resolved by the same methods of demonstration as were available in other fields of social judgement.'[4]

There are two distinct elements in this line of argument. First, there is the question of the inherent impossibility of interpersonal comparisons. In support of his position Robbins quotes Jevons as saying: 'I see no means whereby such comparison can be accomplished. Every mind is inscrutable to every other mind and no common denominator of feeling is possible.'[5] I do not wish to go here into the somewhat solipsistic implications of this position, nor into the undoubted fact that every mind is *not* inscrutable to every other (not even oriental minds, as Maine and Robbins bear out), nor into the relevance of the 'common humanity' of men for the evaluation of social arrangements, illuminatingly analysed by Bernard

[4] Robbins (1938), p. 636.
[5] Robbins (1938), p. 637.

Williams.[6] For our purpose it is sufficient to note that we have been interpreting interpersonal comparisons of welfare in terms of choices of being in the position of one person rather than that of another. Under this system 'the common denominator of feeling' is not far to seek, and systematic thinking about it seems perfectly possible.[7]

The second element in the argument arises not from the alleged impossibility of making interpersonal comparisons but from the possibility that it might in fact be held that Maine's Brahmin was indeed ten times as capable of happiness as the other man. Two questions arise here, viz., (i) why so? and (ii) what then? Taking the second question first, if Maine's Brahmin were right and if his statement were interpreted to mean that he indeed had ten times as much welfare as the untouchable for any given income level, then the Weak Equity Axiom would immediately recommend that the Brahmin be given *less* income than the untouchable! Maine's Brahmin got away with his argument (if argument it was), only because he was facing a Benthamite and only because Robbins paid the ultimate compliment to his utilitarian adversaries by being

[6] 'That all men are human is, if a tautology, a useful one, serving as a reminder that those who belong anatomically to the species *homo sapiens*, and can speak a language, use tools, live in societies, can interbreed despite racial differences, etc., are also alike in certain other respects more likely to be forgotten. These respects are notably the capacity to feel pain, both from immediate physical causes and from various situations represented in perception and in thought; and the capacity to feel affection for others, and the consequences of this, connected with the frustration of this affection, loss of its object, etc. The assertion that men are alike in the possession of these characteristics is, while indisputable and (it may be) even necessarily true, not trivial. For it is certain that there are political and social arrangements that systematically neglect these characteristics in the case of some groups of men, while being fully aware of them in the case of others; that is to say, they treat certain men as though they did not possess these characteristics, and neglect moral claims that arise from these characteristics and which would be admitted to arise from them.' (Williams, 1962, p. 112.)

[7] I am not sure that 'the same methods of demonstration' does not apply here 'as were available *in other fields of social judgement*' (Robbins 1938, p. 636; italics mine). The distinction that is being made is not particularly clear especially since Robbins admits into his framework of 'scientific foundations' both 'observation' and 'introspection' (pp. 637 and 640).

able to think of no way of handling individual utilities except by *adding* them.

Probabilistic egalitarianism

But even *within* the utilitarian framework and even after noting that people may indeed have different utility functions, it can be asked: Why is it more likely that the Brahmin has a greater capacity for satisfaction than the untouchable? What if we assume that it is as likely that this is the case as that the opposite holds? What then? It is to this question that Abba Lerner (1944) had addressed himself in dealing with distributional problems in a socialist economy. Lerner's answer for distributing a given total income was that the right solution in such a situation was to divide it equally. Since doubts have been raised from time to time as to what precisely Lerner's theorem amounts to and whether it is valid,[8] a somewhat formal presentation of the result is called for. This is not very difficult to give, and I have in fact presented such a formulation elsewhere (Sen 1969b). What is much more important is to rescue Lerner's result from its reliance on the utilitarian framework which we have found to be objectionable (see Chapter 1), and to look for a theorem that would be valid not only for the utilitarian case but also for others. Such a generalization is indeed possible.[9]

Assumption 4.1 (Total Income Fixity): There is a fixed income y^* to be divided among n individuals, i.e., $y_1 + \ldots + y_n = y^*$.

Assumption 4.2 (Concavity of the Group Welfare Function): Social welfare W, a symmetric and increasing function of individual welfare levels $W(U_1, \ldots, U_n)$, is concave.

Assumption 4.3 (Concavity of the Individual Welfare

---

[8] See Friedman (1947), Samuelson (1964), Breit and Culbertson, Jr. (1970).

[9] We are sticking to n possible individual welfare functions. It is easy to drop this requirement (see Sen 1969b), but the intuitive aspect of the Lerner problem is caught rather well by the case in which there are n persons and n individual welfare functions but it is not known *who* has *which* function.

Functions): There are n individual welfare functions $U^1(y), \ldots, U^n(y)$, and each of them is concave.

Assumption 4.4 (Equi-probability): If p^j_i is the probability that person i has the welfare function U^j, then for all j, $p^j_i = p^j_h$, for all individuals i, h.

Theorem 4.1

Given Assumptions 1, 2, 3, and 4, the mathematical expectation of social welfare is maximized by an equal division of income.

Thanks to the symmetry of W, we can define a group welfare function $W = F(y^1, \ldots, y^n)$, in which y^j is the income going to the person with the j-th welfare function U^j. For any income distribution $(y_1, \ldots, y_n)$, any reordering of it $(y^1, \ldots, y^n)$ essentially reflects a particular assignment of individual welfare functions to the persons in the group. For any distribution vector y, there are $n!$ such reorderings $\tilde{y}(k)$, $k = 1, \ldots, n!$, and corresponding to each k, there is a specific value of social welfare given by $F(\tilde{y}(k))$. Since Assumption 4.4 implies that each of the possibilities are exactly equally likely, the mathematical expectation E of social welfare is given by:

$$E(y) = \frac{1}{n!}\Sigma^{n!}_{k=1}F(\tilde{y}(k)). \qquad (4.1)$$

If x is an equal-distribution vector, i.e., $x_1 = \ldots = x_n$, then clearly:

$$E(x) = F(x) \qquad (4.2)$$

By Assumption 4.1 it is obvious that:

$$x = \frac{1}{n!}\Sigma^{n!}_{k=1}\tilde{y}(k). \qquad (4.3)$$

By Assumptions 4.2 and 4.3, $F(.)$ is a concave function, and therefore from equations (4.1), (4.2), and (4.3), it must be the case that:

$$E(y) \leq E(x) \qquad (4.4)$$

Since (4.4) holds for all y, evidently Theorem 4.1 must be true.

Note that this result is not subject to the criticism that Milton Friedman (1947) made of Lerner's welfare function by considering the case in which there is no ignorance:

Suppose, further, that it is discovered . . . that a hundred persons in the United States are enormously more efficient pleasure machines than any others, so that each of these would have to be given an income ten thousand times as large as the income of the next most efficient pleasure machine in order to maximize aggregate utility. Would Lerner be willing to accept the resulting division of income as optimum . . . ?[10]

Happily, Lerner does not have to express such a willingness. In fact, he can even confine himself to the class of concave group welfare functions satisfying the Weak Equity Axiom, which would rule out the possibility that Friedman suggests and in fact ensure that the more efficient pleasure machine would be handed out *less* income. Even then the right distribution in a state of ignorance would be the equal one. Lerner's probabilistic egalitarianism need not be based on the utilitarian framework at all (though it does happen to hold for that case as well).[11]

Maximin egalitarianism

The equi-probability assumption has been subjected to some severe criticism. It can indeed be argued that not to be sure who has which utility function is not the same thing as assuming that every possible assignment is equally likely. Perhaps a more interesting assumption than Assumption 4.4 is the following.

Assumption 4.4* (Shared Set of Welfare Functions): For any person i and any utility function j, it is possible that i has j.

Since nothing is now said about probability, the mathematical expectation of social welfare cannot any more be defined. But there are other criteria one can use, and in particular the

---

10 Friedman (1947), pp. 310–11.

11 It may be wondered whether maximization of the mathematical expectation of social welfare would not be senseless in the non-utilitarian case. But this is not so. The simplest case to consider is a non-utilitarian F which is still additively separable, e.g., taking strictly concave transforms of people's utilities and then adding them.

'maximin' policy of maximizing the minimal level of social welfare. To guarantee that the minimum exists for each assignment, we need some additional assumption, and this we do with a simple requirement (though it is, in fact, unnecessarily strong).

Assumption 4.5 (Bounded Individual Welfare Functions): Each individual welfare function U^j is bounded from below.

What kind of a distribution policy would the 'maximin' strategy recommend? Once again an equal distribution, as was shown for the utilitarian case in Sen (1969b), but the result is easily generalized for all concave group welfare functions (indeed also for all quasi-concave functions as well).

Theorem 4.2

Given Assumptions 1, 2, 3, 4*, and 5, the maximin strategy for social welfare is to distribute income equally.

Consider the set of all $\bar{y}(k)$ for $k = 1, \ldots, n!$. Since F is quasi-concave and x is a weighted average of all such $\bar{y}(k)$, clearly:

$$F(x) \geq \text{Min}_k F(\bar{y}(k)). \qquad (4.5)$$

And this establishes the theorem since, x being an equal division, $F(x)$ is invariant with respect to interpersonal permutations of individual welfare functions.

Thus not only is the equal distribution an optimal policy to be followed if the mathematical expectation of social welfare is to be maximized in a situation of ignorance under the assumption of equi-probability, it is optimal also for the 'maximin' strategy completely independently of the relative probability distributions.[12] Since there are people who seem

---

[12] It is important to avoid confusion between the 'maximin' criterion of Rawls (1971), in which the level of welfare of the worst-off individual is maximized with no uncertainty about who has which welfare function, and the 'maximin' strategy referred to in Theorem 4.2, in which the minimal level of social welfare, which can be any concave function of individual welfares, is maximized in a situation of ignorance as to who has which welfare function. Since Rawls's 'maximin' rule yields a concave group welfare function, it is covered by Theorems 4.1 and 4.2, and the results apply to the 'maximin' conception of social welfare and to the use of the 'maximin' strategy within that conception. The maximin–maximin policy is still an equal distribution.

to like paradoxes, I leave it to them to chew over the idea that a 'conservative' policy like the 'maximin' yields a 'radical' conclusion like absolute equality in income distribution, but I fear I cannot recommend it as a very juicy paradox.

It appears that egalitarianism may be optimal under ignorance about relative needs (and therefore about individual welfare functions), and not merely under perfect certainty with the same welfare function being shared by all. Results of the type presented in Theorems 4.1 and 4.2 have to be contrasted with our observations on *identified* differences of welfare functions, e.g., the case of the cripple. Being sure about unequal needs would certainly push us in the direction of an unequal division of income corresponding to relative needs, thanks to the Weak Equity Axiom and similar requirements, but these axioms do not seem to provide a justification for departing from equality of incomes when we are not sure about relative needs. The two generalizations presented here of Lerner's pioneering result in this field permit us to combine Lerner's egalitarian conclusion with adherence to the Weak Equity Axiom and other requirements of equity.

Needs principle versus the works principle

I referred earlier to the contrast between the principle of distribution according to needs and that of distribution according to desert. The usual interpretation of desert is in terms of some conception of value of work done. The Marxian notion of 'exploitation' is based on the concept of 'surplus value', viz., the difference between the value added and the wages paid, and the ratio of the surplus value to the wages bill is taken to be the rate of exploitation. As a general approach this certainly falls in the category of being desert-based rather than needs-based.

While exploitation has played an important part in Marxian economics, it would be a mistake to think that deserts took priority over needs in the Marxian analysis of distribution, or that Marx was not clear on the distinction. In fact he made the distinction very sharply and accepted the ultimate superiority of the needs principle. In his *Critique of the Gotha Programme* of 1875 he took the German Workers' Party very severely to task for confusing the two principles. Pointing out the contradiction displayed in the *Gotha Programme* between the principle of the worker's right to get 'the undiminished proceeds of labour' and that of giving 'equal rights to all members of society' to the output of the society, Marx went on to associate the two principles with two different phases of socialism. Since this analysis has been the starting point of many debates in the socialist literature, and since—as I would argue later—the same set of issues recurs systematically in the technical literature on optimal allocation of resources, I take the liberty of quoting Marx in some detail:

What we have to deal with here is a communist society, not as it has *developed* on its own foundations, but, on the contrary, just as it *emerges* from capitalist society; which is thus in every respect, economically, morally and intellectually, still stamped with the birthmarks of the old society from whose womb it emerges. Accordingly, the individual producer receives back from society—after the deductions have been made—exactly what he gives to it. . . . He receives a certificate from society that he has furnished such and such an amount of labour (after deducting his labour from the common funds), and with this certificate he draws from the social stock of means of consumption as much as costs the same amount of labour. . . .

Hence, *equal right* here is still in principle—*bourgeois right*, although principle and practice are no longer at loggerheads, while the exchange of equivalents in commodity exchange only exists *on the average* and not in the individual case.

In spite of this advance, this *equal right* is still constantly stigmatized by a bourgeois limitation. The right of the producers is *proportional* to the labour they supply; the equality consists in the fact that measurement is made with an *equal standard*, labour.

But one man is superior to another physically or mentally and so supplies more labour in the same time, or can labour for a longer time; and labour, to serve as a measure, must be defined by its duration or intensity, otherwise it ceases to be a standard of measurement. This *equal* right is an unequal right for unequal labour. It recognizes no class differences, because everyone is only a worker like everyone else; but it tacitly recognizes unequal individual endowment and thus productive capacity as natural privileges. *It is, therefore, a right of inequality, in its content, like every right.* Right by its very nature can consist only in the application of an equal standard; but unequal individuals (and they would not be different individuals if they were not unequal) are measurable only by an equal standard in so far as they are brought under an equal point of view, are taken from one *definite* side only, for instance, in the present case, are regarded *only as workers*, and nothing more is seen in them, everything else being ignored. . . .

But these defects are inevitable in the first phase of communist society as it is when it has just emerged after prolonged birth pangs from capitalist society. . . .

In a higher phase of communist society, after the enslaving subordination of the individual to the division of labour, and therewith also the antithesis between mental and physical labour has vanished; after labour has become not only a means of life but life's prime want; after the productive forces have also increased with the all-round development of the individual, and all the springs of cooperative wealth flow more abundantly—only then can the narrow horizon of bourgeois right be crossed in its entirety and society inscribe in its banners: From each according to his ability, to each according to his needs![13]

The two principles contrasted by Marx correspond to two ways of evaluating income distribution, and while the analysis of 'exploitation' deals with *desert*, the analysis of equality and crossing 'the narrow horizon of bourgeois right' relate to the concept of *needs*. The historical sequencing of the two phases of socialism with the two respective principles of distribution became the standard theory of socialist evolution and was not re-examined very critically until the recent Chinese attempts at building communes on the principle of needs at an early stage of socialism. The Chinese debate on the subject I shall comment on later, and I turn first to the relationship of all this to the academic literature on optimal allocation of resources.

Lange–Lerner systems

While much of the literature of optimal allocation is concerned with the achievement of only Pareto optimality (and therefore

[13] Marx (1875), pp. 21–3.

abstains from distributional questions), the two contributions on decentralized resource allocation that pioneered the study of the optimality aspects of price mechanism, viz., the works of Oscar Lange and Abba Lerner, were much concerned with the problem of right distribution. How did they face the conflict of the two principles outlined by Marx?

Lange (1936–37) noted the contrast between the two conditions involved in satisfying (i) distribution according to relative needs, i.e., 'the distribution has to be such that the same demand price offered by different consumers represents an equal urgency of needs', and (ii) the efficiency requirement 'to make the differences of the value of the marginal product of labour in the various occupations equal to the differences in the marginal disutility involved in their pursuit' (p. 101). But, Lange thought that any contradiction between the two principles would be 'only apparent'. The former required an equal distribution of income if needs were equal, but so did the latter after taking note of the fact that 'the disutility of any occupation can be represented as opportunity cost'.

Lange seemed to be assuming equality of educational opportunity and training facilities which would explain much of the difference in productive abilities of different persons. As far as 'exceptional talents' were concerned, which formed a 'natural monopoly', he noted that they could be paid 'incomes which are far below the value of the marginal product of their services without affecting the supply of those services'.[14]

While this last point is of some importance—and we shall return to this question again later on in this chapter—there is little doubt that Lange was over-simplifying a complex picture. As Dobb (1933) had pointed out in an early critique of market socialism, there are questions of relative scarcity in any given market equilibrium and 'both costs and needs are precluded from receiving simultaneous expression in the same system of market valuations' (p. 37). Lange emphatically rejected Dobb's argument that these conditions were contradictory (p. 102), but Lange's market equilibrium seemed to

[14] Lange (1936–37) pp. 101–2. The last of these remarks was in response to a criticism by Dobb (1933).

assume (i) the absence of short-run scarcities, (ii) complete
equalization of educational and training opportunities, including in the selection process, (iii) the absence of indivisibilities
in the educational structure, and (iv) successful avoidance of
payment of any 'rent' to natural talents. He also largely
ignored the problem of incentives for intensive work effort,
which had worried Marx.

Lerner (1944) was less optimistic and felt that 'the principle
of equality would have to compromise with the principle of
providing such incentives as would increase the total of
income available to be divided' (p. 36). But where should the
line of compromise be drawn? This is undoubtedly one of the
more basic problems of socialist planning faced with the conflict between efficiency and equality.

Can taxes help in resolving the conflict? The question has
cropped up in different forms repeatedly. In particular, it has
been asked whether one can base pre-tax incomes in line with
efficiency and post-tax incomes in line with needs. The answer
is: Surely one can, but then why should the people in question
take their decisions on efforts, leisure, etc., on the basis of
their pre-tax incomes rather than on post-tax incomes? After
all, pre-tax income is just a façade, and post-tax income is all
that matters.[15] And then the conflict is back again—now
related exclusively to post-tax incomes.

This recognition led to a search for a 'non-distorting' tax. Is
there such an animal?[16] In principle it seemed that 'lump-sum
taxes' could do the trick. A lump-sum tax is unrelated to income, work, expenditure, consumption, saving, or anything
else that a person can vary. By construction, therefore, lump-
sum taxes cannot 'distort' allocation. Is this a fable? To discuss
this I begin with a slight detour, viz., what goes wrong with
the income tax.

[15] If pre-tax incomes have some 'prestige value', the picture will be more
complex, but since men don't live by prestige alone, post-tax incomes will
continue to influence individual decisions.

[16] This is an ancient issue in public finance, and the poll-tax has been much
analysed. In the context of its use for socialist allocation and redistribution,
see Samuelson (1947) and Dobb (1969) among others.

The income tax

The underlying problem can be explained in terms of a very simple model involving one commodity, i.e., homogeneous income. The following notation is used:

$y_i(t)$ = pre-tax income of person i under tax system t;

$y_i(0)$ = pre-tax income of person i in the special case of a no-tax system;

$y_i^*(t)$ = post-tax income of person i.

In the Lange–Lerner system, in the absence of externalities, increasing returns, and such things, $y_i(0)$ would correspond to the marginal productive contribution of each person's economic resources. A tax system may distort the person's decisions on work, leisure, etc., and the pre-tax income $y_i(t)$, in the presence of a system of taxes and subsidies, would represent a different equilibrium from that reflected in $y_i(0)$, because of the distortion of the reward system implicit in the taxes. On the other hand, $y_i^*(t)$, the income after taxes and subsidies, would presumably reflect *the* evaluation of needs and other distributional values used in the planning system.

Let w_i be the marginal income of worker i from a unit of effort, the hardship of which he evaluates as equivalent to α_i units of income at the margin. Let β_i be the value that worker i attaches to a unit of income going to others, measured in units of his own income. In the no-tax system, the worker will put in effort to the extent that:

$$w_i = \alpha_i \qquad (4.6)$$

But with an income tax at the marginal rate of t per unit, $0 < t < 1$, he will equate:

$$w_i[(1 - t) + t\beta_i] = \alpha_i \qquad (4.7)$$

(4.6) and (4.7) will be equivalent if and only if:

$$either\ \alpha_i = 0,\ or\ \beta_i = 1 \qquad (4.8)$$

These conditions correspond respectively (i) to the case in which the person does not mind expending effort and sweat, and (ii) to the case where the person values the marginal income of others just as much as the marginal income of himself. Either of these conditions must be fulfilled for income tax to be non-distorting. But if $\alpha_i > 0$ and $\beta_i < 1$, then the income tax will distort allocation.

Lump-sum taxes

Can this problem be avoided? Are there taxes that will not have this distorting effect? First consider a relatively simple case in which a person's relative preference for income and leisure are not affected by his overall prosperity, though variations of the rate of remuneration for work would of course affect his work decisions.

Consider a fixed tax, t_i, on person i such that he must pay t_i no matter what else he does (works or not, eats a lot or a little, or anything else):

$$t_i = [\Sigma_i \, y_i(0)/n] - y_i(0) \qquad (4.9)$$

Since the tax is fixed, the person cannot gain anything from varying his amount of work. Since his income–leisure preference is not affected by his level of prosperity, these lump-sum taxes leave everything completely unchanged as far as work and production are concerned. But the taxes (or subsidies since t_i can be positive, negative, or zero) take the system from one of distribution according to work to one of distribution according to needs.

The planners have to estimate the set of $y_i(0)$, which involves estimating the real capabilities of each person. There are two problems here, viz., (i) the cost of collecting the information, and (ii) the deliberate misinformation which person i might try to convey to the planners. The former can be quite serious, and it is of particular relevance to a system geared to achieving economy of information in the process of optimization. The decentralized system of the Lange–Lerner kind aims at reaching the optimum iteratively through trial and error with extreme parsimony in the transfer of detailed information. This problem is all the more serious when the assumption of invariance of income–leisure preference with respect to net prosperity is dropped. The non-distorting character of the lump-sum taxes still survives, but in calculating t_i from (4.9) one would have to interpret $y_i(0)$ valued not as it would be in the absence of all taxes, but after taking note of the impact of lump-sum taxes through being on a different part of the leisure–income indifference map. The marginal equilibrium given by (4.6) would still hold, and the lump-sum taxes would not interfere with the achievement of efficiency, but the calculations for (4.7) and (4.9) would be particularly complex, since α_i would depend on the level of income after the lump-sum tax.

The second problem would be an equally serious difficulty. It would be in the interest of each person to pretend to be less productive than he is and then to take things easy. By producing less oneself one reduces total output by a relatively small amount, and under egality the impact on one's net income is minute.

Hence with lump-sum taxes the distortion comes in not in the form of insufficient work effort *given* the tax system, but in that of giving wrong signals to the planners about one's productive ability, thereby influencing the tax system itself in one's favour. If person i can convince the planners that he is worthless and capable of no greater effort, then the value of t_i will be relatively smaller and he may be spared the necessity of exerting himself much. Such deliberate misinformation may bedevil the Lange–Lerner iterative procedure quite severely. Given a personal-gain oriented approach, this barrier is not easy to cross.

Work motivation

Underlying all this is precisely the problem of work motivation with which Marx was concerned. Marx saw no escape from it in the early phase of socialism in which the society and the people are 'economically, morally and intellectually, still stamped with the birthmarks of the old society from whose womb it emerges', and conceived of an ultimate solution to this problem in 'the all-round development of the individual', 'after labour has become not only a means of life but life's prime want'.[17] However, as we noted, he saw this only as a distant prospect.

The Soviet wage system reveals a concentration on work rewards and incentive payments,[18] which Marx had associated with the first phase of socialism. There are, of course, exceptions to this,[19] but the big point of departure can be associated with the Chinese attempt at communized agriculture with a deliberate move to achieve now what Marx had foreseen for the distant future. The Chinese experience on this is worth investigating in the context of the conflicting claims of the works principle and the needs principle.

During the so-called 'Great Leap Forward', which was launched in China in 1958, there was a strong move in the direction of non-material incentives, especially in agriculture. The proportion distributed according to work done was severely reduced, and the 'supply portion', which was distributed on some non-work criteria, including considerations of 'needs', was correspondingly raised. Sometimes even 80 to 90 per cent of the net product came to be distributed as the supply portion.[20]

In an economy like China there are several advantages in using a non-work basis of payments. First, as is well recognized in the literature on economic development, an important barrier to the utilization of surplus manpower is the wage system, which requires a prior supply of wage goods before under-utilized labour can be mobilized.[21] A non-wage system would reduce the need for a *prior* surplus of wage goods, and labour could be rewarded by the fruits of its own output after the production lag. The Chinese were embarking on a vast programme of labour mobilization which included a remarkable amount of physical movement and migration.

[17] Marx (1875), pp. 21–3.
[18] See Dobb (1951), Nove (1961), Wiles (1962), Bergson (1964), and Ellman (1971).
[19] A system of free medical facilities, educational opportunities and social security, and subsidized housing and other services, does involve indirect use of the needs principle.
[20] See Hoffman (1964), (1967), and Riskin (1971).
[21] See Nurkse (1953), Robinson (1956), Sen (1964), and Marglin (1966).

Second, given the nature of the Chinese revolution and its predominant values, a system of 'material incentives' was regarded with considerable suspicion, and the Soviet concentration on an incentive system of rewards was the subject of much criticism. Thus philosophically and in terms of effective utilization of surplus manpower, the Chinese were poised for a move towards reliance on 'non-material incentives'. The 'leap' was taken in 1958.

During 1958–60 this experiment was carried out with much zeal along with other features that characterized the 'Leap Forward'. As is well known, the movement as a whole ran into several serious problems, but it is difficult to dissociate the difficulties generated by the use of non-material incentives from those caused by other features of the Leap Forward. It is certainly significant that as the movement came to an end the proportion distributed according to work was substantially raised and the use of the 'needs' principle was conceded to have been premature.[22] However, the emphasis on non-material incentives was not entirely abandoned and was partly revived later.[23] In fact, this feature of the substantial use of non-material incentives is recognized to be one of the remarkable aspects of the Chinese economy.

A game-theoretic presentation
of the problem of work motivation

The problem of incentives that had bothered Marx was undoubtedly relevant to the Chinese experiment. It is, in fact, a basic question in collectivist allocation. The logic of the problem can be analysed in terms of some elementary games of the non-zero-sum variety. Interesting insights seem to come from contrasting games like the 'Prisoners' Dilemma'[24] with other games (like the 'Assurance Game'[25]) that differ from it

[22] Cf. 'But they [the communes] had been formed very hastily; the necessary psychological preparation had not everywhere been made, and some extreme ideas, such as abolishing private plots and distributing food according to needs rather than on work points, proved to be far ahead of the times. During the bad years reorganization took place and the extremist policies were abandoned.' (Joan Robinson 1969, p. 35.)

[23] Riskin (1971).   [24] See Luce and Raiffa (1957).

[25] See Sen (1967a), (1969a).

in some essential respects. While it is a trifle pompous to brandish little 'games' in analysing homely situations, I think there are substantial advantages in putting the analytical contrasts sharply to catch the precise motivational differences.

Suppose that a typical member of a cooperative considers two alternatives, viz., to work hard (I_1) and not to work hard (I_0). He may make two assumptions about others in the cooperative, viz., that they will work hard (R_1) or that they will not (R_0). Consider a system in which people are paid according to needs (and not work), whereas their main concern is with their own welfare. A typical ranking of alternatives may then take the form (in decreasing order of preference): I_0R_1, I_1R_1, I_0R_0, I_1R_0. By working hard oneself one adds very little to one's income since the principle of distribution is not work but needs, but there is still the hardship of toil. So given the actions of others, everyone may prefer not to work hard, i.e., prefer I_0 to I_1 no matter whether the others do R_0 or R_1. But at the same time they may each prefer everyone working hard to no one working hard, since the latter may be disastrous for all. In such a situation, however, guided by rational calculus everyone ends up not working hard, i.e., doing I_0, which is a strictly dominant strategy. But each would have preferred that all had worked harder. Individual rational calculations would seem to lead all to disaster.

This game—the Prisoners' Dilemma—has been much used in recent years to explain the rationale of an enforceable collusive solution in such fields as taxation, collective savings, etc.[26] However, since a collective contract with provision for enforcement may be extremely difficult to devise for labour efforts, the lesson to be drawn here has to be different. Work supervision to ensure adherence to a 'sincere effort' contract involves many problems,[27] and this is precisely where an

[26] See Baumol (1952), (1970), Sen (1961), (1967a), Marglin (1963), Ellman (1966).

[27] Work supervision of this kind may also bring out some of the most dislikeable features of 'alienation'—a major source of Marxian concern—'in the sense of labour "for somebody else", under the supervision and orders of somebody else'. (Mandel 1968, p. 680.)

incentive system of wages has an advantage.[28] The feasibility of using payments according to needs combined with vigorous supervision of work done is profoundly doubtful.

It is in this context that the question of cultural orientation of work motivation becomes crucially relevant, since the preference ordering in the Prisoners' Dilemma reflects a specific cultural pattern. Consider the following variation of the ranking of the alternatives: I_1R_1, I_0R_1, I_0R_0, I_1R_0. This produces a game ('the Assurance Game') in which each party would work hard (I_1) given the assurance that others would too (R_1) but would prefer not to put in the effort (I_0) if the others would not (R_0). The basic principle here is 'reciprocity', and this game can lead to an optimal solution in a situation of mutual confidence. If people's preferences are more 'socially conscious' in the sense of actually preferring to do the right thing whether or not others do the same, e.g., ranking the alternatives as I_1R_1, I_1R_0, I_0R_1, I_0R_0 everyone would automatically do his 'duty' and the question of supervision or even of confidence would not arise.

That the Prisoners' Dilemma could disappear if people had different preferences is true but hardly interesting. What is, however, quite significant is the fact that even if the people involved continued to have the same Prisoners' Dilemma type preferences, but behaved as if their preferences were as in the Assurance Game (or better still *as if* they had the 'socially conscious' preferences discussed above), they could be better off *even in terms of their true preferences*. This is precisely where the question of cultural orientation comes in, and it may provide a social case for encouraging values that reorient a person's choices and actions even if his personal welfare functions remain unaltered. In a sense, this is a matter of morality, and there are of course many other spheres of life as well in which a society throws up moral values that attempt to dissociate choice from individualistic rational calculus. Indeed this is a common phenomenon for 'homely virtues' like

[28] There are, however, allocational problems for a pure system of distribution according to work as well, on which see Ward (1958), Domar (1966), and Sen (1966).

honesty, keeping promises, etc., but what is important to recognize here is the relevance of all this to the problem of work motivation and therefore to income distribution.

Economic roots of the 'cultural revolution'

This dichotomy between choices on the one hand and preferences (and welfare) on the other has disturbing implications for the theory of 'revealed preference' and also has some bearing on theories of 'moral behaviour', neither of which I intend to pursue here.[29] What is of relevance here is the relation of all this to the conflict between the needs principle and the works principle, and in particular the light that this throws on the concentration on cultural reorientation that characterized China shortly after the end of the Leap Forward which had included the problem-ridden departure from payment according to work.

The economic roots of the Chinese 'cultural revolution' need careful attention. There were, of course, diverse forces involved in that movement, but certainly one strain in the discussion (and agitation) was closely related to the alternative principles of payment and to the question of work motivation. The official pronouncement on the subject explained that 'the aim of the Great Proletarian Cultural Revolution is to revolutionize people's ideology and as a consequence to achieve greater, faster, better and more economical results in all fields of work. . . . [it] is a powerful motive force for the development of social productive forces in our country'.[30] Using words reminiscent of those with which Marx had taken the *Gotha Programme* to task for ignoring the problem of work incentives in the early stages of the socialist economy when it was 'in every respect, economically, morally and intellectually, still stamped with the birthmarks of the old society' (Marx

[29] I have tried to pursue the latter question in my paper for the Bristol Conference on 'Practical Reason', Sen (1972).

[30] 'The Decision of the Central Committee of the Chinese Communist Party Concerning the Great Proletarian Cultural Revolution,' adopted on 8 August 1966, reproduced in Robinson (1969), p. 95. This is the so-called 'Sixteen Points'.

1875, p. 21), the programme of 'cultural revolution' pleaded for 'an education to develop morally, intellectually and physically and to become labourers with socialist consciousness and culture'.[31]

The question of dissociating choices from individualistic preferences and individual welfare seems to have been fairly central to the Chinese experiment on work motivation and the cultural revolution.[32] The recurrent emphasis on acting 'without calculation of loss or gain' and the persistent attack on the pursuit of personal gains relate to this. It is a characteristic of the Prisoners' Dilemma type situation that the consequence of everyone acting rationally according to his true preferences and individual welfare is an inferior social outcome for all, and acting in a morally dogmatic way (*as if* one's preferences were different, whether or not they actually are so) can produce a superior outcome for all (even in terms of individual welfare functions, whether or not they take note of the welfare of others).

This type of consideration seems to have characterized an aspect of the cultural revolution and links it up not only with the Chinese experiments on payment methods in the Leap Forward period and later, but also with the mainstream of the socialist debate on the works principle *versus* the needs principle, involving diverse authors from Marx (1875) to Lerner (1944).

It is not my object here to assess the successes and failures of the Chinese experiment in trying to shift the emphasis of distribution policy from work to needs. What is important for our purpose is to place this experiment in the perspective of the chain of thought linking the Marxian analysis of socialist distribution on the one hand with the literature on optimal allocation and distribution on the other. This is of obvious relevance to the whole question of economic inequality in a socialist society, and the Chinese experiment crystalizes a significant aspect of it.

[31] 'The Sixteen Points', in Robinson (1969), p. 93.
[32] See Riskin (1971).

Desert and productivity

I should like to end the discussion with some remarks on the concept of desert itself. There are several alternative interpretations of desert that can be found in the economic literature. The marginal productivity theory has sometimes been viewed as a theory of deserts. This is explicit in the writings of some, e.g., J. B. Clark (1902), but its implicit presence can be felt in many other discussions of income distribution.[33]

In contrast, Marx's theory of exploitation provides an alternative theory of desert, giving labour the right to the whole of the net produce. The normative aspect of Marx's approach to the question has got somewhat overshadowed by debates on its descriptive features (e.g., the so-called 'transformation problem'), but there is no doubt that Marx saw his theory of value partly as a theory of desert.[34] This was not based on a denial that machinery can be productive—very much the contrary—but on the idea that labour in a direct *plus* 'embodied' form as 'the ultimate source of all value' deserves to enjoy the whole of the net output, and profits merely reflect a particular social arrangement of private ownership of means of production.[35]

The concept of 'exploitation' as developed by Joan Robinson (1933) took departures from the competitive value of the marginal product as indications of exploitation and two kinds were distinguished, viz., (i) 'monopolistic exploitation', given by the difference between the marginal revenue product and the competitive value of the marginal product (reflecting monopolistic elements in the product market), and (ii) 'monopsonistic exploitation', given by the difference between the wage rate and the marginal revenue product (reflecting monopsonistic elements in the labour market). The concept of desert here was a variant of the marginal productivity theory

[33] Paul Samuelson notes: 'To my astonishment I find that the arbitrariness of J. B. Clark's views on the deservingness of competitively determined rewards is not universally recognized' (Samuelson 1950a, p. 1577).

[34] See especially Part III of *Capital*, Volume I (Marx 1887).

[35] Marx did, however, treat 'nature' as an ultimate source of value as well (see Marx 1875, p. 17).

and was presented within that framework of thought, which she did, of course, subsequently reject.[36]

Sometimes desert has been viewed in terms of the appropriate prices p 'associated' with an optimal programme. These are prices that would 'sustain' that programme in the sense that the people involved would on their own make the choices appropriate for that optimum if they did their gains-maximizing calculations at those prices.[37] Such 'associated' prices need not always exist even when an optimum exists with respect to the objective function and the constraints, and much depends on the nature of the economic assumptions made (e.g., whether there are increasing returns to scale, external economies, etc.).

A special case of such an optimization exercise is that of achieving Pareto optimality. Given certain assumptions, any set of prices emerging in a competitive equilibrium would do for this purpose.[38] Since in the neo-classical framework the competitive price of factors of production would equal the respective marginal productivities, this could provide another approach to viewing marginal productivity as an interpretation of desert. However, since Pareto optimality is a very limited objective (see Chapter 1), the normative appeal of this approach may not be particularly great even within the neo-classical framework.[39]

Productivity and ability

A more full-blooded concept of desert than prices 'associated' with an optimum is based on the notion of 'ability'. Two distinctions between this idea and that of productivity must be noted. First, the productivity idea relates to all factors of production while the notion of ability relates essentially to labour. There are 'fertile' pieces of land but not 'able' pieces,

[36] Robinson (1956), (1960).
[37] See Dorfman, Samuelson and Solow (1958), Arrow and Hurwicz (1960), and Malinvaud (1967).
[38] See Debreu (1959) and Arrow and Hahn (1972). For an illuminating informal presentation, see Koopmans (1957).
[39] See Meade (1965).

nor do we run into 'able' machines. Thus the framework of ability does not directly apply to the question of property incomes. Second, even within labour, productivity can be distinguished from ability as such, since (i) opportunities for the use of one's abilities may not arise in a particular situation, and (ii) 'innate abilities' may be distinguished from derived competence reflecting education, training, and opportunities of learning.

It is this last distinction that has come much into focus in the context of the recent emphasis on 'equality of opportunities', which is in fact a desert-based concept. While educational expansion in modern Western societies has often been put forward as evidence of growing equality of opportunities, serious doubts about the achievements in this field have been raised in a number of studies.[40] It is not my intention here to go into the empirical correctness of the thesis, but to see this approach as falling within the corpus of desert-based normative theories.

A distinction between a system of rewards according to ability and that related to 'associated prices' with an optimum programme is also worth noting here. Natural talents are one thing to which the question of incentives is irrelevant, since people cannot set their natural talents aside in response to a price cut. Given an inflexible supply of talents, there will not be a *unique* 'optimal' price associated with it, since the same supply of talents will obtain at different rates of reward.[41]

It is difficult to justify rewarding talents on grounds of efficiency. We find here two alternative concepts of desert locked in combat with each other. One demands—on grounds of 'merit'—a higher reward for natural ability and does not

[40] See, in particular, OECD (1971) and Bowles (1972). See also Klappholz (1972).

[41] In the short run the inflexibility assumption is clearly appropriate. In the long run variations of the population size could be relevant, and it might be argued that there would be incentive effects if (i) a lower reward to talents were to reduce the propensity of the talented to procreate, and if (ii) talented parents had a greater than average probability of giving birth to talented children. While (ii) seems to be under much discussion today, the argument holds only if (i) is also correct, and there is, in fact, very little evidence for it.

accept the claims of acquired competence which reflects social arrangements. The other points towards rewarding acquired abilities—on grounds of 'incentives'—but provides no case for rewarding natural talents. Both, of course, conflict with the notion of needs.

Desert and needs

In this book my emphasis has been primarily on needs, and the analytical framework presented here is biassed in that direction. There are a number of reasons for this. First, as we have just now seen, there are alternative interpretations of the concept of desert and they can conflict sharply. There seems to be more unity in interpreting the concept of needs.

Second—and here I reveal my bias—it seems to me arguable that needs should have priority over desert as a basis for 'distributional' judgements as such, to which the concept of 'inequality' belongs. Of course, as argued earlier, inequality evaluation involves *non-compulsive judgements*, but *within that sphere* none of the conceptions of desert seem more appropriate.

(1) Taking up first the *incentive-oriented* interpretation of desert, a system of incentives would appear to be a means to an end rather than an end in itself, whereas the fulfilment of needs would be usually taken to be a good thing in itself. If an incentive-oriented unequal distribution—unrelated to needs—is defended, it seems reasonable to describe it as something defended on 'non-distributional' grounds, e.g., the total size of income. If, on the other hand, relative needs are manifestly different and an unequal distribution corresponding to differences in identified needs is recommended, the defence of this position would seem to be on 'distributional' grounds themselves.

(2) Coming now to the *merit-oriented* system of desert, giving more income to the naturally talented people does, of course, amount to giving less to those without talents. The latter includes the Thalidomide babies of today who will be adults tomorrow, the old and the infirm stripped of their talents by the natural process of aging, and—of course—the

genetically defective. A system based on needs would seem to have greater use for the complex idea that we call humanity. Even for limited application of the merit principle—giving more than the 'norm' to the specially meritorious but not less than the 'norm' to the demented—it can be argued that the measure of merit is culture-specific. While many of us may be content to live in a society which values the ability to lecture more than it values, say, the ability to make loud, shrill noises by blowing sharply through one's nose, we might be perfectly able to give long lectures about possible societies in which the latter quality would be the more desired virtue. Merit is a bit of an accident not only in its origin, but also in its being treated as merit.

(3) The Marxian principle of desert based on the value of labour has been a powerful mover of mankind in providing a focus of attention on inequalities arising from class differences in the ownership of means of production, but—as we saw—Marx himself regarded this right to the 'fruits' of labour as a 'bourgeois right' to be supplanted by the principle of needs when the opportunity arose. As a critique of property income, this notion of labour 'getting its value' has an obvious appeal, but it is difficult to defend it as a 'principle' against that of distribution according to needs, if feasible. And the question of feasibility takes us back to incentives, cultural values, and the question of tolerating inequality on 'non-distributional' grounds; these questions have been discussed earlier in this chapter.

(4) It is not easy to interpret the neo-classical marginal productivity theory as a normative theory, as was pointed out earlier, and if it does have a place it is a part of an incentive system corresponding to prices associated with an optimal programme. But even in the neo-classical model the only optimality such 'competitive prices' guarantee is merely Pareto optimality, which is in itself a very limited goal. Furthermore, as shown earlier, the presence of 'rent' elements in the high payments to the talented, productive people also makes the incentive problem less straightforward.

It is with this general outlook that I have concentrated in

this work on analysing the evaluation of inequality mainly from the point of view of needs rather than that of desert. While relatively little help could be obtained from the main avenues of welfare economics—'old' and 'new'—we have used a broad framework of interpersonal comparisons (formalized in $\bar{R}$) and have analysed principles of evaluation and statistical measures of inequality in that light. Because of the mixture of descriptive and normative considerations in the concept of inequality and the inherent incompleteness of that concept, inequality evaluation has been seen in terms of non-compulsive, evaluative judgements expressed as quasi-orderings. The alternative approaches explored would all fall within this general framework.

On *Economic Inequality* after a Quarter Century

JAMES FOSTER AND AMARTYA SEN

A.1 Review and Motivation

A.1.1 Prologue

The 1973 version of this book (to be called *OEI-1973* in this annexe) began by noting that the idea of inequality was 'both very simple and very complex'. While the perception of serious inequality moves people 'with an immediate appeal hardly matched by any other concept', the evaluation of inequality involves much economic, social, political, and philosophical complexity. The book attempted to analyse these complexities, and to relate them to issues involving principles that have intuitive interest.

This annexe is concerned with making the book (1) analytically more contemporary and inclusive, and (2) substantively more responsive to the practical issues of on-going concern. We discuss some of the more important developments that have taken place in the subject of inequality evaluation and the related welfare-economic analysis since the publication of *OEI-1973*. We also take up some new problems which have emerged as important in contemporary discussions—in policy-related practical debates as well as in political philosophy and political economy.

We shall come to these developments presently, but before that—in the first section of the annexe—we shall briefly review the main lines of analysis pursued in *OEI-1973*. This should help to relate the motivation and perspectives underlying this book with the analytical and substantive concerns of the contemporary literature. The page references are all to the 1973 edition, but since the old chapters have been left quite unchanged in this enlarged edition (aside from correcting a few typos), those references coincide, nearly always, with the pages in the present extended edition.

A.1.2 The 1973 themes

The issues selected here from *OEI-1973* do not attempt to summarize the book, but highlight some of the points of departure and also some arguments that ended up being closely related to subsequent works in this area.[1]

(1) *Welfare economics and the inadequacy of utilitarianism*: The 1973 book began with the necessity of welfare economics in evaluating economic inequality, and focused particularly on the need for systematic treatment of distributional value judgements. It emerged that traditional welfare economics provided rather little guidance to the judgement of inequality (see Chapters 1 and 2). Utilitarianism, which had been the mainstream approach to welfare economics, is profoundly unconcerned with inequalities precisely in the variable on which it focuses (and to which it attaches overwhelming importance), to wit, *individual utilities*. All that matters in the utilitarian view is the sum total of these utilities representing the respective individual advantages, independently of their distribution.

This problem can arise even when everyone has the same utility function, but it is especially counter-intuitive when some people are better 'utility producers' than others are. Utilitarian calculus takes no account of the *total* utility enjoyed by a person—only of the impact on utility at the margin, so that a person who is much worse off in terms of overall well-being or utility receives no particular consideration for that reason. In fact, the *levels* of utility and their interpersonal correspondence can be arbitrarily changed—for example, by adding a constant to one person's utility function but not to another's—without altering the utilitarian social ordering in any way whatsoever (*OEI-1973*, pp. 43–6). Consequently, the utilitarian ordering can be quite perverse in dealing with distributional inequality when distinct per-

---

[1] Good accounts of the contemporary literature can be found in Love and Wolfson (1976), Kakwani (1980a), Eichhorn and Gehrig (1982), Atkinson (1983, 1989), Foster (1985), Jenkins (1989), Lambert (1989), Chakravarty (1990), Cowell (1995), and Silber (1996).

sons have different utility functions. The utilitarian maximand discriminates against a person who is uniformly handicapped in converting income into utility (since she would be seen as an 'inefficient' utility maker, with a low utility-generating ability). The utilitarian logic is insensitive to the fact that giving her less income would *compound* the lowness of her utility-generating capacity: she would get a lower total income in addition to having lower utility *per unit* of income (pp. 15–23).[2]

Simple utilitarianism can be factorized into three components: (1) 'consequentialism' (judging the rightness of all choice variables, such as actions or rules or institutions, only by the goodness of the consequent states of affairs), (2) 'welfarism' (judging the goodness of states of affairs only by utility information), and (3) 'sum ranking' (judging utility information, for a given population, simply by summing utilities).[3] The indifference to the distribution of utilities is due entirely to the third factor (sum ranking), and the reach of utility-based reasoning can be broadened well beyond utilitarianism, by specifically rejecting the exclusive reliance on sum totalling of utilities. This possibility of dropping sum ranking, while retaining consequentialism and welfarism, was pursued in *OEI-1973* (see particularly pp. 15–23, 43–6, 77–87), taking 'social welfare' (or the goodness of states of affairs) to be based on distribution-inclusive judgements of the set of individual utilities.[4] This broader framework was then applied in *OEI-1973* to such issues of inequality evaluation as (1) using 'equity axioms' that are sensitive to utility differences to

[2] Utilitarianism is, in fact, an extreme case of low equality preference in aggregating utilities of different people. Taking the more general formula of adding concave transformations of the respective individual utilities (a formula to be discussed later), the reach of equality preference in the space of utilities turns on the extent of this concavity. The utilitarian formula corresponds to the case in which there is no strict concavity at all—only linearity.

[3] The factorization of utilitarianism is more fully discussed in Sen (1979a) and Sen and Williams (1982).

[4] See also the egalitarian welfare-economic framework developed by James Meade (1976) in his far-reaching exploration of the nature of the 'just economy'. Also see Baumol (1986) and Young (1994).

assess economic inequality (pp. 18–22),(2) generalizing the Atkinson-type evaluation of inequality to take explicit note of inequalities in utility distribution in a not necessarily additive framework (pp. 38–42), (3) making welfare-economic interpretation of Lorenz dominance include concerns about utility distributions (pp. 49–56), and (4) incorporating preference for less inequality of utilities in Lerner's framework of 'probabilistic egalitarianism' (pp. 83–7).

The critique of utilitarianism in *OEI-1973* was largely confined to sum ranking, even though criticisms of welfarism and consequentialism already figured both in the social choice literature (e.g., in Sen 1970a, 1970c) and, of course, in ethics and moral philosophy (see particularly the powerful critiques of Rawls 1971, Williams 1973, Nozick 1974, Scanlon 1975, among others). In later discussions on the assessment of economic inequality, welfarism in particular has come under fire, and the question has been specifically raised as to whether the 'utility' of the individual under any of the standard interpretations (i.e., pleasure, or happiness, or desire fulfilment, or the binary relation of choice) provides enough of a basis for judging the person's overall advantage. That question, which was only briefly considered in *OEI-1973* (pp. 77–9), and more specifically discussed in Sen (1979a, 1980), has been pursued a great deal in the recent literature on justice and equity (see section A.7 below).

(2) *Need for interpersonal comparisons*: The hold of utilitarianism on neoclassical welfare economics had declined, following the methodological critiques presented by Lionel Robbins (1932, 1938) and others, disputing the scientific status of interpersonal comparisons. Since 'interpersonal comparisons' had by then come to stand for comparisons of *utilities* only, the eschewal of utility comparisons led, in effect, to abstention from all comparisons of interpersonal advantages.[5]

_____

[5] Robbins's position was not entirely accurately stated in *OEI-1973* (pp. 12–13). It was not so much that Robbins was recommending that we should 'avoid' interpersonal comparisons, but rather that he believed that such comparisons did not have any scientific status. William Baumol (1975) pointed this out in his review of *OEI-1973*. Since Foster has no responsibility for *OEI-*

The 'new' welfare-economic theories refrained altogether from invoking interpersonal differences in well-being (or opportunities, or freedoms). There was going to be no interpersonal comparisons whatever—either of *levels* or of *gains and losses* of individual advantages. The response of standard welfare economics to the critique of interpersonal comparisons of utilities was, thus, to produce normative approaches that were even less concerned with distributional problems than utilitarianism is, and this development can only be described as a robust move from the frying pan into the fire.

With a little axiomatic help, it was demonstrated in *OEI-1973* that a welfare-economic rule that demands completeness of the weak social preference and transitivity of strict social preference based on individual preferences, but admits no interpersonal comparisons, would make *all* Pareto-incomparable states socially indifferent to each other (*OEI-1973*, Theorem 1.1, pp. 7–12; see also Sen 1970a, Chapters 8 and 8*). For example, in this perspective, *each* distribution of a given cake among a number of cake-loving people must be declared to be exactly as good as any other (from the social

---

1973, the following remark is specifically Sen's: 'My summary of Robbins's important and influential position on utility comparisons, made on pages 12–13, was clearly in error, exactly for the reasons that Baumol mentions (even though the critique presented on pages 81–3 stands, but should have been less combatively worded). In fact, Robbins's pointer to the difficulties in comparing different persons' utilities provides one significant ground for basing inequality comparisons on *non-utility* information. My own argument for moving to non-utility information was based instead on the normative inadequacy of the utility-based approach (discussed in Sen 1980, 1992, and in section A.2 below), as opposed to the epistemological arbitrariness of utility comparisons, emphasized by Robbins himself. There is, however, a real *complementarity* between Robbins's early critique of utilitarianism and my proposal to move away from the utility space to the non-utility space of functionings and capabilities (including the valuing of equality of basic capabilities). Indeed, Robbins's strong defence of the case for reducing inequalities in educational opportunities fits well into a general case for "basic capability equality" (on related issues, see also Majumdar 1983). This was powerfully incorporated in the philosophy underlying the momentous—and radical—"Robbins Report" on British higher education. My critique of Robbins on pages 12–13 of *OEI-1973* was, thus, not only misplaced, it was also quite unfair.'

point of view). This was scarcely a fine beginning for a theory of inequality evaluation.[6]

Thus, the revival of a basically utilitarian perspective in evaluating inequality (as proposed earlier by Pigou 1912 and Dalton 1920) proved to be a very productive move. This happened primarily through the classic paper of Atkinson (1970a).[7] A significant part of *OEI-1973* was, in fact, Atkinson-inspired. While the welfare economics of utilitarianism is seriously limited, that format can be broadened—a challenge that was taken up in the generalizations that followed (retaining welfarism and consequentialism, but dropping the reliance on simple summation of untransformed utilities). We shall come back to these questions in sections A.2 and A.3.

(3) *Social welfare functionals and distributive judgements*: Recent work in social choice theory—a subject pioneered by Kenneth Arrow (1951)—has opened up various ways of conceptualizing interpersonal utility comparisons for use in social aggregation and public decisions. The original formulation of the social choice problem in the Arrovian 'social welfare function' (SWF) admitted no interpersonal comparisons of utility, and suffered, in this respect, from much the same difficulties as the bulk of the 'new' welfare economics. Indeed, it can be shown that Arrow's 'impossibility result' is strongly grounded on the absence of such comparisons (on this see Sen 1970a). This recognition itself has contributed, to a considerable extent, to the development of a substantial literature exploring the possibility and consequences of using interpersonal comparisons of various types. The format of social welfare functions can be suitably broadened to make room for the systematic use of interpersonal comparisons, and a 'social welfare functional' (or SWFL) can be defined over combinations (strictly, n-tuples) of utility functions, with alternative 'in-

---

[6] Contrast the constructive approach explored in the literature on 'fairness'. See particularly Foley (1967), Varian (1975), Baumol (1986), Moulin (1988), and Young (1994). See also Jorgenson, Lau, and Stoker (1980) and Jorgenson and Slesnick (1984).

[7] Kolm (1969) had covered very similar ground, and this too was, rightly, influential.

variance conditions' reflecting different possibilities of inter-personal comparison.[8]

The distinction between different types of utility comparisons (e.g., of level comparability, unit comparability, cardinal full comparability, ratio scale comparability) has a clear bearing on choosing between different approaches in evaluating inequality. For example, utilitarianism requires comparisons of units but not of levels, whereas maximizing the position of the worst-off person (in line with Rawls's 1971 reasoning) requires comparisons of levels but not of units.[9] These differences were examined in the specific context of inequality evaluation in *OEI-1973* (pp. 22–3, 43–6), and the underlying distinctions proved to be crucial for the choice of approach in evaluating inequality. Even though the arguments in *OEI-1973* were conducted *within* a generally 'welfarist' framework, much of that discussion can be translated to other ways of judging individual advantage (on which more presently).

(4) *Distributional badness versus inequality*: As stated already, *OEI-1973* was much influenced by the writings of Atkinson (1970a), and also by the works of Pigou (1912), Dalton (1920), and Kolm (1969). Pigou and Dalton had, however, used the purely utilitarian approach to welfare economics, and were thus unconcerned about the inequality of utility distribution; their interest in income distribution related to their focus on the maximization of the sum total of utility. Thus their evaluation of what they called 'inequality' was really

[8] On the basic structure of SWFLs, see Sen (1970a), which also presented a typology of interpersonal comparisons that can be used in social choice problems; see also Hammond (1976), d'Aspremont and Gevers (1977), Arrow (1977), Sen (1977), Roberts (1980a, 1980b), Blackorby, Donaldson, and Weymark (1984), d'Aspremont (1985), among other contributions. Various intermediate types of interpersonal comparisons were also characterized, with a metric on the extent of 'partial comparability' (see Sen 1970a, 1970b), on which see also Blackorby (1975), Fine (1975), Basu (1981), and Osmani (1982).

[9] The analytical issues involved in these differences were quite extensively discussed in Sen (1970a, 1974, 1977, 1979b), Hammond (1976a, 1976b, 1977), d'Aspremont and Gevers (1977), Arrow (1977), Blackorby and Donaldson (1977, 1978, 1984), Gevers (1979), Roberts (1980a, 1980b), Blackorby, Donaldson, and Weymark (1984), d'Aspremont (1985), Elster and Roemer (1991), among others.

concerned with assessing 'distributional badness', judged—
in their particular case—by the loss of total utility sum
(irrespective of the distribution of utilities).

Atkinson's approach was not exclusively utilitarian, even
though it invoked an additively separable framework, with the
individual values of u_i adding up to the total social welfare
(without the necessity to see the u_i values as individual
utilities). In some of the discussions in this annexe (particularly, in sections A.2–A.5), this Atkinsonian device will be
much used, and it would be important to remember that while
this form is restrictive in terms of imposing additive separability, there is nevertheless no necessity to be entirely
'utilitarian', in taking u_i to be individual utility. That would be
one possible interpretation, but in general u_i would stand for
the individual component of social welfare that is associated
with person i.[10]

Since an explicit attempt was made in *OEI-1973* to require
that the value of social welfare should take note of distributional inequalities in individual utilities, there were two
distinct reasons for regarding income inequality to be 'distri-
butionally bad' and for preferring a more equal distribution
of a given total income:

(1) the *inefficiency* of income inequality in generating *aggregate* utility (reflecting the loss of utility sum total due to
inequality in individual incomes), and

(2) the *inequity* of income inequality in leading to *unequal
utilities* (reflecting the loss of social welfare from inequality in
individual utilities associated with inequality of incomes).

---

[10] Indeed, each u_i can be seen as a concave transformation of the respective
individual i's utility (a framework consistent with Atkinson's 1970a analysis
and explicitly invoked by Mirrlees 1971 and developed by Roberts 1980b). See
also Jorgenson, Lau, and Stoker (1980) and Jorgenson and Slesnick (1984).
If the same strictly concave transform is used for all individuals, then the aggregative form based on summing the set of u_i will also be equality preferring
in the space of utilities. On a more technical point, the use of an isoelastic
function defining social welfare over individual utilities (as in Mirrlees 1971
and *OEI-1973*, Ch. 1) would require that individual utilities must be all positive or all negative (on this and related issues, see Anand and Sen 1996).

Utilitarianism is concerned only with the former, whereas a 'welfarist' interpretation of Rawls's (1971) 'difference principle' would be inclined towards the latter. *OEI-1973* was much concerned with showing that inequality evaluation can be based on taking full note of *both* these considerations, and that they can be accommodated together within the general approach of inequality measurement developed by Atkinson by changing the formulations appropriately.[11]

(5) *Description and prescription*: *OEI-1973* insisted that inequality has both descriptive and prescriptive aspects (pp. 2–3, 61–5, 71–6). The interpretational differences were illustrated with different ways of seeing some of the standard measures of inequality (Chapters 2 and 3). A specific measure of inequality (such as the Gini coefficient of the income distribution based on the Lorenz curve) could be seen in either mainly descriptive, or mainly prescriptive terms.

Even the basic criterion of Lorenz dominance can be seen either in clearly *normative* terms, or in mainly *descriptive* perspectives. Consider a distribution A of a given total of income, over a given population, that is Lorenz dominant over another distribution B (i.e., A has a higher Lorenz curve than B). In the former line of interpretation, it can be shown that any symmetric social welfare function that is strictly quasi-concave in individual incomes (i.e., which yields diminishing marginal rates of substitution between individual incomes) must generate more social welfare with A than with B.[12] Several different relationships can be established on properties of income distribution, based on social welfare functionals, to bring out the relevance of Lorenz comparisons for making normative social judgements of alternative distributions (see pp. 48–58). Furthermore, if inequality is identified with social

---

[11] The formulational variations received more definitive exploration in the works of Blackorby and Donaldson (1977, 1978). See also section A.4 below, and the recent survey of the literature on the normative analysis of inequality by Blackorby, Bossert, and Donaldson (1995).

[12] In fact, the required condition can be weakened to strict S-concavity (*OEI-1973*, pp. 55–6), which is a very weak kind of concavity (and does not require diminishing marginal rates of substitution in general).

welfare loss for a given total of income (as in Pigou's approach), or with equivalent income loss for given social welfare (as in Atkinson's framework), then a higher Lorenz curve can be seen as indicating less inequality, for a large class of criteria of social evaluation.

However, there is also, at the same time, a largely descriptive—and rather simpler—sense in which A, with a higher Lorenz curve, has less inequality than B: to wit, we can move from B to A through a sequence of income transfers always going from a richer to a poorer person (see pp. 55-8). The two approaches based respectively on (1) the use of normative values to avoid loss of social welfare, and (2) the descriptive features of reducing income differences between richer and poorer persons, provide two different ways of seeing the linkage of Lorenz comparisons and inequality evaluation. Neither can be said to be uniquely important to the exclusion of the other.[13]

While the normative and descriptive comparisons of inequality are congruent in many cases, they need not invariably be so. For example, consider a given vector of unequal individual incomes, and an identical individual utility function shared by all but parametrically varied in different exercises. What happens, now, if we take the 'normative' measure of inequality as being given by the loss of aggregate utility from inequality (or correspondingly, by an Atkinsonian measure of equivalent income loss)? As the individual utility function—shared by all—is made more and more strictly concave (keeping the mean utility fixed), the gaps between individual utilities *diminish*, whereas the social welfare loss—given by aggregate utility loss—from a given income distribution *increases*. Thus, the alterations specified yield simultaneously:

(1) *decreasing* utility inequality,

(2) *unchanging* income inequality, and

(3) *increasing* inequality index as evaluated by an Atkinson-

[13] There are other reasons for resisting any claim that inequality comparison must be either 'entirely evaluative and ethical', or 'entirely descriptive and observational'. On this see *OEI-1973*, Ch. 3.

type normative criterion based on aggregate welfare loss.[14]

They are not, of course, inconsistent with each other in any way, but the contrasts show that our standard descriptive understanding of inequality may conflict sharply with the 'normative measurement' of inequality. Even when we are convinced of the correctness of that normative approach for the making of policies, we can continue to doubt that this is a good way of 'measuring' inequality (as opposed to the *loss* from inequality).

One minimal message to emerge is the possibility of retaining a serious epistemic interest in the descriptive content of inequality comparisons, without presuming that this must somehow get *subsumed* by the ethics of the standard normative criteria.

(6) *Axiomatic analysis*: The influence of social choice theory was partly responsible for the extensive use of formal axioms in evaluating inequality in *OEI-1973*. The axiomatic approach has some drawbacks, particularly when the content of a particular axiom is not altogether transparent.[15] On the other hand, that approach does give some concreteness to evaluative analysis where the underlying principles might be otherwise less clear. This applies, for example, to different interpretations of Lorenz comparisons, and to a whole collection of other analytical results, varying from the demonstration of the evaluative impasse that follows from the absence of interpersonal comparisons (Theorem 1.1) to egalitarian conclusions that result from informational lacunae of particular types (Theorems 4.1 and 4.2).

One of the axioms used, the 'weak equity axiom' (WEA), gave priority, in a particular way, to reducing distributional inequality in total utility levels (pp. 18–22, 43–6). If for every

[14] See Sen (1982a, pp. 416–22). The 'contrariness' of the ethical indicators of inequality was identified and well discussed by Bengt Hansson (1977), and further pursued in Sen (1978).

[15] Rae (1981), See Yaari and Bar-Hillel (1984), Temkin (1986, 1993), Broome (1987), Le Grand (1991), Amiel and Cowell (1992), Fields (1993), Tungodden (1994), Foster (1994a), and Thomson (1996), among others, for related discussions.

given level of individual income, person 1 has less total utility than person 2, then WEA demands that person 1 should have more income than 2 in an optimal distribution of a given total income among n people, including these two. This is, in some ways, a very strong demand, since it is a move towards egalitarianism in utilities, taking no note of the efficiency aspects of income distribution in generating high total utilities. It is, in some ways, a push in exactly the opposite direction to utilitarianism which concentrates exclusively on the efficiency of utility generation (and neglects altogether the argument against substantial inequalities in personal utilities). The merit of WEA is mainly as a dialectical counterpoint to the utilitarian focus.[16]

(7) *Partial orderings*: While the axiomatic approach permits some precision in formulating the principles underlying any approach to inequality evaluation, it also brings out the possible conflicts between different principles. One of the procedures extensively used in *OEI-1973* is that of looking for partial congruence of different principles or measures and then confining overall comparisons only to the 'intersection' rankings. This procedure tends to yield incomplete orderings (or 'quasi-orderings'). The Lorenz comparisons themselves—including the exercises initiated by Atkinson's pioneering paper—can be seen in this light, but the 'intersection' ap-

[16] Not surprisingly, the main criticisms of WEA have tended to come from utilitarian authors (see, for example, Brandt 1979, and Griffin 1981, 1986). These attacks, engaging as they are, have typically misinterpreted the demands of WEA—the alleged counterexamples do not really fit. For example, both Griffin and Brandt took WEA to apply to distributions of *particular* resources, such as specialized medical care, and they resisted—sensibly enough—the awarding of resources for medical care to a person with less need of that care (though generally more deprived). In fact, WEA operates on the allocation of total incomes (a generalized resource), and does not demand that more of any *specific* resource (such as medical attention) be given to the person who gets less out of that resource, even if she is generally more deprived. The issue of compensation relates to giving a person who is more disadvantaged *altogether* (for every given level of shared income) a greater income (a *general* resource, or a 'primary good' as Rawls would call it), not more of some specific resource which another person may need more acutely (for further discussion of this issue, see Sen 1981). On related questions of fair compensation, see Roemer (1993) and Fleurbaey (1994, 1995a, 1995b).

proach can be used in many other contexts as well. This search for a 'common ground' is one of the uniting features of the analyses presented in *OEI-1973*, and the book even ended on that note (p. 106). Quite a lot of the more recent work on inequality assessment has been in terms of a partial ordering, and this literature will receive attention in subsequent sections.

This methodological outlook can be defended in pragmatic terms, related to the need to 'get on', without waiting to solve all the problems which may not readily—or even at all— happen. But there is a bigger issue here of descriptive methodology, which was briefly considered in *OEI-1973* (pp. 5–6, 47–8), but which has been discussed more fully in Sen (1992, pp. 46–9). If a concept has some basic ambiguity (as ideas of what constitutes 'inequality' tend to have), then a *precise* representation of that ambiguous concept must *preserve* that ambiguity, rather than try to remove it through some arbitrarily completed ordering. This issue is quite central to the need for *descriptive accuracy* in inequality assessment, which has to be distinguished from fully ranked, unambiguous assertions (irrespective of the ambiguities in the underlying concept).[17]

(8) *Incentives and inequality*: Arguments in favour of tolerating inequality are often based on incentive grounds. That issue was addressed in Chapter 4 of *OEI-1973*. The connection between the incentive issue and the nature of individual motivation was discussed there, relating the analytical issues to the political literature on different 'distribution principles' (explored, for example, by Marx 1875, 1887). The distinction between incentive-based arguments for inequality and desert-based arguments also received some analysis (pp. 102–6).[18] This annexe does not take up this general issue as a specific field of investigation.

[17] The recent work on fuzzy sets and fuzzy preferences applied to the measurement and evaluation of inequality fit well into this general methodological approach; see Basu (1987b) and Ok (1995).

[18] These and related distinctions have been further examined in Sen (1992).

(9) *Variable population and welfare standard*: When inequality measures are compared for different societies, it is typically the case that we are comparing two different population sizes. But the welfare economics invoked in the standard theory of inequality evaluation is geared to a given population, and taking a more liberal view, at least to an unchanged size of population. The population-constancy assumption can be dropped, and replaced by some specific way of taking note of size variations in comparing welfare standards. The simplest case is, of course, size neutrality, in the sense of invariance of the welfare standard with respect to replication, and this was used in *OEI-1973* (and also in Dasgupta, Sen, and Starrett 1973). The symmetry axiom for population formalizes this, and given that condition, the welfare standards (and the inequality measures derived from them) can be made comparable over different population sizes through appropriate replication of each to make the population sizes congruent (*OEI-1973*, pp. 59–60). These procedures make the welfare-economic results of constant-population exercises extendable to variable-population sizes.

There is an asymmetry here between the evaluation of inequality and the assessment of social welfare, and this deserves some clarification. Since inequality is a *relative* concept, it may be reasonable enough to think that there is no change in inequality if a three-person society is replicated a hundred times to produce a society with 300 people in which a hundred people share the fate of each person in the original situation. But to assume that social welfare is also unchanged is far less plausible. Of course, 'aggregate utilitarians' (such as Bentham or Sidgwick or Edgeworth or Pigou) as opposed to mean utility maximizers would find replication to be a good thing (if the sum total of utilities is positive), but they would not be alone in finding number neutrality to be deeply problematic. Anyone with some interest in the totality of human experiences and lives—not just aggregate utility maximizers—would identify a substantial issue here.

There is, thus, some asymmetry between the implications of size variations (and replication, in particular) respectively on (1) the evaluation of social welfare, and (2) the appraisal and normative measurement of inequality. This may look like a problem since the close association between inequality evaluation and welfare assessment is quite central to the Atkinson approach and to the normative part of inequality evaluation pursued in *OEI-1973*. The correspondence between the two was preserved in *OEI-1973* by talking not about aggregate social welfare, but about 'mean welfare' (p. 59), or what can be sensibly called 'welfare standard' (in the same way as one considers 'the standard of living'). It is less implausible to assume that a replication of population without changing the proportional distribution of different individual experiences should leave the 'welfare standard' unaffected, just as it would also leave the inequality index unaltered.[19]

A.1.3 Further issues

The listing, in the previous section, of problems that received attention in *OEI-1973* is, of course, quite incomplete, but it captures some of the focal concentrations in that project. However, some of the issues briefly identified in *OEI-1973* did not receive any substantial exploration there, and some important matters were not even identified. A substantial part of this annexe will be devoted to explorations that have occurred since then in these fields. These issues include, among other problems, the implications for inequality evaluation of variations of mean income (briefly referred to on pp. 36–7, 60–1 in *OEI-1973*), requirements of transfer sensitivity (discussed generally, but not in an axiomatically systematic way, on pp. 27–33 in *OEI-1973*), and demands of decomposability and subgroup consistency (briefly considered and rather rapidly 'dismissed' on pp. 31–4, 39–41 in *OEI-1973*). These problems

[19] Coming back to the contrast between the two types of utilitarians, viz. (1) those who maximize aggregate utility, and (2) those who take the maximand to be per capita utility, we do not have to take sides on this dispute to be able to use the invariance of 'welfare standard' with respect to replication. The aggregate utilitarians will take the social maximand to be the *product* of the welfare standard and the population size, whereas the per capita utilitarians will see the welfare standard *itself* as the appropriate maximand. Various 'intermediate' positions are, of course, also possible.

are not only important in their own right, they also relate to the general strategy of inequality evaluation pursued in *OEI-1973*. In sections A.2–A.5 these issues will be considered, *inter alia*, in the context of general discussions of the post-1973 literature.

There is also the related subject of poverty evaluation, which was not explicitly taken up in *OEI-1973*, even though the discussions on the measurement and appraisal of inequality have a clear bearing on poverty studies. In Sen (1976b) some of the considerations involved in inequality evaluation, as discussed in *OEI-1973*, were applied to the measurement and appraisal of income poverty, and many interesting and important contributions in this general field have occurred in contemporary poverty studies. Section A.6 will examine the main lines of work.

A major problem that received only indirect attention concerns the implications of the variability of needs between different people. This subject made recurrent appearances in *OEI-1973* (see, for example, pp. 16–23, 77–91), but did not get translated into a decisive move away from judging inequality only in the space of *incomes* or *utilities*. Further, the characterization of needs may require us to go beyond the *utility-oriented* framework to which the 1973 book was more or less entirely confined. In particular, the 'space' in which inequality is to be assessed becomes specifically important to consider.

These matters are of central relevance to concepts of justice and equity, and they lie very close to the normative measurement of inequality. Different ways of judging individual advantage other than incomes (including 'primary goods', 'resources', 'functionings', 'capabilities', 'opportunities for welfare', and so on) have received much attention in the contemporary theories of justice, and their bearing on the evaluation of inequality and poverty will be considered in section A.7.

A.2 Inequality and Welfare

A.2.1 Welfare as a basis for inequality measurement

Basing inequality judgements on the traditional tools of welfare economics was one of the two main approaches pursued in *OEI-1973*.[20] As was mentioned earlier, this 'normative' line of investigation was pioneered by the classic paper of Atkinson (1970a).[21] There were two major understandings in this Atkinsonian perspective. The first is the 'Atkinson Theorem' about Lorenz dominance, which shows how the Lorenz ranking can be interpreted as a welfare ranking of income distributions, assuming a fixed total income, the same needs and other non-income characteristics, additively separable social welfare functions, and strict concavity of individual utility functions—and thus of their sum (the last two requirements can be relaxed, to considerable extents, on which see Chapter 3 of *OEI-1973* and section A.3 below).

The second achievement of this Atkinsonian perspective was an intuitive method of converting welfare functions into inequality measures, and vice versa. Not only does this close correspondence serve the purpose of constructing new measures of inequality, but it also helps in uncovering the implicit value judgements in inequality indicators that are used without specifying any welfare assumptions. This important

[20] The other approach looks for descriptive cogency in terms of traditional understanding of inequality; for example, noting that a transfer of income from a poorer to a richer person must increase income inequality, quite irrespective of welfare. The distinction and the overlap between the two approaches were discussed in *OEI-1973*, pp. 61–3, 71–2, and also here in section A.1.2, issue (5).

[21] A similar approach was also developed by Kolm (1969), with more of a focus on justice and less specifically on the measurement of inequality.

relation is quite central to the work that has followed in this field, and we should pause to clarify this linkage.

It may be useful to present briefly an intuitive understanding of the Atkinson approach in terms of a simple diagram. Diagram A2.1 portrays a world of two identical individuals who share a given total income OJ; the line JK represents all possible distributions of this given total, with C as the point of equal division and CE as the mean income. Each of the social

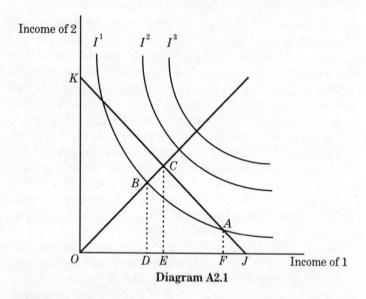

Diagram A2.1

indifference curves such as I^1, I^2, I^3, represents a particular level of social welfare as an increasing and symmetric function of individual incomes, but with diminishing marginal rates of substitution (or strict quasi-concavity of the social welfare function).[22] If the actual distribution of income is the one

[22] This corresponds, in fact, to a not-necessarily additive social welfare function, and thus represents the more general case of (2.16) and (2.17) in *OEI-1973* (p. 42) rather than the original Atkinson case of (2.14) and (2.15) (p. 38). Note also that the indifference maps represent the case in which social welfare is strictly quasi-concave on individual incomes; in fact a more general case would involve the weaker requirement of strict S-concavity (on this see Dasgupta, Sen, and Starrett (1973), and *OEI-1973*, pp. 56–8).

reflected in A (with persons 1 and 2 getting respectively OF and AF), then this is 'equivalent' in terms of social welfare to each receiving the equal income of BD, since A and B lie on the same social welfare indifference curve. BD is, thus, 'the equally distributed equivalent mean income' of the actual income distribution A (corresponding to equation (2.16) on p. 42 of *OEI-1973*). The generalized Atkinson measure of inequality is given by the difference—appropriately normalized— between the actual mean income (CE) and the equally distributed equivalent mean income (BD), and it can be sensibly indexed by $(1 - BD/CE)$, which corresponds to equation (2.17) in *OEI-1973*.

This class of inequality measures is, thus, completely determined by the social welfare functions (given by the respective indifference maps). It is easily seen that the converse is also true, in the sense that if the inequality level for every pair of incomes (like the point A) were known, we could immediately deduce the equally distributed mean equivalent income level and draw the entire indifference map of social welfare on that basis. This normative approach thus locks the problem of inequality measurement and that of welfare evaluation in a very tight relation. What the diagram illustrates for the two-person case holds generally for n persons.

It must, however, be noted that the relationship between social welfare and inequality measures is not that of a one-to-one correspondence. If, for example, everyone's income is doubled, then the measure of inequality, which is basically *relative*, may well remain unchanged; this would definitely be the case with most descriptive measures (such as the coefficient of variation, or the Gini index), and would also apply to normative measures given homotheticity of the social welfare function (on which more in the next subsection A.2.2). On the other hand, it is reasonable to presume that there would be some *increase* in social welfare as a result of an all-round increase in everyone's income. The one-to-one correspondence would apply only for a given mean income (i.e., for movements along the distributional line JK in the two-person case in Diagram A2.1).

A.2.2 From welfare to inequality

The equivalent income function has the property of being *linearly homogeneous*—doubling all incomes doubles the equivalent income—whenever the original welfare function is *homothetic*.[23] Intuitively, homotheticity makes the indifference curves 'radial copies' (blow-outs or blow-ins) of each other. In this case, the resulting inequality measure is definitely mean independent.[24] Atkinson noted that additivity in the presence of homotheticity restricts consideration to the single-parameter family:

$$
A_\varepsilon(\mathbf{x}) = \begin{cases} 1 - \left[\dfrac{1}{n_x} \sum_{i=1}^{n_x} \left(\dfrac{x_i}{\mu_x} \right)^\varepsilon \right]^{1/\varepsilon} & \text{for } \varepsilon \le 1 \text{ and } \varepsilon \ne 0 \\[2ex] 1 - \prod_{i=1}^{n_x} \left(\dfrac{x_i}{\mu_x} \right)^{1/n} & \text{for } \varepsilon = 0 \end{cases}
$$

which is now known as the Atkinson family.[25]

What happens if welfare is not homothetic? We lose the property of mean independence in the normative inequality measure, and this can thus introduce an 'absolutist' element in what is standardly thought of as being a *relative* concept (that of inequality). Blackorby and Donaldson (1978) present an alternative procedure which yields *relative inequality* measures for non-homothetic social welfare functions.

Recall that the welfare indifference curves of non-homothetic functions are not all radial copies of one another. Blackorby and Donaldson (1978) pick a 'reference' curve which is used to generate an ersatz (or an 'as if') welfare

[23] A function is homothetic if it is an increasing transform of a linearly homogeneous function. Note that a welfare function and its equivalent income function are increasing transforms of one another.

[24] If each income in x is doubled, $I = (\mu_x - e_x)/\mu_x$ is unchanged since both μ_x and e_x are doubled (where μ_x and e_x are the mean and equivalent incomes, respectively). It is interesting to note that Dalton's (1920) approach (*OEI-1973*, p. 37) yields the same inequality measure as Atkinson's when welfare itself is linearly homogeneous.

[25] As discussed in *OEI-1973*, removing the requirement of additivity significantly broadens the range of welfare-based relative inequality measures.

function that is linear homogeneous. Applying Atkinson's transformation then yields a relative measure or, more precisely, a different relative measure for *each* reference level of welfare. If the original social welfare function is homothetic, the ersatz welfare functions and relative inequality measures are all 'reference free' and we are back to the original Atkinson territory.

Blackorby and Donaldson's alternative transformation nicely extends Atkinson's line of analysis. The generalization is, however, achieved at some inescapable cost. As Blackorby and Donaldson have pointed out, the derived inequality index, while relative, need not be 'normatively significant'. Away from the reference level, the ersatz and true welfare functions can disagree. Consequently, a particular redistribution of income can simultaneously lead to higher inequality *and* higher (true) welfare, breaking the inverse relationship (for a given mean income) underlying the classical Atkinson approach. The Blackorby–Donaldson results identify the trade-offs inherent in measuring 'relative inequality' through the social welfare approach when homotheticity cannot be presumed.

A.2.3 From inequality to welfare

To get a sense of the value judgements underlying a given inequality measure for *fixed mean* comparisons, any negative transformation of the inequality values will do, even simply the negative of the inequality measure itself. But to make welfare comparisons across different means, we must *assume* a specific transformation linking up inequality measures I for different mean incomes μ. One obvious alternative when the index I takes values between 0 and 1 is the reverse of the Atkinson transformation. For a mean-independent I, this yields the linearly homogeneous welfare function:

$$W = \mu(1 - I).$$

This transformation is indeed quite natural, and the resulting welfare function has the intuitive interpretation as the size of the pie (μ), corrected downwards by the extent of inequality $(1 - I)$.

This formulation of W has clear similarities with the Gini-based welfare indicator $\mu(1 - G)$, derived in Sen (1976a), but that uses a rather different—and specifically multicommodity—approach.[26] In that multicommodity analysis, for any commodity distribution vector (specifying the amount of each commodity going to every person), the value $\mu(1 - G)$ identifies a 'bounding hyperplane' in the commodity distribution space below which social welfare is definitely less than in x, but above which there is ambiguity (depending essentially on the exact slopes of the indifference surfaces, which are not known beyond the fact that they are concave; that is, the social welfare function is quasi-concave). There is, thus, no exact fit but a signficant similarity between:

(1) the derivation of the welfare function $\mu(1 - I)$ through the reverse of the Atkinson transformation in a one-commodity world (with homogeneous income), and

(2) the use of $\mu(1 - G)$ as a hyperplane that asymmetrically bounds the set of superior points thereby identifying a partial ordering of social welfare.

The distinction does not lie only in the use of a specific inequality indicator (viz. the Gini coefficient G) in the latter with a parametric use of any inequality index I in the former; indeed, the latter exercise can be extended to cover inequality indicators other than G. The main difference is in the admission of a multicommodity world in the latter approach with the use of a general approach of concavity (or quasi-concavity, to be exact). The partial orderings generated by the latter approach avoid the constraining simplification of a one-commodity world, and do not require the arbitrary specification of a *particular* commodity-based utility function.[27]

Closer to the Atkinson exercise, Blackorby and Donaldson (1978) have constructed a welfare function $\mu(1 - I)$ for each of

[26] On related results, see also Fisher (1956), Graaff (1977, 1985), Hammond (1978), Blackorby and Donaldson (1978, 1984), Jorgenson, Lau, and Stoker (1980), Roberts (1980c), Osmani (1982), Jorgenson and Slesnick (1984), Kakwani (1986), among other contributions.

[27] On this, see Sen (1976a) and in the related work by Osmani (1982).

the commonly used inequality measures I. They illuminate the implicit value judgements in each case through depicting indifference curves in the three-income simplex of constant total income (see *OEI-1973*, pp. 56–8).[28] Much can be learned about inequality measures from these simple diagrams, and the understanding of the relation between social welfare and the normative measurement of income inequality has been much advanced by Blackorby and Donaldson's characterizations.[29]

[28] We might call this three-income simplex the 'Kolm triangle', since Kolm had made such pioneering use of that representation (Kolm 1969, p. 190).

[29] See also Blackorby and Donaldson (1980a, 1980b, 1984) on related issues.

A.3 Welfare Functions:
Unanimity and Dominance

A.3.1. Partial rankings and intersection quasi-orderings

Any specific statistical measure of income inequality (such as the Gini coefficient, the coefficient of variation, or the Theil measure) generates a 'complete' ranking that orders every pair of income distributions. So does any fully articulated complete welfare function defined over the space of income vectors. In contrast, a relation devised as a partial ordering, like the Lorenz relation, can be silent on many pairs and only record unambiguous comparisons. The very basis of its comparison, to wit, one Lorenz curve being higher everywhere (or at least, higher somewhere and lower nowhere), makes the ranking relation potentially incomplete (depending on whether the Lorenz curves to be compared cross or not).

In contrast to a designed partial order, it is also possible to arrive at a partial order on the basis of the rule of going by the *congruence* of different complete orderings; for example, the shared rankings of distinct complete orders generated by different statistical measures of income inequality. *OEI-1973* was much concerned with derived incomplete relations based on 'intersections' of complete orders—what were called 'intersection quasi-orderings' (pp. 72–4). Intersection quasi-orderings are based on *unanimity* according to a given set of criteria, or—equivalently—on the intersection of the orderings generated by these criteria. If the multiple criteria are welfare functions (or, alternatively, inequality measures), the intersection quasi-ordering offers verdicts that are independent of the choice of a specific welfare function among the admitted ones (or of a particular inequality measure in the acceptable class of inequality indicators). In this section the 'intersection approach' will be discussed in the context of welfare functions, and later on—in section A.4.2—the approach will be applied to the class of relative measures of inequality.

The 'Atkinson Theorem' regarding Lorenz dominance, for fixed mean comparisons, can itself be seen as linking up two intersection quasi-orderings. Indeed, Lorenz dominance, which reflects the intersection of a class of inequality comparisons, coincides with the intersection quasi-ordering generated by permissible classes of welfare functions (such as the sum total of individual utilities with a strictly concave individual utility function shared by all—the class considered by Atkinson himself).[30] Subsequent work has explored important aspects of these quasi-orderings, particularly how each treats cross-mean comparisons and how each can be strengthened or made 'more complete'. We now know, for example, that the Lorenz ranking is the intersection quasi-ordering generated by all 'relative' inequality measures, and that the welfare intersection quasi-ordering has its own 'generalized' Lorenz curve which indicates when that intersection ranking holds.

The additive welfare functions of Atkinson's Theorem have the form:

$$W(\mathbf{x}) = \frac{1}{n_x} \sum_{i=1}^{n_x} u(x_i)$$

for income distribution vectors $\mathbf{x}$ of arbitrary length n_x (i.e., any number of people n_x), where $u' > 0$ and $u'' < 0$. Each member of this class of welfare functions is clearly (1) symmetric, (2) replication invariant, (3) monotonically increasing, (4) strictly concave, and (5) additive.[31] Atkinson's result shows

[30] The additive case based on the sum total of individual utilities is a special application of summing individual $u(y_i)$ for all individuals i, where the u function is strictly concave, whether or not it is interpreted to be the individual utility of person i. This broader case was the one with which Atkinson himself was concerned. The result can be shown to be obtainable from other classes of not necessarily additive social welfare functions (on which see *OEI-1973*, Ch. 3).

[31] Strict concavity, monotonicity, and additivity are well-understood general properties of such real-valued and vector-argument functions. Replication invariance was discussed earlier, and requires that if $\mathbf{x}$ is obtained from $\mathbf{y}$ by

that for all welfare functions satisfying these properties, if the Lorenz curve of **x** is higher than that of **y**, then (for distributions with the same mean income) $W(\mathbf{x})$ is larger than $W(y)$. For such comparisons, Lorenz dominance is equivalent to the intersection of orderings generated by these welfare functions.

The theorems presented in Chapter 3 of *OEI-1973* effectively show that to get the former result, additivity is not needed, and that strict concavity can be relaxed to strict S-concavity.[32] This generalizes this part of the Atkinson result to a much broader class of welfare functions for which the Lorenz ranking is decisive.[33] While this *sufficiency result* about what Lorenz ranking entails is clearly a generalization of Atkinson's theorem, the converse—that is, the *necessity result* which tells us what entails the Lorenz ranking—is subsumed by Atkinson's Theorem. It is redundant to check that all strictly S-concave welfare functions give the same ranking before pronouncing that there is a Lorenz dominance here, since unanimity over the strictly smaller—additive and strictly concave—class ensures the same conclusion, viz. that it is a case of Lorenz dominance (see *OEI-1973*, pp. 54–5). One of the implications of this relationship is that unanimity over the smaller, additive, and strictly concave class of welfare functions ensures unanimity over the larger, general class of welfare functions—without additivity and with only strict S-concavity. Consequently, for the special case of *unanimous* welfare judgements across different welfare functions, additivity and strict concavity represent no additional restriction at all.

a replication of any length (so that $\mathbf{x} = (\mathbf{y}, \ldots, \mathbf{y})$), we have $W(\mathbf{x}) = W(\mathbf{y})$. This effectively ensures that W reflects welfare in per capita terms. Finally, symmetry requires that $W(\mathbf{x}) = W(\mathbf{y})$ whenever **x** is obtained from **y** by a permutation.

[32] Strict S-concavity is a weaker requirement, given symmetry, than not only strict concavity but also strict quasi-concavity. In fact, strict S-concavity is as far as we can go; it is equivalent to the Pigou–Dalton transfer condition, with symmetry. The Pigou–Dalton transfer condition is satisfied if any transfer from a poorer to a richer person reduces social welfare W (see *OEI-1973*, pp. 56, 64).

[33] The covered class includes many that were not specifically discussed in *OEI-1973*, including for example the generalized Gini functions of Weymark (1981) and Donaldson and Weymark (1980), which can also be viewed as non-expected utility functions (see Yaari 1988).

A.3.2 Generalized Lorenz dominance

The fixed-mean comparisons addressed by Atkinson's Theorem are not the only comparisons over which these welfare functions can agree. Extending this line of analysis, a complete characterization of 'unanimity of welfare' quasi-orderings can be obtained with the help of Shorrocks' (1983) *generalized Lorenz curve*, *GL*, defined as the Lorenz curve L scaled by the mean μ (i.e., $GL(p) = \mu L(p)$ for each population share p).[34] Generalized Lorenz dominance is then defined analogous to Lorenz dominance: x dominates y by the generalized Lorenz criterion, written x*GL*y, if GL_x lies above GL_y (or at least above somewhere and not below anywhere). Diagram A3.1 illustrates comparisons of generalized Lorenz curves.

Shorrocks (1983) shows that x*GL*y is equivalent to $W(\mathbf{x}) > W(\mathbf{y})$ for all welfare functions W satisfying the requirements

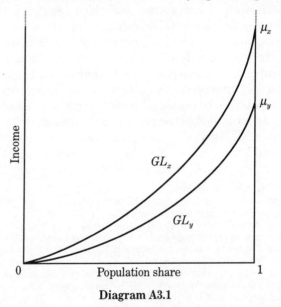

Diagram A3.1

[34] While Shorrocks was the first to identify the exact conditions and to establish precisely how they operate, there were earlier discussions of this general issue, particularly by Blackorby and Donaldson (1977).

mentioned earlier.[35] Consequently, for this class of welfare functions, GL is the appropriate indicator of unanimously higher welfare when means differ. In the special case in which means are the same, xGLy coincides with xLy, which leads us back to the Lorenz theorems of Atkinson and related results (as in *OEI-1973*, Chapter 3).

Even though generalized Lorenz rankings extend welfare comparisons quite radically by removing the requirement of fixed means, they too are incomplete (in the way the entire Lorenz approach is). For example, if x has the higher mean, while y has the higher of the respective smallest incomes, then x and y cannot be ranked by GL. However, Shorrocks and others have provided many empirical examples for which GL applies and welfare functions agree, and this extension is of much practical importance indeed.

The Shorrocks (1983) result suggests an alternative characterization of the welfare functions satisfying the required properties, to wit, *GL-consistent* (since they agree with the generalized Lorenz ranking when it applies). The approach also suggests one specific GL-consistent welfare function that concentrates on the area below the Lorenz curve, analogously to the Lorenz interpretation of the Gini coefficient. And that can then be linked to the Gini-based 'corrections' for inequality in 'distribution-adjusted real national income' $\mu(1 - G)$ as proposed in Sen (1976a).[36] Let W be twice the area below the generalized Lorenz curve. W ranges between 0 (approximated

[35] Actually, the Shorrocks result concerns the weak definition of generalized Lorenz dominance; hence the welfare dominance he obtains has a weak inequality. See also Marshall and Olkin (1979, p. 109).

[36] In fact, as was discussed earlier (in section A.1.2), $\mu(1 - G)$ is not the welfare function itself, but represents a supporting hyperplane that bounds from below all the superior points in the multicommodity characterization analysed in Sen (1976a). However, $\mu(1 - G)$ can be used as a welfare function itself, consistently with that analysis, for the special case of a one-commodity world (or *as if* one-commodity world with fixed substitution rates) and linear interpersonal weights. It is in that simpler form that $\mu(1 - G)$ has been most used in actual empirical work for intercountry comparisons; for example, in the United Nations' *Human Development Report 1990* (UNDP 1990, pp. 11–13). See also Sen (1973b) and Kakwani (1980a, 1981, 1984b, 1986) for uses of this and related measures.

when GL is near the horizontal axis) and μ (approximated when GL is near the diagonal of complete equality), and is clearly GL-consistent. It is easy to verify that W is $\mu(1 - G)$, corresponding exactly to the Gini-based social welfare criterion used in Sen (1976a).[37] Its simple graphical representation as well as its interpretation as the mean income modified downward by the Gini inequality adds to its attraction as an intuitive and usable welfare indicator.

A.3.3 Stochastic dominance

A variety of unanimity quasi-orderings are extensively used in the analysis of behaviour under risk and that approach corresponds closely to the use of congruence of different orderings in assessing inequality and welfare. In risk analysis, one distribution is said to *stochastically dominate* another if it yields higher expected utility for all utility functions in a given class.

There are three common stochastic dominance relations—'first, second, and third order'—denoted respectively as FSD, SSD, and TSD. The FSD relation holds whenever all persons with *positive* marginal utility prefer one distribution to another; SSD applies when all persons with *positive and decreasing* marginal utility share a preference ranking; TSD requires congruent preference among those with *positive, decreasing, and convex* marginal utility.[38] As we move to increasingly narrower classes when we go from the first to the second to the third order of stochastic dominance, the three

---

[37] Note that even though $\mu(1 - G)$ is fully GL-consistent (and indeed corresponds to twice the area under the generalized Lorenz curve), not all of the welfare functions of the form $\mu(1 - I)$, using other measures of inequality I, are GL-consistent. See Blackorby and Donaldson (1978) for examples of violation.

[38] Each relation can be captured in a simple condition on the cumulative distribution function (*cdf*), which indicates the proportion of the population $F(s)$ with income no greater than s. In that representational framework, FSD compares the *cdf*s directly; SSD evaluates integrals of the *cdf* (the integral condition of Rothschild and Stiglitz 1970 corresponds to this); and TSD uses double integrals of *cdf*s. See, for example, Bawa (1976).

unanimity quasi-orderings are nested. The least complete ranking FSD entails SSD, which in turn entails TSD.

By appropriately reinterpreting expected utility as group welfare, the three can also be interpreted as intersection quasi-orderings of welfare. In fact FSD indicates unanimity for all symmetric, replication-invariant, and monotonically increasing welfare functions. Adding the Pigou–Dalton transfer condition generates SSD, the original welfare quasi-ordering (or generalized Lorenz dominance).[39] An additional condition of 'transfer sensitivity' (belonging to a class of properties to be discussed presently), which requires that a fixed-sized income transfer should have a greater effect on social welfare when it occurs at lower income levels, takes us to TSD.

Two important inequality quasi-orderings are produced when SSD and TSD are applied to normalized distributions (where incomes are divided by the mean), and these will be examined further in section A.4. The stochastic dominance relations have also proved fruitful in poverty analysis (see Foster and Shorrocks 1988a, 1988b, and Atkinson 1987), as discussed in section A.6. In addition, stochastic dominance has been extended to distributions of more than one variable. Atkinson and Bourguignon (1982) have made good use of these results in their dominance approach to multidimensional welfare comparisons.[40]

---

[39] The integral condition integrates *cdf*s along the income axis; generalized Lorenz curves are constructed by integrating the inverse of *cdf*s along the population axis. A simple change of variable converts the integral condition into generalized Lorenz dominance. See Foster and Shorrocks (1988a, 1988b).

[40] Different approaches to multidimensional inequality and welfare comparisons can be found in Kolm (1977), Maasoumi (1986, 1995), Dardanoni (1992), Tsui (1995), and others. Foster, Majumdar and Mitra (1990), in particular, revisit the Atkinson Theorem in a market setting, and show how generalized Lorenz comparisons of expenditure distributions (which include *inter alia* Hicksian comparisons of national income) can signal higher total welfare.

A.4 Relative Inequality: Measures and Quasi-Orderings

A.4.1 The class of relative inequality measures

In this section, we are concerned with the properties of inequality measures and the quasi-orderings that can be obtained from their congruence. We focus particularly on the *relative* aspect of inequality comparisons. Most of the commonly used numerical measures of inequality are replication invariant and mean independent; that is, they are invariant to changes in population size or mean income which leave the *relative* distribution unchanged. Lorenz comparisons also have these invariance properties. For example, if the income levels in distribution x were replicated arbitrarily to obtain the distribution (x, . . .,x), or if they were rescaled by a positive k to obtain the distribution kx, the Lorenz curve would be unaltered.[41]

Inequality measures that satisfy (1) symmetry, (2) replication invariance, and (3) mean independence (these three stand, respectively, for invariance under permutations, population replications, and scalar multiplication), and also (4) the Pigou–Dalton condition (inequality increases as a result of a regressive transfer), are called *measures of relative inequality*

---

[41] This relies on the standard definition of Gastwirth (1971), which, for discrete distributions like x, amounts to plotting the income share of the poorest l persons against their population share (for each $l = 0, 1, \ldots, n_x$) and connecting the points with line segments. More generally, where F is any cumulative distribution function (indicating the proportion of the population $F(s)$ with income no greater than s), and F^{-1} is its inverse (or 'generalized' inverse if F has jumps), the Lorenz curve of F is defined for $0 \le p \le 1$ as:

$$L(p) = \int_0^p F^{-1}(q)\mathrm{d}q/\mu, \text{ where } \mu = \int_0^1 F^{-1}(q)\mathrm{d}q \text{ is the mean of } F$$

(or simply *relative measures*).[42] Prominent examples include the coefficient of variation C, the Gini coefficient G, and the Theil measure T, each described in *OEI-1973* (pp. 27–36).

Two other families are also worth considering, which are generalizations of the Theil and Gini measures respectively. The first is the *generalized entropy* class of measures, defined for values α other than 0 and 1 by:[43]

$$I_\alpha(\mathbf{x}) = \frac{1}{\alpha(1-\alpha)} \frac{1}{n} \sum_{i=1}^{n} \left[1 - \left(\frac{x_i}{\mu} \right)^\alpha \right]$$

with I_1 being the Theil measure:

$$I_1(\mathbf{x}) = T(\mathbf{x}) = \frac{1}{n} \sum_{i=1}^{n} \frac{x_i}{\mu} \ln\left(\frac{x_i}{\mu} \right)$$

and I_0 being Theil's 'second' measure, also known as the mean logarithmic deviation:

$$I_0(\mathbf{x}) = D(\mathbf{x}) = \frac{1}{n} \sum_{i=1}^{n} \ln\left(\frac{\mu}{x_i} \right)$$

Note that I_2 is a multiple of the squared coefficient of variation C^2.

It may seem odd to generalize the Theil measure which itself is 'not exactly overflowing with intuitive sense' (*OEI-1973*, p. 36). The primary justification for I_α relates to the decomposition properties to be considered in the next section, but there are also some other merits. For example, the measures in the range $\alpha < 1$ are seen to be Dalton indices—measuring the percentage social welfare loss due to inequality—where social welfare is utilitarian and the individual utility function takes a particular form with constant relative risk aversion (or 'isoelastic', of the type discussed by

[42] Anand (1983), who investigated the shared properties of these measures, called them the Lorenz class of inequality indices (pp. 339–40).
[43] See Shorrocks (1980), Cowell (1980), Cowell and Kuga (1981b), who defined the family as such, and Bourguignon (1979) who did nearly the same.

Atkinson 1970a).[44] Indeed, each I_α in this range is a monotonic transformation of an Atkinson measure, and the parameter α can be seen as an indicator of 'inequality aversion' (more averse as α falls).[45] The parameter also indicates the measure's sensitivity to transfers at different parts of the distribution. For each I_α, the effect of a small regressive transfer depends not only on the incomes of the giver and receiver, and on the mean income, but also on the parameter α (the specific relations are identified in a formula characterized by Cowell 1995). I_2, for example, exhibits 'transfer neutrality', since a given size of transfer between two persons who are a fixed income distance apart has the same effect at high and low incomes. T, D, and all measures with $\alpha < 2$ (including those satisfying Atkinson's condition of $\alpha < 1$) favour transfers at the lower end of the distribution.[46]

The second class of measures, the *generalized Gini* measures, also have the merit of being able to exhibit different amounts of transfer sensitivity to transfers along the distribution. To understand what is involved, it is important to recall that the unmodified Gini has the property that the effect of a transfer depends on the relative ranks or positions of the two persons between whom the transfer takes place, and not on the actual incomes. In fact, since the effect on the Gini depends only on the *difference in ranks*, or equivalently, on the *number of people* who have intermediate incomes in between the two persons, and not on their specific ranks, the Gini exhibits a special type of 'positional transfer neutrality'.

One can retain the focus on position without requiring the

---

[44] See Bourguignon (1979, p. 913) who sketched this argument. We must be careful to take absolute values when needed, since utility and hence social welfare can be negative as the formulae stand. Cowell (1995) interprets I_α as measuring the distance from complete equality.

[45] See Atkinson (1983) for an illuminating discussion of this interpretation.

[46] Properties of 'transfer sensitivity' are discussed in section A.4.3. The measures beyond $\alpha = 2$ stress transfers at higher incomes in a kind of 'reverse sensitivity'—which calls into question I_α's usefulness for this range. Note that all the generalized entropy measures have the property that the effect of a transfer between two persons is independent of the distribution of income among the remaining persons—a rather strong restriction on the information used in judging distributional changes (on this more later).

Gini's strict neutrality. For example, to emphasize transfers at the lower end, one might alter the weights on incomes in the definition of the Gini (see equation (2.8.3) in *OEI-1973*). Alternatively, the Lorenz distance $[p - L_x(p)]$ used to calculate the Gini area could receive different (positive) weights $\theta(p)$ at different p, yielding the generalized Gini class defined by Shorrocks and Slottje (1995) as:

$$G_\theta(\mathbf{x}) = \int_0^1 [p - L_x(p)] \theta(p) \, dp \Big/ \int_0^1 p\theta(p) \, dp$$

Notice that the numerator is the weighted area between the 45° line and the Lorenz curve, while the denominator is the weighted area below the 45° line, so that when $\theta(p)$ is a constant, $G_\theta(\mathbf{x})$ reduces to the normal Gini. By choosing a decreasing weighting function $\theta(p)$, for example, one can ensure that transfers between persons who are a given 'distance' apart (measured by the number of people occupying intermediate positions) have greater effect at the lower part of the income distribution (i.e., when the people involved in the transfer are poorer). Consequently, $G_\theta(\mathbf{x})$ can be made to conform with 'positional transfer sensitivity' and other desired forms of positional sensitivities through the specification of the weighting function.[47] It should also be noted that the effect of a small transfer between two persons is independent of the distribution of income among the remaining persons—so long as the respective rankings of the two remain the same. This is a restriction on the type of information that is allowed to count, but of a different category from the informational invariance imposed by the generalized entropy measures.

A.4.2 Lorenz dominance and relative inequality

While distributional judgements based on a single-inequality measure are frequently used in public debates, these judgements can be quite arbitrary in the sense that another

---

[47] Papers with generalizations of the Gini include Mehran (1976), Pyatt (1976, 1987), Donaldson and Weymark (1980), Kakwani (1980a, 1981), Weymark (1981), Nygård and Sandström (1982), Yitzhaki (1983), among others, although not all of the indices considered are 'relative' in the sense defined earlier.

measure could have led to a very different conclusion. Considerations of this kind led *OEI-1973* to argue for relying not on the ranking generated by any one inequality measure but by the intersection of the class of measures each of which has some interest and plausibility (pp. 72–6). If a particular distribution *A* were to be ranked higher in terms of inequality than another *B* by *every* inequality measure in the plausible class, then there would indeed be a powerful argument for taking *A* to be more unequal than *B*. That intersection approach has already received attention, earlier on in this annexe (in section A.3.1), starting from the welfare end and looking for inequality rankings that would conform to a whole class of welfare functions. The intersection approach is now to be examined for classes of inequality measures with specified properties—without explicitly invoking any welfare function.

The practical usefulness of the intersection depends on the feasibility and convenience of checking whether all of the members of the class of plausible inequality measures agree. When there is a small class of such measures, it may be quite straightforward to check this directly (see, for example, *OEI-1973*, pp. 72–3), but when the class is very large, and especially when it is infinite, the direct approach can be intractable. An alternative strategy is to identify the common thread of analytical requirements underlying the plausible class of measures, and then to use them to identify a convenient test for unanimity or, perhaps, to construct the intersection quasi-ordering itself.

Consider, now, the class of 'relative' inequality measures: those satisfying the four basic axioms requiring symmetry, replication invariance, mean independence, and the Pigou–Dalton condition. What intersection quasi-ordering does this class generate? The answer, as shown by Foster (1985), is precisely the *Lorenz quasi-ordering*, which characterizes all comparisons over which the relative inequality measures agree.[48] If one relative measure contends that x has more

[48] See also Anand (1983), who shows that all the relative measures are Lorenz consistent. He also emphasizes what this result shows about the relevance of Lorenz comparisons for 'inequality in a positive or descriptive

inequality than y, checking the Lorenz criterion will confirm whether this verdict is robust in the relative class, or simply measure specific. If Lorenz dominance holds, then all relative measures agree with the original verdict; but if it fails, then some relative measure will rank the distributions differently from the original measure. This also gives us an alternative characterization of the class of relative measures, to wit, they are exactly those measures that are *Lorenz consistent* (i.e., the measures that agree with the Lorenz quasi-ordering when it applies).

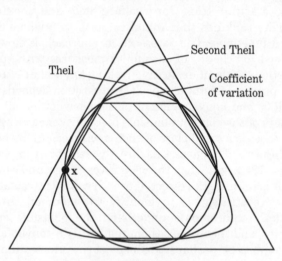

Diagram A4.1

These characterization results can be depicted diagrammatically in the three-person income simplex (as in *OEI-1973*, pp. 56–8). In Diagram A4.1, the shaded set of distributions more equal than x according to the Lorenz criterion lies within

sense', aside from their normative relevance (pp. 339–40). See also the related results of Fields and Fei (1978) and Schwartz and Winship (1980). Shorrocks and Slottje (1995) investigate whether *subclasses* of the relative measures might generate the Lorenz quasi-ordering. They establish that while the generalized Gini measures do, the generalized entropy measures do not.

the 'more equal' sets for all three of the relative inequality measures depicted (namely, the two Theil measures and the coefficient of variation). This illustrates the Lorenz consistency of these particular measures. As additional 'relative' measures are taken up, not only does the Lorenz set of greater equality lie within each of these new 'more equal' sets, but, furthermore, the intersection of the 'more equal' sets for all 'relative' measures tends to converge to the Lorenz 'more equal' set. This illustrates how Lorenz dominance can be seen as the unanimity quasi-ordering of the relative measures.

A.4.3 Transfer sensitivity

The Pigou–Dalton transfer principle is egalitarian, in the sense that any transfer from a poorer to a richer person must be seen as an increase in inequality and regarded as a worsening. But it has little to say about the relative strengths of the effects of transfers at different parts of the income distribution vector. Some Lorenz-consistent measures are more sensitive at the top of the distribution; others emphasize the lower end; and the coefficient of variation is the knife-edge measure for which such a transfer has the same effect all along the distribution.[49]

Atkinson (1970a,1973) suggested that a given income transfer should have the greatest effect at the lower end of the distribution, and in an immediate, intuitive sense, this requirement seems reasonable. After all, why should a transfer between two millionaires have the same (or a greater) effect than the same transfer at the lower end of the distribution? It turns out that the specific impact of this requirement depends rather crucially on how this intuition is translated into analytical requirements—for example, on whether it is 'income based' or 'position based' (a distinction discussed at greater length below). While the status of this additional requirement is still to some extent an open issue, it is

[49] There are, of course, other relative measures that fall outside this classification altogether either because their sensitivity to transfers is not monotonic, or because there is no clear link between the magnitude of the effect of a transfer and its location.

important to investigate the exact analytical form and the specific implications of accepting the sensitivity requirement identified by Atkinson.

Shorrocks and Foster (1987) have formalized this notion with the help of a transformation they call a 'favourable composite transfer', which is made up of a progressive transfer at one part of the distribution and a regressive transfer of 'equal size' higher up (i.e., while there are two equal-sized redistributions respectively from a richer to a poorer person and from a poorer to a richer person, those involved in the former redistribution are poorer than those involved in the latter).[50] A 'transfer-sensitive' inequality measure is one which must regard such a 'favorable composite transfer' as inequality reducing. If transfers have a larger impact at lower incomes, then the inequality-diminishing effect of the progressive transfer among relatively poorer people should outweigh the inequality-augmenting effect of the regressive transfer among the relatively richer lot, resulting in a lower level of inequality overall.

This axiom, if enforced unconditionally, would remove a number of measures from consideration, including the generalized entropy measures for $\alpha \geq 2$ and all generalized Ginis. Yet a rather broad range of transfer-sensitive, relative measures remain. Shorrocks and Foster (1987) investigate the intersection quasi-ordering generated by this subset of the relative measures and obtain a general characterization of the corresponding ranking. Recall that for *constant-mean* comparisons, Lorenz dominance is equivalent to second-order stochastic dominance (SSD), so that by the mean independence of the Lorenz curve, Lorenz dominance between arbitrary distributions is SSD applied to the respective *normalized* distributions (where the incomes are divided by the mean). The new and more complete quasi-ordering generated by the transfer-sensitive subset of the Lorenz-consistent measures

[50] More formally, a favourable composite transfer involves a transfer of size $a > 0$ from person j to person i and another of size $b > 0$ from person k to person l, where i, j, k, and l are arranged in ascending income order and where, as a result of the transfers, the overall variance is unchanged.

can be expressed as third-order stochastic dominance (TSD) applied to normalized distributions. The gain in reach mirrors exactly the extension of coverage of TSD over SSD for constant-mean comparisons. Particularly sharp sufficient conditions can be given in the case where Lorenz curves cross exactly once (and hence the Lorenz criterion is silent): if the Lorenz curve of y is initially higher than that of x *and* the coefficient of variation of y does not exceed that of x, then all transfer-sensitive measures must agree that x has more inequality than y.[51]

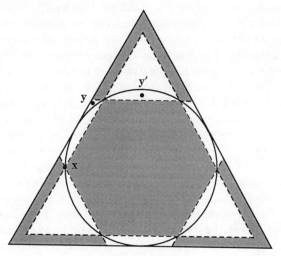

Diagram A4.2

The resulting extension of comparability can be illustrated using the Kolm triangle of income simplex (Diagram A4.2). Note that the set of distributions with the same coefficient of variation as x is the circle through x; that with the same lowest income as x (whose Lorenz curves initially coincide) is the equilateral triangle through x. As before, the four shaded

[51] Davies and Hoy (1995) generalize this result to cases where Lorenz curves have multiple crossings.

areas depict the Lorenz comparable points. There are six additional regions of comparability under the new quasi-ordering, including distributions (like y) outside the triangle and on or outside the circle, and distributions (like y') that are inside the triangle and on or inside the circle. The added requirement of transfer sensitivity renders comparable a portion of the previously non-comparable set of the Lorenz ranking.

These findings have great analytical and practical interest, particularly since transfer sensitivity clearly appeals to many people as a general principle to follow. However, some issues should be borne in mind before insisting on measures that are transfer sensitive. The income-based nature of the requirement disallows many measures that may satisfy the intuitive requirements of 'greater sensitivity at the lower end of the distribution'—for example, the generalized Gini measures with a decreasing weight function. In fact, the transfer-sensitivity axiom immediately dismisses all generalized Gini measures, irrespective of their relative sensitivites, because of their reliance on *positions* rather than *incomes* to determine the impact of transfers. There is, thus, a conflict of approaches—not of relative sensitivities *per se*—between the Gini outlook which attaches importance to the placing of people relative to others and the transfer-sensitivity principle that is guided by the income levels of the parties to a transfer.

It is also clear that the reliance on higher-order comparisons (judging the relative effects of two 'equal' transfers) makes transfer sensitivity somewhat less compelling than other basic axioms (such as the Pigou–Dalton transfer principle, which gauges the direct effect of a single transfer). This aspect was briefly mentioned in *OEI-1973*: while 'it is possible to argue' in the direction of transfer sensitivity, 'by now we are dealing with areas in which our intuitive ideas of inequality are relatively vague' (p. 28). Consequently, it may be best to regard transfer sensitivity as an interesting 'additional' property, rather than as a fundamental requirement for inequality measurement.

A.5 Composition and Consistency

A.5.1 Decomposability

In *OEI-1973* an aggregation property for subgroups of populations is briefly mentioned in discussing Theil's entropy measure of inequality (pp. 35–6). The general property of additive separability is also discussed later on, in the context of welfare measurement (*OEI-1973*, pp. 39–41), paying particular attention to an independence axiom due to Hamada (1973). These two types of conditions, now known as 'decomposability' and 'subgroup consistency', have come to play a central role in inequality analysis, in terms of theory as well as practical application.[52] These conditions have also been used to classify inequality indices in terms of their acceptability. Several key characterizations of well-known measures of inequality are based on these requirements (seen as axioms). Other measures, including most notably the Gini coefficient (still the most commonly used measure of inequality in empirical work), have been criticized for their failure to satisfy them. We now turn to these developments.[53]

The main idea behind decomposability of inequality measures can be traced to the *analysis of variance* (or ANOVA), a

[52] See, for example, the analytical explorations in Bourguignon (1979), Cowell (1980, 1988a, 1988b), Shorrocks (1980, 1984, 1988), Cowell and Kuga (1981a, 1981b), Foster (1983), Kanbur (1984), Russell (1985), as well as such empirical studies as Mookherjee and Shorrocks (1982), Anand (1983), Cowell (1984). A strong case can also be made for decomposing inequality according to income *source* (e.g., earned and unearned income). Shorrocks (1982) has provided a definitive study of the alternative methodologies.

[53] In his classic study of economic inequality and poverty in Malaysia, Anand (1983) presents an excellent example of the power and cogency of decomposition analysis for descriptive and prescriptive investigations. The monograph also contains a set of extremely useful Appendices (pp. 302–54) on 'the measurement of income inequality', from which we have freely drawn.

traditional method of evaluating 'how much' of the variance in a variable (such as income) can be 'explained' by relevant characteristics (such as age, sex, race, schooling, or work experience). The key formula of ANOVA links overall income variance to 'between-group' and 'within-group' variances. The 'between-group' term B is the variance that would exist if each observation were replaced by the mean income of the group sharing the same characteristics, so that we concentrate only on variations *between* these groups. The 'within-group' term W, on the other hand, is the weighted average of the variance *within* each group, where the weight is the 'population share' or the share of total observations in the respective group. In the two-group case this may be written as:

$$V(\mathbf{x},\mathbf{y}) = [W] + [B]$$
$$= [w_x V(\mathbf{x}) + w_y V(\mathbf{y})] + [V(\bar{\mathbf{x}},\bar{\mathbf{y}})]$$

where $w_x = n_x/n$ and $w_y = n_y/n$ are 'population-share' weights (the shares of total observations in the respective groups), $V(\cdot)$ the variance of the respective vector, while $\bar{\mathbf{x}}$ and $\bar{\mathbf{y}}$ are the 'smoothed' group distributions (with each member of the respective group having the mean income of that group). The ratio of the between-group term to the total variance, B/V, is then interpreted as the contribution of that group classification (or the characteristic on which the classification is based) to total variance; W/V is similarly interpreted as the within-group contribution.[54]

Note, though, that the variance is an absolute measure of dispersion, not a *relative* inequality indicator (see *OEI-1973*, p. 27). Indeed, if each income is doubled, the overall measured dispersion is quadrupled. There are two common ways of converting the variance into a mean-independent measure, either through taking the variance of logarithms, or through

[54] For example, in a simple regression model if each group is taken to share the same value of the independent variable, R^2 measures the between-group contribution, while $1 - R^2$ is the proportion left unexplained, which corresponds to the within-group contribution (i.e., owing to variations in other variables with the same value of the chosen independent variable). The analogy with regression analysis is discussed further in Anand (1983, pp. 222–3).

going for the coefficient of variation.[55] Both these ways can be interpreted as using the variance over a *transformation* of incomes that makes them mean independent.

The *variance of logarithms* is obtained by applying the variance to the distribution of log-incomes. In fact, following the important and influential work of Mincer (1958, 1970), there has been considerable use of the income variable in logarithmic form in wage-determination models. The resulting 'semi-log' regression equation yields an ANOVA decomposition invoking a population-share-weighted within-group term (like the variance), but a rather different between-group term.[56] However, the variance of logs, like the variance itself, is not Lorenz consistent. The variance of logs satisfies mean independence, but the basic Pigou–Dalton condition is violated. Such violations arise only when relatively high incomes are involved (*OEI-1973*, pp. 28–9).[57] Even so, this does not mean that the problem is a minor one. As demonstrated by Foster and Ok (1996), the likelihood of violations is significant, and the extent of the disagreement between the variance of logs and the Lorenz criterion can be surprisingly large.[58] These difficulties do not necessarily remove the variance of logs from consideration, but they do provide an incentive to explore other possibilities.

The second procedure applies the variance to the *normalized*

[55] See *OEI-1973* (pp. 27–9), for discussions of the coefficient of variation, and of the standard deviation of logarithms (the square root of the variance of logarithms).

[56] Instead of using the arithmetic mean in the smoothed distribution, the geometric mean (the m-th root of the product of m incomes) must be used to preserve the exact decomposition. Alternative notions of 'representative income' in the between-group term are explored in Blackorby, Donaldson and Auersperg (1981) and Foster and Shneyerov (1996b). The latter paper characterizes a two-parameter family of additively decomposable measures which includes the variance of logs and all generalized entropy measures.

[57] See also Cowell (1977) and Creedy (1977).

[58] Foster and Ok (1996) show the existence of distributions x and y for which xLy, with L_x being arbitrarily close to the line of complete equality and L_y being arbitrarily close to the edge of complete inequality, and yet the variance of logs judges x to have *greater* inequality than y. They also show that the likelihood of violations of the transfer principle is much higher than previously suggested (see, for example, Creedy 1977).

(or unit mean) distribution of incomes to obtain the squared coefficient of variation, C^2. This is indeed Lorenz consistent as well as mean independent, and its decomposition has a standard between-group term. However, the population-share weights w_x on the within-group term have to be altered from (n_x/n) to $(n_x/n)(\mu_x/\mu)^2$ to account for the difference in the subgroup normalization factor μ_x and the overall normalization factor μ. This adjusts the population share upward or downward depending on whether the subgroup mean is higher or lower than the overall mean.[59]

Theil's 'entropy' measure T also has an additive decomposition, but its formula has weights of the form $w_x = (n_x/n)(\mu_x/\mu)$, or the share of the group in the total income. The population share is still adjusted in favour of richer subgroups, but to a lesser extent than the previous measure.[60] Theil's second measure D returns to the pure population-share weighting $w_x = n_x/n$ of the variance. All three of the measures C^2, T and D have decompositions of the form:

$$I(\mathbf{x},\mathbf{y}) = [W] + [B]$$
$$= [w_x I(\mathbf{x}) + w_y I(\mathbf{y})] + [I(\bar{\mathbf{x}},\bar{\mathbf{y}})]$$

generalizable to any number of groups, where all weights are positive and depend only on the means and the population sizes of the group relative to the overall distribution. A measure satisfying these requirements can be called an *additively decomposable* inequality measure.

Shorrocks (1980, 1984) established the following strong link between this form of decomposition and the generalized entropy class:

I is a Lorenz-consistent, normalized, continuous, and additively de-

---

[59] Interestingly, the within-group and between-group *contribution* terms are the same for C^2 as they are for V; while V is not mean independent, its constitutive terms are.

[60] The Theil index is derived from the Shannon entropy measure, which also has a useful decomposition as a measure of information. Khinchin's (1957) axiomatic characterization of the Shannon measure can be converted directly into a characterization of the Theil measure (on this, see Foster 1983, 1985), yielding a characterization that is a bit more transparent than Theil's (1967) own—somewhat cryptic—story.

composable inequality measure if and only if it is a positive multiple of a generalized entropy measure.[61]

The 'if' portion of the proof follows immediately, since each generalized entropy measure I_α can be additively decomposed with weights $w_x = (n_x/n)(\mu_x/\mu)^\alpha$. The 'only if' part of the proof is quite challenging, since it requires the derivation of a specific functional form (viz., I_α) from the assumed general properties. This is accomplished using methods from the study of functional equations, which, like differential equations, offers up an entire function as a solution, but from equations that do not involve derivatives.[62]

This characterization theorem shows how drastically the requirement of additive decomposability limits the permissible inequality measures. However, it should be noted that other types of breakdown are also available, and the issue can be characterized differently and less exactly. An important example is the Gini coefficient which can be given an additive but somewhat artificial form of 'decomposition': $G(\mathbf{x},\mathbf{y}) = [W] + [B] + [R]$, where W is a weighted average of within-group Ginis (with weights $w_x = (\mu_x n_x^2)/(\mu n^2)$), B is the Gini applied to the standard 'smoothed' distribution, and R is a non-negative *residual* term devised to balance the equation. For instance, if $\mathbf{x} = (0,8)$ and $\mathbf{y} = (4,20)$, then $G(\mathbf{x},\mathbf{y}) = 1/2$ is overall inequality, and $W = 3/16$ and $B = 1/4$ are the respective component values, so that $R = 1/16$ is left unaccounted for by the breakdown. The Gini measure cannot be decomposed neatly into the 'within' and 'between' group terms required

[61] Here normalization is taken to include the requirement that the inequality measure I be zero at equality. Continuity is the usual 'no-jump' assumption. Actually, Shorrocks (1984) proves a more powerful result. Let us call a measure I *aggregative* if it can be expressed as a function of subgroup means, population sizes, and inequality levels alone. Then I is a Lorenz-consistent, normalized, continuous, and aggregative inequality measure if and only if it is a continuous, increasing transformation of a generalized entropy measure.

[62] The interested reader may consult the classic work of Aczel (1966) and the survey of applications in economics by Eichhorn (1978). There have been, by now, quite a few works employing this approach; see Chakravarty (1990) and the references cited there.

by additive decomposability, which may lessen its appeal in certain applications.

While the presence of R makes the Gini coefficient less suitable for decomposition analysis, the R term does have value from another perspective in giving useful information that decomposable indices must, by definition, ignore. Recall that the weights in the Gini formula depend on all incomes in the distribution. Consequently, when a subgroup's incomes are evaluated *without* reference to the entire distribution (as in the construction of the within-group term), or when they are replaced with *subgroup means* (as in the between-group term), some information on the rankings of individuals is lost. The residual term conveys the lost information in a natural way: R indicates the extent to which the various subgroup distributions *overlap*.[63] In the special case where subgroup distributions are *non-overlapping*, R vanishes and the two standard terms account for all of the inequality. As an example of this, note that each income in $\mathbf{x}' = (0,4)$ is below each income in $\mathbf{y}' = (8,20)$, and that $G(\mathbf{x}',\mathbf{y}') = 1/2$ is indeed the sum of $W' = 1/8$ and $B' = 3/8$. In general, though, subgroup distributions tend to overlap, and hence all three terms—the overlap term as well as the standard within-group and between-group terms—are required to reconstruct the Gini inequality value.

Blackorby, Donaldson, and Auersperg (1981) have presented another way of altering the decomposition formula, for the Atkinson family of measures. They use a different form of between-group term based on 'equivalent incomes' of group distributions rather than *subgroup means*. In contrast to the Gini decomposition, the residual term here is *negative* (or non-positive), indicating that the formula's within-group and

---

[63] Where $\mathbf{y}$ is the subgroup with the higher mean, R can be expressed as the sum of the differences $|y_i - x_j| - (y_i - x_j)$, over all i and j, divided by μn^2. A non-zero entry in this sum corresponds to the case where an income from $\mathbf{y}$ (the higher mean distribution) falls below an income from $\mathbf{x}$, and hence where the subgroup distributions overlap. For other interpretations of this term, see Bhattacharya and Mahalanobis (1969), Pyatt (1976), Love and Wolfson (1976), Silber (1989), Lambert and Aronson (1993), and especially Anand (1983, pp. 311–26).

between-group terms account for *more* inequality than is present in the original distribution. This is, thus, not an exact—residual-free—decomposition, but Blackorby, Donaldson, and Auersperg's investigation moves the analysis of between-group inequality more in line with the general Atkinsonian approach of using 'equally distributed equivalent incomes'.[64]

When additive decomposability is imposed as a strict requirement, there is, as mentioned earlier, the class of generalized entropy measures I_α to choose from. While, on the one hand, this restriction would eliminate many potential inequality measures, there is still, on the other hand, quite a range of measures from which a choice can be made. This selection can be approached from several directions. The property of transfer sensitivity, for example, may be invoked, which immediately limits consideration to the range $\alpha < 2$. The form of decomposition—or more specifically, the weighting structure—also helps distinguish between measures. For instance, we have noted that the within-group weights for the (squared) coefficient of variation ($\alpha = 2$) and Theil's entropy measure ($\alpha = 1$) emphasize the inequality within richer subgroups. Ruling this out would select a measure in the range $\alpha \leq 0$. Alternatively, note that Theil's two measures are the only ones with weights that sum up exactly to 1. The sum of weights for the other measures exceeds or falls short of unity by an amount proportional to the between-group term, clouding the interpretation of the within-group term (on this, see Shorrocks 1980). Consequently, only $\alpha = 0$ or 1 would be fully endorsed by this criterion.

The 'standardization' analysis of Love and Wolfson (1976) suggests one more way of deciding. The traditional approach defines B through using an 'as if' distribution $(\bar{x}, \bar{y})$ where within-group inequality has been removed. An alternative is to construct the within-group term W' first by rescaling group

---

[64] See also Foster and Shneyerov (1996a, 1996b) who present exact additive decompositions which base the within-group weights and the between-group 'smoothed' term on a 'representative income function' potentially different from the arithmetic mean.

distributions to remove between-group inequality, and then define the between-group term $B' = I - W'$. Is there a generalized entropy measure which gives the same answer both ways? As noted by Shorrocks (1980, p. 629) and Anand (1983, p. 200), only the second Theil measure D among the generalized entropy measures satisfies this independence property.[65] The precise form of decomposition may, therefore, exercise a powerful influence on the selection of an inequality measure from a generally plausible class.

A.5.2 Subgroup consistency

There is no denying that decomposability as a property is useful for addressing certain distributional problems. The practical convenience of having additively decomposable inequality measures is strong enough to make them much in demand in policy-oriented circles. But even if one accepts the *usefulness* of decomposability, one might still wonder about its *acceptability* as a general condition. Many interesting questions do not require inequality to be broken down by population subgroups, while others can be approached using a simple comparison of subgroup and overall inequality levels.

To be sure, some form of decomposition is needed to answer such questions as: how much of income inequality in the United States could be attributed to differences between whites and non-whites and how much to differences among whites and among non-whites respectively? As a word of caution, though, we might note that sometimes questions that are plausibly asked may not be sensibly answerable. (For

---

[65] This leaves open the question raised by Anand (1983) whether there are any measures *outside* the generalized entropy class that yield a decomposition that is independent of the route taken (the 'smoothed' or 'standardized' approach). Foster and Shneyerov (1996a) have shown that Theil's second measure is indeed the unique 'path-independent' decomposable measure in the usual mean-based world. But when the scope of decomposition is broadened to allow arbitrary 'representative income' functions (in defining standardized and smoothed distributions), the possibilites expand to a single-parameter family of measures containing the variance of logs, among others.

example, 'how much of the breakdown of this marriage was the responsibility of the husband and how much of the wife, adding up exactly to a total responsibility of 100%?') If there is even a modest amount of interdependence between groups in society, an exact separation into between-group and within-group terms may not be attainable. A residual term (as in the Gini breakdown) or some other modification to additivity may be needed to account for overflow or undercounting inherent in the problem.

There is, however, a related property—'subgroup consistency'—which seems to have much immediate appeal as a general axiom for inequality measurement. It is a condition of positive responsiveness of the overall inequality measure to changes in the inequality levels of constituent subgroups. By way of illustration, suppose that a population is divided into two groups, say men and women, and the income distribution changes while the group populations and mean incomes remain constant. *Subgroup consistency* requires that if male inequality rises with female inequality unchanged, then overall inequality must likewise register an increase. More formally, if means and population sizes are unchanged in going from $\mathbf{x}$ to $\mathbf{x}'$, and from $\mathbf{y}$ to $\mathbf{y}'$, then:

$$I(\mathbf{x}') > I(\mathbf{x}) \text{ and } I(\mathbf{y}') = I(\mathbf{y}) \text{ entail } I(\mathbf{x}',\mathbf{y}') > I(\mathbf{x},\mathbf{y}).$$

Note that this property says nothing about the *size* of the overall increase in inequality relative to the change in the subgroup—it is only a *directional* correspondence. Indeed, the increase in subgroup inequality could be precipitous and the increase in aggregate inequality very small, without violating the precept. And unlike additive decomposability, subgroup consistency admits the possibility of interactions between subgroups—so long as the overall effect of an increase in $I(\mathbf{x})$, with an unchanged $I(\mathbf{y})$, is an increase in $I(\mathbf{x},\mathbf{y})$.

The theoretical motivation for subgroup consistency can be easily understood. In fact, there are also practical grounds for seriously considering the adoption of this principle. First, there is the pragmatic question of how to ensure the coherence of regional and national policies designed to reduce inequalities. For if a policy to reduce the dispersion of incomes in a given region—call it a regionally progressive policy—can be regressive at the national level, this can lead to confusion among policy-makers, and also to apparent conflicts between state and national interests.

At a more formal level, there is an obvious similarity between subgroup consistency and the transfer principle. For if **x** is made up of two persons and the incomes in **y** are left undisturbed, then an increase in inequality in **x** must be echoed by an increase in inequality overall, owing to the transfer principle. Subgroup consistency carries the requirement two steps further, to cases where **x** has more than two persons and where the incomes outside **x** may change, while maintaining their subgroup inequality level. It should be noted that these steps that take us beyond the transfer principle are actually quite substantial, since the distributional changes that raise $I(\mathbf{x})$ and maintain $I(\mathbf{y})$ may involve a whole series of regressive and progressive transfers (rather than the single transfer and no change, respectively, required by the transfer principle).

There are, thus, serious arguments in favour of requiring subgroup consistency from inequality measures, but there are considerations on the other side as well. They relate mainly to the way in which interdependences between individuals work across the boundaries of *different* partitions of the total population. We postpone taking up that general question until the next subsection.

A more immediate question to be addressed now is: which measures satisfy this property? It is clear that any additively decomposable measure—and hence any generalized entropy measure—is subgroup consistent. With the between-group term and within-group weights held fixed (owing to the constant subgroup means and populations), any increase in a single subgroup's inequality is reflected in a higher level of inequality overall. However, the converse proposition (that subgroup consistency leads to additive decomposability) is certainly not true, as evidenced by the Atkinson family of measures.[66] Replacing decomposability with subgroup consistency surely yields a larger class. But how much larger?

In another powerful characterization, Shorrocks (1988) has shown that the only continuous and normalized relative inequality measures that are subgroup consistent are the generalized entropy measures (or some transformation thereof—such as the Atkinson family).[67] This then provides an interesting justification for the generalized entropy class in particular and decomposability in general. For if the possibility of subgroup consistency is regarded as essential, then one is, by implication, constrained to choose from the decomposable class of relative indices (or a suitable transformation thereof).

A.5.3 Consistency and interdependence

Subgroup consistency and related properties impose rather strict restrictions on what kind of information can be considered in measuring inequality. In particular, one must be willing to accept that a change in a subgroup's distribution which happens to raise inequality in the subgroup must lead to an increase in overall inequality, no matter how that change influences the relative positions of the remaining population (so long as their own incomes remain unchanged). Is that rather 'separatist' view justified?

Consider the following example. Group 1 has the distribution $(1,3,8,8)$ which then changes to $(2,2,7,9)$, while group 2 has the completely equal distribution (a,a). Subgroup consistency would require the direction of change in overall

---

[66] Each member of the Atkinson family is subgroup consistent as a transformation of a generalized entropy measure, but does not itself exhibit an exact additive decomposition.

[67] The Shorrocks axiom is actually slightly weaker since it assumes strict inequalities for both subgroup comparisons and only a weak inequality overall. Repeated application of the axiom in the text yields '$I(x') > I(x)$ and $I(y') > I(y)$ entail $I(x',y') > I(x,y)$' and this, in turn, yields the Shorrocks version.

inequality in going from (1,3,8,8,a,a) to (2,2,7,9,a,a) to be independent of the level of a. Indeed every generalized entropy measure exhibits this independence, with measures in the range $a > 2$ consistently ranking (2,2,7,9,a,a) above (1,3,8,8,a,a) in inequality terms and measures with $a < 2$ consistently ren-

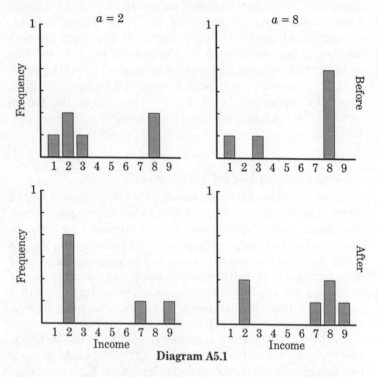

Diagram A5.1

dering the contrary judgement. Now focus on the two cases obtained when $a = 2$ and $a = 8$: the respective pairs of frequency distributions depicted in Diagram A5.1. After examining the distributions, one might be prepared to argue that instead of requiring consistent judgements across the two cases, the verdicts should run *opposite* to one another. Indeed, the Gini coefficient exhibits this pattern: the distributional change is *inequality reducing* for the case $a = 2$, when we move from

(1,2,2,3,8,8) to (2,2,2,2,7,9), and *inequality enhancing* for the case $a = 8$, when we move from (1,3,8,8,8,8) to (2,2,7,8,8,9). In determining the overall effect of a distributional change, the Gini index, like many other Lorenz-consistent indices, takes more into account than just the incomes of the affected parties.[68] Subgroup-consistent measures, on the other hand, render judgements on the basis of a much smaller information set—the subset of altered incomes—and the judgements are unaffected by the presence of other (unchanged) incomes.

The property of subgroup consistency, then, forces an inequality measure to ignore certain types of potentially relevant information in making comparisons. Since inequality is quintessentially a relative concept, it seems odd that the overall judgement in particular must be independent of information on the relative positions of the subgroups as measured by, say, the subgroup means. Why must a change that, on balance, appears to increase inequality when the second group is much poorer than the first, necessarily have the same effect in the presence of a much wealthier second group? As illustrated by the example given earlier, the answer is not altogether obvious.[69]

The potential difficulties with subgroup consistency are perhaps more troubling when its implications are considered

---

[68] As discussed earlier, the weights in the Gini formula depend on the distribution of people over the income levels, and in particular on the number of people in between the persons who are directly involved in the transfer. The persons with income levels 1 and 3 are separated by two persons when $a = 2$, but not when $a = 8$, and similarly the persons with income levels 7 and 9 are separated by two persons when $a = 8$, but not when $a = 2$. To see the same matter in another way, when a person's sense of deprivation depends on her *relative* rank in the overall distribution, then it does matter where the value of a places the two persons with incomes (a,a), relative to the others. See also Mookherjee and Shorrocks (1982), Cowell (1988b), and Subramanian (1995) for related examples and discussions.

[69] An interpretation is also possible using the Gini breakdown. While the change from (1,3,8,8) to (2,2,7,9) leaves both B and W unchanged, the 'overlap' term R rises when $a = 8$ (since (1,3,8,8) and (8,8) are non-overlapping while (2,2,7,9) and (8,8) intersect) and falls in the case $a = 2$ (by analogous reasoning). The source of the 'inconsistency' is the shifting relative positions of the subgroups as reflected in R.

with informational details that a real-world setting provides. Suppose that the population is divided into subgroups according to some criterion (such as race, community, gender, location, class), and people interact with, and also compare themselves with, others 'like' them. Then no matter which single criterion is selected, there can be considerable interdependence between the predicaments, well-beings, and perceptions of people in different subgroups. It is quite possible that a partitioning according to one criterion (say, location) may lead to the dominant relations being *inside* the respective subgroups (in this case, locational groups), which triumph over any contrary influences that may come from other identities (say, race). But for this reason itself, it is plausible to expect that the dominance of 'internal' connections need not hold for subgroups classified according to *another* criterion (this time, race), overwhelming the influences of other identities (including locational connections). For subgroup consistency to hold, it must come out right for *every* partitioning of the population. The presumption of the 'overall' inequality being in 'directional correspondence' with the change in the inequality of *any* subgroup—given no change in incomes in other subgroups—is very demanding indeed when *all possible partitions* have to be considered, some of which would leave a lot of interconnections in the perceptions and well-being of people in *different* subgroups (classified according to *some* criterion).[70]

It must also be remembered that it is possible to use subgroup consistency and also decomposability in a *contingent* way. An illustration is provided by the immunity of subgroup

[70] What is under fire here is not, of course, only subgroup consistency. Interdependences of certain types can also lead to violations of *symmetry* and can make even the *transfer principle* less compelling. Once the complications of interdependences are considered, many of the widely used axioms may lose their credibility. In certain cases the tension between interdependence and these axiomatic requirements can be resolved by adjusting the income variable to take into account the various (perhaps non-symmetric) spillovers. See Basu and Foster (1996) for a related approach to the measurement of literacy. The requirement of subgroup consistency may then be more tenable as applied to the transformed variables.

consistency from the relativist interdependences of the kind that the Gini coefficient concentrates on *when* groups have non-overlapping ranges of incomes; even the Gini coefficient would be subgroup consistent then.[71] The bottom line is not the total acceptance or the total rejection of subgroup consistency or of decomposability, but their discriminating use, depending on the purpose at hand.

[71] See Anand (1983, pp. 320–2). See also Anand (1993) on the relevance of the nature of the partition for making decompositional addition plausible or not plausible.

A.6 Inequality and Income Poverty

A.6.1 Poverty: identification and aggregation

While *OEI-1973* considered the varying importance of inequality in different parts of the distribution of incomes, it did not specifically investigate poverty. Concentration on poverty in particular as opposed to inequality in general would require a very specific focusing on the predicament of the poor. In addition, any assessment of poverty cannot be entirely 'relative', since absolute incomes (and absolute opportunities in general) must have a bearing on what we take to be the prevalence of poverty in a particular society. Thus, the study of poverty cannot really be seen to be a matter of studying inequality only.

Yet there is a close connection between evaluating poverty and assessing inequality (including inequality among the poor), and this connection has received much attention recently. In Sen (1976b), there was an attempt to integrate the two sets of concerns (i.e., poverty and inequality), and this line of investigation has been very extensively explored in the subsequent literature.[72] We shall present some of the main issues that have emerged. Most of the work has been conducted in the context of a unidimensional indicator of individual income, with poverty being seen as inadequately low income; this may be called 'income poverty'. This emphasis is in line with the view of advantage and deprivation investigated in *OEI-1973*, and its reflection in the distribution-sensitive measure of poverty proposed in Sen (1976b). Recently this view of poverty has been seriously questioned by the argument

[72] The literature on distribution-sensitive measures of poverty is now quite large; see the critical assessments (in addition to new results) presented in Foster (1984), Kakwani (1984a), Seidl (1988), Atkinson (1987), Ravallion (1994), and Zheng (1996).

that the exclusive reliance on 'income poverty' can hide crucial aspects of economic deprivation (in Sen 1980, 1983, and other works). An alternative view will be discussed in section A.7, after considering the more general issue of the relevance of 'space' in judging inequality *as well as* poverty. The present section focuses on 'income poverty' only.

Evaluation of poverty can be broadly divided into two steps:

(1) *identification*: we have to identify the poor among the total population in the community;

(2) *aggregation*: the diverse characteristics of the poor would have to be put together to arrive at an assessment of the level of aggregate poverty in that community.

In the context of 'income poverty', the identification exercise is primarily one of choosing a 'poverty line income' below which people are counted as poor. The aggregation exercise would consist, in this case, of choosing a way of ranking communities with different vectors of individual incomes, and— more ambitiously—of choosing a functional form that maps different income vectors (and poverty lines) into a numerical index of aggregate poverty.

It is the latter exercise—aggregation—that relates most immediately to issues of inequality evaluation, and this will occupy much of the discussion. But distributional concerns can be important even in the determination of the poverty line income. The identification of the level of income at which people can be cogently described as poor may well depend on the pattern of affluence and deprivation that others experience, and this can be affected by both the mean income and the actual distribution around the mean. Indeed, a 'relativist' view of income poverty can take us forcefully in the direction of making the poverty line responsive to the distribution of incomes as well as the mean income (e.g., the poverty line may be fixed at half the median income level of that community).[73] The sensitivity of the poverty standard to the pattern of

---

[73] On this and related issues, see the classic papers of Victor Fuchs (1965, 1976).

distribution relates *inter alia* to taking a 'relative' view of poverty. The extent to which a person falls behind other individuals can be checked only with the detailed pattern of distribution—not just the mean income. The issue depends, thus, on the merit of seeing poverty in mainly relative rather than absolute terms, and this issue will reappear in the discussion that follows (and again in section A.7).

There is another question of some practical importance in the choice of the 'poverty line'. Is the choice to be viewed primarily as a 'descriptive' exercise (e.g., what is the level of income below which a person would be regarded as 'poor' and seriously deprived in a given society?), or mainly as a 'prescriptive' exercise (e.g., what is the level of income below which no one should be allowed to fall in that society?)? While the two types of questions are interconnected (since the prevention of significant deprivation can plausibly be regarded as one of the ethically important objectives of the society and the state), they are not identical questions and need not obtain the same answer (on this see Sen 1979a, 1981).

One reason for a difference between the two interpretations of poverty (aside from the somewhat 'foundational' distinction that a description need not by itself induce a prescription) is that the overall ethical objectives of a society can include concerns *other than* the elimination of economic deprivation. For example, no decision to 'supplement' the incomes of all the people below a descriptively relevant line of deprivation (or 'poverty line') follows *automatically* from the fixing of that poverty line, which merely recognizes that some people *are* poor. Even if a country did not have the means to supplement the incomes of the people thus identified as poor, that would not wash away their 'poverty'.[74]

---

[74] The distinction was extensively discussed in Sen (1979a, 1981). It may be true that even in most cases of serious famine, the victims can be helped to survive *within* the aggregate means of the poorest of economies through sensible economic policy (on this see Sen 1981 and Drèze and Sen 1989), but there is still an important conceptual distinction between (1) the recognition of economic deprivation and (2) the political and economic feasibility of eliminating it.

While descriptive poverty lines ('who are the poor?') have been officially specified—and have been periodically revised—in a number of countries (this includes the United States, even though the actual lines chosen there have been subjected to much criticism), in other countries (such as the United Kingdom or Italy) there is no specified descriptive line at all—only an identification of the level of income below which a person has the legal right to receive assistance from the state ('who ~~entitlement~~ are eligible to receive assistance?').[75] Equating the two can lead to some confounding of distinct issues. For example, a country's ability to pay for income support and the competing demands on scarce resources may radically restrict the number of people who can be assisted, even when some of the people not assisted are recognized as being seriously deprived and poor.

There are, thus, strong arguments for distinguishing between (1) the diagnostic poverty line and (2) the immediately imperative income-support line. The latter exercise is, of course, clearly ethical and value based, but even the former—mainly descriptive—subject cannot be seen as being 'value free'. Indeed, valuation does come into deciding what is to count (or not count) as 'serious deprivation' or 'poverty'. However, in so far as the former exercise takes the form of recording the values that happen to be prevailing in a particular community at a given time, the principal task for the investigator is one of description of what values are actually and widely held. This is an old subject, which has been much discussed, and need not be pursued further here.[76] But the nature of social understanding and public discussion can be

---

75 On this issue, see Atkinson (1996).

76 The distinction has been important in the classical writings on 'subsistence' and 'necessities' (see, for example, Smith 1776 and Marx 1887) on what counts as 'necessity' in a particular country at a given moment. As Marx (1887) put it, discussing the notion of 'subsistence', the concept of 'the so-called necessary wants' have 'a historical and moral element', but 'nevertheless in a given country, at a given period, the average quantity of the means of subsistence is practically known' (p. 150). The relation between values and description, and in particular the need to see 'description as choice', are discussed in Sen (1982a, Chs. 19 and 20).

helped by giving a specific role to the description of poverty (in terms of contemporary standards), even when the prescriptive links with remedying may not be immediate.[77]

If the specification of a poverty line has an inescapable dependence on values, the same applies to the exercise of aggregation in 'putting together' the diverse information on the deprivation of different people in a community, into an aggregate index of overall poverty in that community. The aggregation exercise, which has received much analytical attention in the literature on poverty in recent decades, involves the use of various competing value systems implicitly present in distinct formulae of composition. The axioms and properties of different aggregation procedures reflect values of various kinds which may be worth scrutinizing explicitly.

A.6.2 Classical poverty aggregation: head count and income gap

Perhaps the most widely used measure of poverty is the so-called 'head-count ratio', which identifies the poverty of the community with the proportion of poor people (i.e., in the case of income poverty, the ratio of total population whose incomes fall below the poverty line). Let x be the vector of personal incomes for the community as a whole, and z the poverty-line income. If the number of people with income less than (or equal to) z in x is given by $q = q(x;z)$, and the number of people in that community is $n = n(x)$, then the head-count ratio H is simply q/n.[78] Clearly, the head-count measure H ignores the 'depth' as well as the 'distribution' of poverty. The marginally poor are counted the same as the truly destitute by this simplest of aggregation methods. While H is surely an important *partial* index of poverty, which along with other such

---

[77] Recently, Atkinson (1996) has argued persuasively for the need to specify an 'official poverty line' in the UK separately from the requirements of 'income support'. This is part of his argument for having regular reporting on the state of poverty in the UK, in ways comparable to the regular 'inflation report' issued by the Bank of England.

[78] If we look at 'distribution functions', the head-count ratio is $H(F;z) = F(z)$, the distribution function evaluated at the poverty line (yielding the proportion of the population with incomes at or below the poverty line).

indices can tell us much about poverty, it is not by itself a convincing *overall* measure of poverty.

The problems with using the head-count ratio as a unique aggregate index of poverty can be illustrated by the recommendations it offers to policy-makers seeking to reduce poverty by a maximum amount given a fixed budget allocation.[79] For any initial distribution, the solution algorithm is to 'save first' the most well-off poor person, then save the second most well-off, and so on, until the redistributive budget is exhausted. Indeed, if income could be extracted from the most destitute person and redistributed to the least destitute person just below (or at) the poverty line (to make her 'cross' the line), this would appear, in terms of the head-count measure, as an efficacious method of reducing poverty. Clearly, the head-count ratio H would need to be supplemented by additional information on the incomes of the poor.[80]

The 'depth' of a poor person's poverty can be measured by the extent of the 'gap' $(z - y_i)$ between the poverty line z and the person's income y_i. One can capture the overall 'distance' of the incomes of the poor by an aggregate *gap* measure, based on the total, or per capita, shortfall of poor people's incomes from the poverty line. When μ_p is the mean income of the poor population, the 'income-gap ratio' $I = (z - \mu_p)/z$ reflects the average shortfall of the incomes of the poor expressed as a share of the poverty-line income z. Gap measures add a second dimension to the picture of poverty, and they can be extremely useful in poverty evaluation. Indeed, they are the second most commonly used measures of poverty.

However, like the head-count measure H, the gap measures too are best seen as partial indicators of poverty. The income-gap ratio does not tell us how many people are poor (a subject on which H exclusively concentrates), and along with H, the income-gap ratio I also ignores the distribution of income among the poor (in particular, how the total income gap is

---

[79] See Bourguignon and Fields (1990) for similar analyses of a variety of poverty measures.

[80] It is, thus, remarkable that most empirical studies of poverty tend, still, to stop at the head-count ratio.

divided among them). For example, if there is a regressive transfer of income from the most destitute person to one who is much richer but still below the poverty line (even after the transfer), then neither the income-gap ratio I, nor the head-count ratio H, would record any change in the state of the poor, and yet the most deprived would have been made poorer still (benefiting a relatively richer person).

The limitations of the head-count ratio and the income-gap ratio, taken separately as well as jointly, led to the proposal of distribution-sensitive measures of poverty. The particular measure proposed in Sen (1973c, 1976b) included distribution sensitivity through a principle of 'relative equity', which gives more and more weight per unit of the income shortfall of poorer and poorer persons.[81]

A.6.3 Relative deprivation and the S measure of poverty

The poverty measure proposed in Sen (1973c, 1976b) is a direct combination of three distinctive characteristics of the interpersonal profile of poverty: (1) the head-count ratio H, (2) the income-gap ratio I, and (3) a measure of distribution of incomes among the poor, namely the Gini coefficient G_p. When the number of poor people q is fairly large, this index amounts to:[82]

$$S = HI + H(1 - I)G_p$$

The original derivation of the 'S measure' in Sen (1976b) was based on welfare-economic ideas, linking the *weights* on income shortfalls to the *ordering* of individual incomes and welfare levels.[83] The weights on income shortfalls are fixed by

[81] While the recent literature on distribution-sensitive poverty measures has tended to respond—by following or extending or disputing—the proposals made in Sen (1973c, 1976b), this issue had also received attention in an earlier, but neglected, paper by Watts (1968).

[82] This is the 'replication-invariant' version of the Sen measure. The original formula included an additional factor $q/(q+1)$ in the second term (which clearly approaches unity for large q).

[83] The expression 'an ordinal approach to measurement' in the title of Sen (1976b) referred to the ordinality of the interpersonal comparison of individual welfares. The weights that were obtained from this by using the rank-

the idea of 'relative deprivation'—how does your income compare with those of others (in ordinal comparisons)? The weight is higher the more poor people there are who are 'ahead' of you (i.e., have a higher income). In fact, the weights are simply given by the rank of the person in the scale of relative poverty (the poorest gets a weight of q).[84] These assumptions, combined with a normalization of the poverty index to the product HI of the head-count measure and the income-gap measure when there is no inequality among the poor (all the poor having the same income), yielded the Sen measure. The Gini coefficient G_p ended up being in the formula for S not because it was explicitly invoked, but as an analytical implication of this weighting procedure (Theorem 1 in Sen 1976b).[85]

The rather large literature that has followed this initial proposal has included several extensions and amendments of—as well as departures from—this way of doing things. We shall consider here only a few of the developments, but the literature has been well surveyed and discussed elsewhere.[86]

What are the axioms that the S measure satisfies? It satisfies (1) *monotonicity*, (2) the *weak transfer condition*, (3) *symmetry*, (4) *replication invariance*, (5) *scale invariance*, and (6) the *focus axiom*. The S measure is clearly *monotonic* on the incomes of the poor, in the sense that any reduction of income of any poor person increases the measure of poverty. Also, it fulfils a *weak transfer condition*, which requires that a rank-preserving transfer of income from a richer poor person to a

ordering procedure (originally devised by Borda in 1781 to get cardinal weights from voters' orderings) do, of course, satisfy greater comparability (as the 'Borda values' do); on this, see Sen (1970a).

[84] This feature, which is exactly comparable with Borda's method of determining weights on votes according to ranks, can be generalized to less specific 'positional' rules, in the same way the Borda procedure has been broadened in the social choice literature; on the latter, see Gärdernfors (1973), Fine and Fine (1974).

[85] To get an intuition about the result, we have to note the Gini coefficient's analytical connection with rank-order weighting. In *OEI-1973* this connection was already noted (pp. 31–3); see particularly the equivalence relation (2.8.3). See also Sen (1976a, 1976b) and Hammond (1978).

[86] See Foster (1984), Kakwani (1984a), Seidl (1988), Atkinson (1989), Ravallion (1994), Tungodden (1994), Subramanian (1996), and Zheng (1996).

poorer poor person must lead to a reduction of the poverty measure. The properties of *symmetry, replication invariance,* and *scale invariance,* which are analogous to the properties discussed in the context of relative measures of inequality (see section A.4), are also fulfilled.[87] Further, it satisfies the *focus axiom* (discussed in Sen 1981 and Foster 1984), whereby the poverty measure is invariant with respect to the incomes of the *non-poor,* since it 'focuses' specifically on the state of the poor.[88]

The S measure does not, however, satisfy some other requirements which have intuitive appeal in many contexts. Principal among such contingent concerns are the requirements of (1) *continuity* and the *strong transfer condition,* and (2) *decomposability* and *subgroup consistency.* Following the introduction of the Sen measure, several classes of distribution-sensitive poverty measures have been proposed to address these and other concerns. In the next two subsections, we will evaluate the relative merits of (1) and (2) along with the measures they have motivated. But first we

[87] Symmetry requires that if an income distribution vector **y** is obtained from another **x** through a permutation of individual incomes, then the poverty measure remains unchanged; $P(\mathbf{x},z) = P(\mathbf{y},z)$. Replication invariance is an axiom, discussed earlier, which says that if **y** is obtained from **x** by the replication of the population k times (with all the incomes correspondingly replicated), this must leave the poverty measure unchanged: $P(\mathbf{x},z) = P(\mathbf{y},z)$. Scale invariance is equivalent to homogeneity of degree zero of the measure of poverty $P(\mathbf{x},z)$ as a function of the vector of incomes **x** and the poverty line z, and it requires that the multiplication of all income variables (i.e., the poverty line z and the income distribution vector **x**) by the same positive number r would leave the poverty measure unchanged: $P(\mathbf{x},z) = P(r\mathbf{x},rz)$.

[88] The motivation behind the *focus axiom* is that 'the state of the poor' depends on the state of *only* the poor, and in particular poverty cannot be seen as reduced as a result of any increase in the incomes of the *non-poor* (no matter how large). This seems reasonable enough for assessing poverty in the *descriptive* sense, but it does not tell us how easy—or difficult—it will be to remove poverty through transfers from the rich to the poor (in the context of policy making). Sudhir Anand (1977, 1983) has discussed this issue, and also pointed out how the concern can be dealt with by a change of normalization, viz. replacing S by zS/μ, where μ is the mean income of the community (with rich and poor taken together). One of the underlying concerns is the proportion of total national income that would have to be devoted to bring everyone above the poverty line through transfers from the rich; on this see Anand (1977, 1983) and Beckerman (1979).

consider a class which directly generalizes the S measure and thus shares many of its characteristics.

The extension of S is based on the possibility, noted and explored by Anand (1977) and Blackorby and Donaldson (1980b), of replacing the use of the Gini coefficient in the measure by some other measure of inequality. The S measure can be seen in terms of Atkinson's 'equally distributed equivalent' income of the poor population, with the evaluation being done through the Gini valuation function, $e_p^G = \mu_p(1 - G_p)$, where μ_p and G_p are, respectively, the mean income and the Gini coefficient of income distribution of the poor. We have then:

$$S = H(1 - e_p^G/z)$$

If the evaluation of the 'equally distributed equivalent' income of the poor is done by some other inequality indicator, we shall get a corresponding modification in the poverty measure, thereby producing a general class of poverty indicators, which generalizes the approach implicit in the S index:[89]

$$Q = H(1 - e_p/z)$$

The assessment of members of the class of poverty measures Q depends in part on the attractiveness of the chosen inequality indicator and, correspondingly, of the axioms they may or may not satisfy. The acceptability of the S measure turns, to a certain extent, on the attractions of the Gini coefficient as an indicator of inequality *vis-à-vis* others (and its corresponding axiomatic properties).[90] On this, different proposals can be entertained, with some gain and some loss (as is true in the choice of inequality indicators in general, as discussed in *OEI-1973*). The variance of logarithms, for example, has the

[89] Blackorby and Donaldson (1980b) provide an illuminating ethical interpretation of this class of measures. Alternative descriptive interpretations are also possible (as in the case of the Sen measure itself, which can be interpreted either in ethical or in descriptive terms).

[90] See *OEI-1973* (pp. 29–34), and also Sen (1976a, 1979d), Pyatt (1976), Hammond (1978), Yitzhaki (1979), Kakwani (1980a), Osmani (1982), Thon (1982), Lipton (1985), Chakravarty (1988), among other contributions. For arguments against rank-order weighting, see particularly Clark, Hemming, and Ulph (1981) and Atkinson (1987).

unfortunate characteristic of violating the Pigou–Dalton transfer principle (as discussed in *OEI-1973*, p. 29, and above), and so a poverty measure based on this index will likewise be defective. An inequality indicator with unattractive properties carries its problems over to the measurement of poverty.

However, it should be noted that even perfectly reasonable inequality measures can have problems in this context, arising from the specific transformation employed by Q to link inequality with poverty. Several standard measures of inequality lead to poverty measures that violate the demands of monotonicity and the weak transfer condition (for specific examples, see Foster 1984). We must, therefore, be careful to select an inequality measure whose 'equally distributed equivalent income' e_p is consistent with these basic requirements. An alternative approach, within the general format of P, is to consider directly a social welfare function whose corresponding e_p has the requisite conditions.[91]

A.6.4 Continuity, transfers, and the S^* measure

We mentioned in the previous section that the S measure of poverty does not satisfy the *strong transfer condition*, which requires that a rank-preserving transfer of income from a poor person to a richer poor person must lead to a reduction of the poverty measure (irrespective of what may happen to the number of the poor). While a transfer of income from a person below the poverty line to one who is richer certainly raises the S measure so long as the number of people in poverty is not affected by this transfer, the result is not clear when the transfer makes the recipient cross the poverty line. S attaches great significance to the poverty line and gives a constitutive role to the head-count ratio, and so the result can then go either way here, depending on the exact circumstances. (The same applies to Blackorby and Donaldson's generalization of S into the broader format of Q.) Had the poverty measure been

---

[91] It is, however, interesting to note that the equally distributed equivalent value may not necessarily be concave on incomes even when the underlying social welfare function itself is concave (on this and related issues, see Anand and Sen 1996).

an index of *inequality* in general, there could clearly be a violation of the Pigou–Dalton transfer condition here.[92]

A possible defence of sticking to the weaker version of the transfer condition (rather than demanding the stronger version) lies in the argument that a poverty measure is not an index of inequality, and if the poverty line is to be taken seriously, it is not a mistake to attach considerable importance, *inter alia*, to crossing this line, without making it the only centre of attention, as in the head-count measure (on this argument, see Sen 1983). A counterargument, presented by Shorrocks (1995a), points out that while this might well be the case in principle, this property of the S measure has the consequence that 'measurement errors associated with incomes close to z will have greater significance than usual' (p. 1227).[93] In fact, the possibility of measurement errors also heightens the significance of another limiting feature of the S measure, viz. its violation of continuity around the poverty line. In the context of actual use of poverty indicators, the possibility of measurement errors is indeed a legitimate and serious concern.[94]

Virtually all measures of poverty, including S, satisfy a

[92] There is another 'transfer' condition that is sometimes used in assessing measures of poverty, viz. what was called 'transfer sensitivity' in subsection A.4.3 earlier: that a given rank-preserving transfer should have more effect on the poverty value when the people involved are poorer. Kakwani (1980b) imposes this condition, and proceeds in that direction by suitably adapting the poverty measures, for example by taking power transformations of the rank-order weights. See also the discussion in Foster (1984a).

[93] Also, the emphasis on the precise value of the poverty line gives much importance to the knife-edge issue of whether or not to include among the poor the people *exactly on* the poverty line; see Donaldson and Weymark (1986) on the distinction between 'strong' and 'weak' definitions of poverty and its implications. We use the more inclusive 'strong' definition throughout.

[94] Of course, the importance in practice will depend crucially on the structure of the error distribution for incomes as well as the shape of the underlying income distribution. With enough symmetry, the likelihood that a poor person will be seen as nonpoor can match the probability of the opposite error. The use of the head count in this instance could entail very little cost. Moreover, errors may be much more important in practice for certain continuous, but transfer-sensitive, measures which amplify errors at the very bottom of the distribution.

restricted form of continuity, which requires a measure to be continuous when the number of poor is fixed. If continuity at the poverty line is also deemed to be a crucial property, there is actually a straightforward way of extending restricted continuity into full continuity. The *censored distribution* **x*** associated with a given distribution **x** replaces each income *above* the poverty line *z* with the *exact poverty-line income z* and leaves all other incomes unchanged.[95] The *continuous version P** of a poverty measure *P* is defined by *P**(**x**;*z*) = *P*(**x***;*z*). In other words, *P** is found by applying *P* to the censored distribution **x*** rather than the distribution **x** itself. The conversion process preserves the underlying motivation of the original measure while enforcing a continuous transition as incomes cross the poverty line.[96]

In general, the continuous version of a measure satisfying the basic axioms (of monotonicity, weak transfer, symmetry, replication invariance, scale invariance, and the focus axiom) will also fulfil these requirements. In addition, the transformed measure now satisfies the strong transfer axiom, since the censoring process ignores any changes in the number of poor brought about by a regressive transfer among the poor, and instead views the transfer as a combination of a transfer (covered by the weak transfer axiom) and a decrement (covered by the monotonicity axiom). Consequently, this process goes far in addressing both of the concerns—continuity at the poverty line and the stronger transfer axiom.

Applying this method to *S* then gives us the *continuous version of the S measure*:

$$S^* = HI + (1 - HI)G^*$$
$$= (1/n^2)\Sigma_{i=1}^{n}(2R_i - 1)g_i$$

where G^* is the Gini coefficient of the censored income distribution, R_i is the i-th person's 'poorness' ranking over the entire population of incomes (with the poorest receiving a

[95] On the idea behind and the relevance of 'censored distribution', see Hamada and Takayama (1977) and Takayama (1979).
[96] The continuous version of the income-gap ratio is the 'gap' measure I^* = HI where the normalized shortfall is now measured in per capita terms.

rank of n), and g_i is i's normalized income gap $(z - x_i^*)/z$ (where $g_i = 0$ for non-poor i). See Shorrocks (1995a), who derives this measure by altering the normalization assumption in Sen (1976b) and by assuming continuity.[97]

The first formula shows that S^* depends exclusively on the per capita poverty gap measure HI and the inequality measure G^*, with the greater emphasis on G^* when the gap is small, and smaller emphasis when the size of the gap becomes large. The second formula for S^* returns to the ranking-based inter-pretation of the S measure, but here the 'relative deprivation' weights R_i use the entire population as a reference group rather than the subset of poor persons. Consequently, when an income crosses the poverty line, the rankings do not change discontinuously, and the strong transfer condition is satisfied (as shown by Thon 1979 for an early version of S^*).

The S^* measure satisfies monotonicity, the weak transfer condition, symmetry, replication invariance, scale invariance, and the focus axiom, but in addition—unlike the S measure—it also fulfils continuity and the stronger version of the transfer condition. In the extended list of properties usually invoked in this literature, the only ones that S^* does not sat-isfy are subgroup consistency and decomposability—but that raises general issues which are discussed later (in subsection A.6.5). In addition, S^* has an interesting representation in terms of the area below a curve used to define a unanimity quasi-ordering poverty analysis, and this interpretation pro-vides a fine analogy with the link between the Gini coefficient and the Lorenz curve.[98] This way of seeing S^* will be con-sidered in subsection A.6.6 when the quasi-ordering approach to poverty comparisons is developed.

Before moving on to these topics, we should mention that a continuous version can be obtained for each of the measures of the form $Q = H(1 - e_p/z)$, discussed above, by applying the

[97] S^* is also the replication-invariant version of the measure given in Thon (1979), who devised it to satisfy the strong transfer axiom. The class of indices studied by Chakravarty (1983a) subsumes this measure (although it is not explicitly presented).
[98] On this, see also Shorrocks (1995a).

measure to the censored distribution. The resulting class of measures is:

$$Q^* = 1 - e^*/z$$

where e^* is the equivalent income of the censored distribution, which is the general form suggested by Clark, Hemming, and Ulph (1981) and extensively studied by Chakravarty (1983a). For any appropriate choice of relative inequality measure (or welfare function), we can thus obtain a poverty measure satisfying the basic axioms as well as continuity and the strong transfer condition.[99]

A.6.5 Decomposability, subgroups, and the P_α measures

It was discussed in section A.5 that the Gini measure of inequality can violate decomposability and the property called subgroup consistency. This characteristic entails that similar violations can occur for the S (or S^*) measure in the present context, since the Gini coefficient is one of its constituent elements. Different views can be entertained on how serious a drawback a failure of one or both of the properties might be (as was indeed discussed in section A.5), and in general one's outlook will depend on the question one is addressing. For example, Anand (1977, 1983) used the S measure in his evaluation of aggregate poverty in Malaysia, but reverted to the decomposable head-count ratio in constructing his 'profiles of poverty' over population subgroups. We shall return to this issue later on in this subsection, but first we discuss a class of poverty measures specifically designed to satisfy both of these properties, and see how it works. The approach follows the line of analysis developed by Foster, Greer, and Thorbecke (1984).

[99] When the Gini coefficient is used, we obtain the S^* measure; when Atkinson's parametric family of inequality measures is used, we obtain the family of poverty measures of Clark, Hemming, and Ulph (1981) defined as $C_\beta(\mathbf{x};z) = 1 - [(1/n)\Sigma_{i=1}^{n}(x_i^*/z)^\beta]^{1/\beta}$ for $\beta \leq 1$ and $\beta \neq 0$, and $C_\beta(\mathbf{x};z) = 1 - \Pi_{i=1}^{n}(x_i^*/z)^{1/n}$ for $\beta = 0$. This class has two special features that deserve mention. First, the parameter β has a useful interpretation as a measure of 'aversion to inequality in poverty', with rising aversion as β falls. Second, while C_β is not itself a decomposable measure of poverty, it is subgroup consistent and has a monotonic transformation that is decomposable—properties that we now will examine more closely.

In contrast to the S and S^* measures, which require the weight on an individual's income shortfall to depend on the incomes of others (since that is how the 'ranks' are determined), Foster, Greer, and Thorbecke (1984) adopt a 'minimalist' view that the weight on person i's shortfall should depend only on the poverty line z and i's own income x_i. Their choice is the remarkably direct structure of weighting the normalized shortfall of person i by a power of the normalized shortfall (possibly just itself).

The P_α family of poverty measures is defined by:

$$P_\alpha(\mathbf{x};z) = (1/n)\Sigma_{i=1}^{q}\, g_i^\alpha \quad \text{for } \alpha \geq 0$$

When α takes on the value 0, the measure becomes $P_0 = H$, the head-count ratio. All the indices in the P_α class, with the exception of P_0, satisfy the monotonicity axiom. At $\alpha = 1$, the index becomes $P_1 = HI$, the per capita poverty gap. The entire class satisfies symmetry, replication invariance, scale invariance, the focus axiom, and also continuity. Further, all indices with α above 1 satisfy the weak and the strong forms of the transfer axiom.

In this family, P_2 can be thought to have the clearest structure of all—the weights on a normalized shortfall are the normalized shortfalls themselves.[100] It is easily established that P_2 can be expressed as:

$$P_2 = H[I^2 + (1 - I)^2 C_p^2],$$

where C_p is the coefficient of variation among the poor.[101]

[100] This particular poverty measure P_2 was also independently identified by Kundu (1981), and he had, in fact, verified several of its properties. Clark, Hemming, and Ulph (1981) derived a family of poverty measures (in addition to the class given above) whose continuous versions are the P_α measures. The parameter α in the P_α family can be interpreted as an indicator of the degree to which inequality among the poor 'matters' in assessing poverty.

[101] This relationship with the coefficient of variation ensures that P_2 has a transfer neutrality property: the effect of a given-sized regressive transfer between two poor persons who are a given 'income distance' apart is the same regardless of the absolute levels of income. It is easy to verify that for α beyond 2, the poverty measures are 'transfer sensitive' (see A.4.3 above); they stress transfers at lower income levels. Shorrocks and Foster (1987) provide the precise definition of transfer sensitivity. Kakwani (1980a, 1980b) was first to discuss this property with respect to poverty measurement. We shall return to this issue in the next subsection.

The main motivation for the P_α indexes is that each exhibits a useful and intuitive decomposition by population subgroups. Let a population of size n be divided into m (mutually exclusive) subgroups according to, say, ethnic community, geographical region, race, or some other characteristic of interest. The overall poverty of the whole community can now be seen as the weighted sum of the poverty level of the respective subgroups, with the weights being given by the ratio of the population of that subgroup to the total population n of the entire community.[102] The P_α measures have proved popular in both applied and theoretical work (see for example Ravallion 1994), owing in part to their comprehensibility, the axioms they satisfy, and in the case of P_2, the direct connection with a well-known inequality measure (viz. the coefficient of variation). However, it is clearly their decomposability which has led to their widespread application in practice.

But why should we particularly want decomposable measures? A key advantage is that it allows the breakdown of total poverty into components, and tells us how much of the overall poverty may be attributed to various population subgroups respectively.[103] Actually, there are two conceptually distinct objectives of this type of analysis. The first objective concerns identifying how intense poverty is for different groups (e.g., for which group is poverty particularly high?). Such identification can be very useful, particularly since the results can be

[102] Unlike the formula for inequality decomposition discussed in section A.5.1, there is no term for 'between-group' poverty here. For decomposable inequality measures, the between-group term represents that part of inequality arising from differences between subgroup means. The standard decomposition formula evaluates the between-group term as the inequality in a 'smoothed' distribution in which all within-group inequality is removed and each person in group j is given group j's mean. When all groups have the same mean, the between-group term vanishes (for normalized inequality measures), and overall inequality becomes a weighted average of within-group terms. By analogy, the poverty decomposability formula has no between-group term because the poverty line—which is the standard against which poverty is evaluated—is taken to be constant across all subgroups. See Ravallion (1994) for a helpful discussion of this issue (p. 61).

[103] For an illuminating and practically important application of decomposition analysis, applied to the three ethnic communities in Malaysia, see Anand (1983). See also Anand (1993) for a decomposition of international inequality into 'within-nation' and 'between-nation' components.

utilized to 'target' better the relatively poor groups.[104] However, decomposability is not strictly needed for this use. One can easily evaluate and compare poverty values across different groups using any poverty measure—whether or not it is decomposable. If such comparisons were the only goal of the analysis, there may not be any real need for the poverty measure to be decomposable.

The real advantage of decomposability lies, in fact, in the second use, to wit, that of consistent *breakdown* of the total poverty of a community to the poverty levels of its subgroup components (considered independently of each other). If the aim is to determine 'how much' a given subgroup contributes to overall poverty, decomposability would really help. The contribution of subgroup j to total poverty can be found by weighting the subgroup poverty value by its population share and by then expressing this as a percentage of total poverty. For decomposable measures, these contributions sum to 100%; for non-decomposable indexes, the sum may exceed or fall short of 100%.

As was discussed in subsection A.5.2 earlier, the property of decomposability in inequality analysis is closely linked to that of subgroup consistency. A similar link for poverty measurement exists and has been investigated by Foster and Shorrocks (1991), who define subgroup consistency in the following way (analogously to the condition in inequality measurement).[105] A poverty index $P(\mathbf{x};z)$ is *subgroup consistent* if for every poverty line z and any distributions $\mathbf{x}$, $\mathbf{x}'$, $\mathbf{y}$, and $\mathbf{y}'$ for which $n(\mathbf{x}) = n(\mathbf{x}')$ and $n(\mathbf{y}) = n(\mathbf{y}')$ we have:

$$P(\mathbf{x}';z) > P(\mathbf{x};z) \text{ and } P(\mathbf{y}';z) = P(\mathbf{y};z)$$
$$\text{entail } P(\mathbf{x}',\mathbf{y}';z) > P(\mathbf{x},\mathbf{y};z).$$

If the poverty measure were not subgroup consistent, one

[104] See Kanbur (1987a), Thorbecke and Berrian (1992), and Ravallion (1994).

[105] This requirement is quite closely related to the 'subgroup monotonicity' axiom presented in Foster, Greer, and Thorbecke (1984), and the related axiom given in Shorrocks (1988) for inequality measures (see also subsection A.5.2.). Notice that the present axiom places no restrictions on mean incomes of subgroup distributions, since the common poverty line assumes the role that the mean income plays in inequality analysis.

might encounter a situation in which each local poverty allevi-
ation effort succeeds in bringing down the poverty level and
yet the measured level of overall poverty *rises*. A measure that
allows this possibility may be seen as problematic in evaluating such an anti-poverty programme. From a conceptual
point of view, subgroup consistency might also be regarded as
an extension of the monotonicity condition. Monotonicity
requires overall poverty to fall when one person's poverty level
is reduced; subgroup consistency ensures that aggregate poverty falls when a subgroup's level is reduced.

The analytical links between subgroup consistency and decomposability mirror the results obtained in the context of
inequality measurement—up to a point. Decomposable
poverty measures are clearly subgroup consistent (since
subgroup levels aggregate to overall poverty for these
measures). And while there are subgroup-consistent poverty
measures that are not decomposable, it can be shown that
every such measure is a monotonic transformation of a decomposable measure. But this is where the analogy with inequality
measurement ends. For while subgroup consistency led to
transformations of a *single* class of decomposable inequality
measures (namely, the generalized entropy class), the
property is much more pluralistic with respect to poverty
measures. The P_α measures are one of many possible forms of
decomposable poverty measures, each of which gives rise to
an extended family of subgroup-consistent measures. For
example, Foster and Shorrocks (1991) show that any continuous, subgroup-consistent poverty measure can be expressed
as a monotonic transformation of 'average deprivation', where
'individual deprivation' is a general function of an individual's
income and the poverty line. Each 'average deprivation'
measure is clearly decomposable.[106]

---

[106] The family of measures explored by Clark, Hemming, and Ulph (1981)
can be transformed into:

$$Q_\beta(\mathbf{x};z) = (1/n)\Sigma_{i=1}^n[1 - (x_i^*/z)^\beta]/\beta \text{ for } \beta < 1 \text{ and } \beta \neq 0,$$
$$= (1/n)\Sigma_{i=1}^n(\ln z - \ln x_i^*) \text{ for } \beta = 0,$$

which represents a decomposable alternative to the P_α class of measures. The

This broadening of the set of possibilities can be traced to fundamental differences in the basic axioms of the two settings—particularly the special role that the poverty line plays in scale invariance and the other axioms. In inequality measurement, scale invariance ensures that the measures are fundamentally relative, with the mean income assuming the role of an endogenous standard of comparison. In poverty measurement, the poverty line, when fixed, is taken as the exogenous standard against which all incomes are compared, and scale invariance applies only when this exogenous standard is made to change correspondingly. The monotonicity and focus axioms further ensure that the 'absolute core' of poverty, which has no exact analogue in the case of inequality, concerns only deviations below the poverty line, with greater poverty arising from greater income shortfalls. These basic differences are the source of the expanded range of possibilities.

Turning now to the basic issues underlying subgroup consistency, we have already discussed (in section A.5) the fact that arguments can be presented both in favour and against subgroup consistency in the measurement of inequality. Since we are now examining distribution-adjusted poverty measures, which marries the measurement of poverty with inequality (particularly among the poor), these conflicting considerations do reappear again here (even though, as we shall presently see, the considerations are not exactly the same in the measurement of poverty as they are in evaluating inequality). We can take one of two broad routes from here in the measurement of poverty. The first is to go for subgroup consistency in an emphatic way, and perhaps even ask for more, viz. decomposability, which certainly makes it easy to relate the poverty of each group to the poverty of its constituent subgroups. The other route is to try to capture the interdependence in people's perception of poverty and perhaps

subset for the range $0 < \beta < 1$ was studied by Chakravarty (1983b), while Q_0 is the measure presented by Watts (1968) (which in addition to being the earliest distribution-sensitive measure, also happens to be decomposable).

even actual well-being, and build these interdependences into the measure of poverty itself. This second route will lose decomposability and may even forfeit subgroup consistency, but the interdependences, if important, can provide a better understanding of relativist elements in the concept of poverty.[107]

We may consider the rationale of each route in turn. Taking up, first, the route of subgroup-consistent and decomposable measures, we may begin by noting that the force of the relativist perspective may be weaker in the measurement of poverty than in the evaluation of inequality. So long as the *same* poverty line z is used for the different subgroups, the deprivation of each person in *any* subgroup is judged in relation to the shared poverty line, and there is an 'absolute' standard here. The measurement of inequality has to be inescapably *relative* (comparing everyone's income with those of others), but this is not so with poverty, since the most basic understanding of poverty is deprivation *vis-à-vis* an externally given poverty line z, and not *vis-à-vis* each other. This makes subgroup consistency, and even decomposability, more plausible in the measurement of poverty than it is in evaluating inequality.[108]

The P_α family of poverty measures proceeds along this line. The deprivation of each person i is made to depend *only* on her own income x_i, relative to the poverty line z, and the poverty measure for each group is built up from the individual deprivation measures *without any interdependence*. The family of P_α is, thus, by its very construction, totally decomposable and *a fortiori* subgroup consistent.[109] The relative position of

[107] Many sociologists have emphasized relativist concerns (particularly 'relative deprivation') in the assessment of poverty. See particularly Townsend (1962, 1979), Wedderburn (1962), and Runciman (1966), and also Dahrendorf (1968) and Béteille (1969). Some economists too have argued for incorporating relativist interrelations in the analysis of deprivation and poverty, most notably Adam Smith (1776). On these issues, see also Sen (1976a, 1976b, 1989). Also Easterlin (1995).

[108] There is, of course, a case for considering different poverty lines for different subgroups.

[109] The same applies to the family C_β and to the 'average deprivation' measures.

person i does not come into the evaluation of her deprivation, nor do the relativities come into the group poverty measures built up from these individual deprivations. The size of poverty for the whole group can clearly be worked out from the poverty of each constituent group, and this decomposability will *inter alia* lead to the satisfaction of subgroup consistency as well.

These decomposable measures are not only convenient to use, and helpful for policy analysis in permitting us to 'split up' the overall poverty of a bigger entity into its constituent components, they also capture the common-sense understanding of poverty very well. As was mentioned earlier, one would find it puzzling, at least initially, if the poverty measure of each subgroup were to go *down* while the measure for the whole group goes *up*. That intuition about subgroup consistency is totally satisfied by the decomposable measures (such as P_α).[110]

Now, considering the other route, we may begin by noting that even though a person's deprivation has to be judged with respect to the poverty line z, her sense of deprivation and the shortfall of her actual well-being *vis-à-vis* an acceptable standard may depend *inter alia* on influences other than her own income x_i and the poverty line z. She could be influenced by the comparison of her own shortfall *vis-à-vis* the shortfall of others. Also, the commodities she needs to have to lead a 'minimally decent life' may depend on the consumption pattern that is standard in that community, which in turn depends on the incomes of others (as Adam Smith had emphasized).[111] These considerations suggest that the poverty line z may be drawn differently for different subgroups. But even if the same poverty line applies to different groups (for example, the 'borderline poor' may be unaffected but people *poorer* than them may be affected by such interdependence),

[110] However, the requirements of subgroup consistency raise many controversial issues, which will be discussed presently.

[111] Smith (1776) put emphasis on the fact that what commodities are treated as 'necessities' must depend on the incomes of others in the community, making some goods 'essential' for avoiding poverty in one community but not in another (see Smith 1776, pp. 351–2).

then too decomposability and subgroup consistency may still be violated.[112]

In the second route, therefore, no fuss is made about satisfying decomposability or subgroup consistency. Rather, interdependences are explicitly incorporated in the conceptualization of individual deprivation, and they can be correspondingly reflected also in the aggregate poverty of a group. This applies particularly to the poverty measure S, and its variants, including S^*. Each person's deprivation is judged by taking into account not only the gap from the externally given poverty line, but also the relative positioning of any poor person *vis-à-vis* others.

The poverty measures of the S class (including S^*) have close linkage with the kind of interdependences that the Gini coefficient reflects. It is, of course, possible that the dropping of subgroup consistency or of decomposability, for reasons already discussed, would call for a different kind of interdependence to be reflected in the poverty measure. We do know, however, from what was discussed in section A.5 that the type of interdependence formalized by the Gini coefficient does have intuitive plausibility (e.g., it provided an effective

[112] The 'Smithian' interdependences work *within* each local community, but not much across them. If the demand that is made by subgroup consistency were to be imposed *only* on a 'community-based partitioning' which internalizes these interdependences, then much sense could be made of that contingent requirement. But subgroup consistency as a general requirement would demand that it must work for *every* possible partitioning: for example, also according to religion, or class, or caste, or even the first letter of one's surname (these differences in non-income features are not even recognized in the analysis of poverty focusing on income information only). The interdependences that are *internal* to each community could run powerfully *across* the subgroups in the partition under consideration (e.g., by the first letter of the surname). This can lead to the violation of subgroup consistency as well as of decomposability. Indeed, depending on how the subgroups are chosen, it is perfectly possible for a poverty measure that is sensitive to Smithian interdependences to go down for each subgroup while the poverty index for the whole group increases. These interdependences will also tend to involve the violation of 'symmetry' as well; they depend on information— about communities—that go beyond anonymous income statistics. Indeed, later on, in section A.7, it will be argued that the most profound impact of the Smithian interdependences is in changing the 'focal variable' for the analysis of economic inequality and poverty (away from incomes).

insight into the judgements of income distribution reflected in Diagram A5.1). But in many other cases we may well have to search for some other kinds of connections.[113] Clearly, no *one* measure of poverty will be able to capture all the different types of interdependences that can be contingently relevant, and if it is good in catching one type of connection and its priority (when relevant), it is likely to be less good in catching another kind of connection and the priority of that (even in a case in which it is the latter priority that is more relevant).

The general conclusion that seems irresistible is that the choice of poverty measure must, to a great extent, depend on the nature of the problem at hand. Also, we are much more likely to get a more reliable judgement on poverty if we were to combine several measures. A fall in poverty in terms of a particular, plausible measure is less convincing as a definitive sign of poverty reduction than a fall that is confirmed by a collection of plausible measures.

Here, we return once again to the strategic merit of the 'intersection approach', which we pursue more fully in the next subsection. The intersection quasi-ordering of, say, S^* and P_α would be less *assertive* than either S^* or P_α (each of which would in fact yield a *complete* order, whereas their intersection will, in general, give us a partial ordering), but those judgements that pass *both* tests would give us stronger grounds for being confident about the shared judgement than what is proposed by either. Individual poverty measures that clearly have demonstrated merits seen on their own (such as S or S^*, or members of the P_α class) can be fruitfully combined, without denying those merits, with other measures with their own merits. Monism does not recommend itself in the art of measurement of poverty, any more than it does in the evaluation of inequality.

---

[113] Unlike the Smithian interdependences, the connections on which S or S^* focuses relate to the ordering of relative incomes in the respective group or subgroup (i.e., on the ranking of 'relative deprivation' in the respective collectivity). These measures thus satisfy symmetry, while violating decomposability and subgroup consistency.

A.6.6 Poverty orderings

The 'intersection approach' discussed in *OEI-1973* and sections A.3 and A.4 above has also received significant application in the poverty measurement literature, with a focus on congruent quasi-orderings. We may recall that there are two steps in the measurement of poverty—identification and aggregation—both of which are likely to entail a degree of arbitrariness in their final selections. The quasi-ordering approach allows one to determine when judgements hold for a range of poverty lines, or a class of poverty measures, thereby making the two steps 'robust' in a way analogous to how the Lorenz criterion removes arbitrariness in the selection of an inequality measure. The resulting 'poverty orderings' are consequently of two main types: *variable-line* poverty orderings, which focus on the identification step, and *variable-measure* poverty orderings which, like the inequality or welfare quasi-orderings discussed above, address aggregation. One interesting finding of this line of enquiry is that the two conceptually distinct forms of poverty orderings are closely related, and link up with other well-known quasi-orderings such as the stochastic dominance relations described in subsection A.3.3. Consequently, this general approach to measurement is a significant unifying theme across welfare, inequality, and poverty measurement.

A variable-line poverty ordering begins with the vexing question faced by the applied researcher: where exactly should the poverty line be set? Even after the conceptual issues discussed above in relation to the identification problem have been solved, one must face the practical problem of deciding where to fix the (arbitrary) cutoff value. And to the extent that a change from one reasonable poverty line to another can affect the poverty evaluation, this may have disturbing consequences.

There is, in fact, no real way round this problem if the purpose is to arrive at an absolute statement about the extent of poverty in a community; that is, pronouncements like '15% of the population here is poor'. However, if the goal is to *compare* poverty levels without focusing on their absolute values ('the percentage of the population that is poor is higher in **x** than **y**'), one can use dominance reasoning, which was discussed earlier to deal with inequality comparisons. We can select that quasi-ordering which is obtained from the intersection of *all* orderings related respectively to *all* reasonable poverty lines.

This is the underlying motivation for the variable-line methodology developed by Foster and Shorrocks (1988a, 1988b).[114] They define the variable-line poverty ordering P generated by the poverty measure P and the range of allowable poverty lines Z as follows: $\mathbf{x}P\mathbf{y}$ if and only if $P(\mathbf{x};z) \geq P(\mathbf{y};z)$ for all z in Z with strict inequality for some z in Z. Results are given for the poverty orderings associated with three members of the P_α family—namely $P_0 = H$, $P_1 = HI$ and the distribution-sensitive measure P_2. In particular, it is shown that when Z places no restrictions on the poverty lines (apart from $z > 0$), the poverty orderings correspond, respectively, to first-, second-, and third-order stochastic dominance.[115]

This finding is of considerable interest. It indicates that these 'poverty orderings' are actually well-known quasi-orderings in the inequality literature; they are, as a result, easy to interpret and use. Moreover, it shows that the poverty orderings have important normative interpretations as 'reverse' welfare quasi-orderings associated with the three classes of welfare functions mentioned in section A.3. In particular, recall that the second of these classes is the original Atkinson class which has the generalized Lorenz ranking GL as its intersection quasi-ordering. It then follows that GL is the variable-line poverty ordering for the gap measure P_1, so that $\mathbf{x}GL\mathbf{y}$ indicates that **y** has more poverty than **x** at some poverty

---

[114] See also Foster (1984) who outlines the Foster and Shorrocks (1988a, 1988b) methodology and results, and Atkinson (1985, 1987) who cites an earlier version of their paper.

[115] For the definitions and characterizations of the stochastic dominance orderings, see A.3.3. The result is easiest to see for the head-count ratio, since $H(\mathbf{x};z)$ is simply the distribution function $F_x(z)$, and hence a higher head count for all z entails a higher distribution function. The second- and third-order characterizations link P_1 to the integral of the distribution function, and P_2 to the double integral. Foster and Jin (1996) derive analogous results for C_β, the Clark, Hemming, and Ulph (1981) measures.

line, and no less poverty at all poverty lines, according to the measure P_1 (with the link extending to the Lorenz ranking when the mean is held fixed).

A less exacting (but perhaps no less reasonable) robustness criterion is to require agreement across all poverty lines lying below some upper bound z^*. Foster and Shorrocks also characterize the resulting *limited range* poverty orderings for these three P_α measures, and find that the new poverty orderings are simply the unlimited range rankings applied to the distributions *censored at z^**. In particular, if the gap measure P_1 is being used, then x^*GLy^* indicates that y has more poverty than x at some poverty line below z^*, and no less poverty at all such poverty lines. In other words, the limited range poverty ordering for the gap measure is simply the 'censored generalized Lorenz ranking' GL^*, where xGL^*y is defined by x^*GLy^*.

The quasi-ordering GL^* (or equivalently, the second-order dominance ranking up to z^*) has another important interpretation as a *variable-measure* poverty ordering, indicating congruence of various measures at the fixed poverty standard z^*. Suppose that P is a continuous poverty measure satisfying symmetry, monotonicity, focus, transfer, and replication invariance. If xGL^*y, where x and y have the same population size, it follows that x^* can be obtained from y^* by a combination of permutations, progressive transfers, and increments among the poor; hence $P(x^*;z^*) < P(y^*;z^*)$, which by continuity and the focus axiom leads to $P(x;z^*) < P(y;z^*)$. Replication invariance extends this conclusion to distributions with arbitrary population sizes. Thus xGL^*y entails that y has more poverty than x according to all poverty measures satisfying these basic properties (along with continuity), and the converse can be verified as well.[116]

---

[116] See Foster (1984) whose partial characterization for a slightly different class of poverty measures (viz., those satisfying monotonicity, symmetry, focus, and transfer) employs an analogous argument. The result given in the text can also be seen as a special case of Atkinson (1987) where the range of poverty lines is taken to be degenerate. See in addition the related results in Spencer and Fisher (1992), Jenkins and Lambert (1993), Howes (1993), and Shorrocks (1994).

Atkinson (1987) has established a fundamental connection between the two dimensions of robust poverty comparisons—effectively tackling both problems at the same time. His results imply that GL^* (or equivalently, second-order stochastic dominance up to z^*) ensures agreement across *all* poverty lines below z^*, for *all* continuous poverty measures satisfying symmetry, monotonicity, focus, transfer, and replication invariance. In addition, if *first*-order stochastic dominance up to z^* holds, then agreement is obtained for an even wider class of poverty measures where the transfer condition need not be satisfied. Consequently, the limited range poverty orderings which were originally developed to address the 'choice of line' question for *specific* members of the P_α family turn out to resolve the 'choice of measure' problem as well.[117] Atkinson's results provide a foundational justification for these poverty orderings, ensuring them a role in poverty analysis comparable to the role the Lorenz criterion plays in inequality analysis.[118]

The discussion up to now has restricted consideration to same-line comparisons of poverty and has thus ignored the property of scale invariance entirely. In fact, this property can extend the reach of the *variable-measure* poverty orderings quite appreciably, by dropping the requirement that poverty lines are the same for the two distributions. Suppose that we want to compare two distributions **x** and **y** which have *fixed*

[117] Note that since the Atkinson (1987) results apply only to fully continuous measures, they exclude the S measure and any other that has a discontinuity at the poverty line. Howes (1993) has shown how the second-order results can be extended to cover these measures by including an extra condition that amounts to a limited form of first-order dominance.

[118] To implement this methodology in practice, Ravallion (1984) has suggested graphing the three 'poverty curves' associated with the three P_α measures, viz. P_0, P_1, and P_2, over a range of poverty lines. The 'poverty incidence curve' for $P_0 = H$ represents first-order stochastic dominance for a range, and hence graphically indicates when this poverty ordering applies. The 'poverty deficit curve' for $P_1 = HI$ likewise represents GL^* and the second-order stochastic dominance criterion. Finally, the 'poverty severity curve' for P_2 represents a criterion which especially emphasizes the lowest incomes. See Ravallion (1994) and the references given there for applications of this approach.

192   INEQUALITY AND INCOME POVERTY

and distinct poverty lines. Scale invariance and the focus axiom together imply that the poverty value for each distribution will be unchanged if each distribution is censored and then normalized (or divided) by its respective poverty line income and evaluated at a poverty line of $z = 1$. Letting x' and y' denote the resulting 'censored–normalized' distributions, then the poverty level of x is simply $P(x';1)$ (and similarly $P(y';1)$ is y's poverty level). Consequently, x has higher poverty than y for all poverty measures satisfying full continuity and the basic axioms (including scale invariance) if y' dominates x' according to second-order stochastic dominance up to an upper bound of 1. In other words, by applying GL^* (with $z^* = 1$) to income distributions *expressed in poverty line units*, we obtain the broadened variable-measure poverty ordering (when scale invariance is assumed).

There is another way of depicting this poverty ordering using the notion of the 'normalized poverty gap' g_i, which is the income shortfall of person i divided by the poverty line if i is poor (and 0 if i is non-poor).[119] Diagram A6.1 represents the 'poverty gap profile' of the income distribution, adding up all the normalized poverty gaps going from the poorest to richer and richer people until the whole population is covered. This is comparable to the way that the generalized Lorenz curve is constructed, except that the slope of the poverty-profile curve keeps falling (or not rising), since the 'gaps' diminish as we move to richer people, whereas the slope of the generalized Lorenz curve keeps rising (or not falling) since the absolute incomes increase as we move to richer persons. The 45° line is the line of maximum poverty, and corresponds to the case in which everyone has a normalized poverty gap of unity (with zero incomes and unit normalized gaps for all).

It can be shown that the vertical distance between the 45° line and the poverty gap profile is just the generalized Lorenz curve of the (poverty-line) normalized distribution, censored at 1. Consequently, by aforementioned result, dominance in

[119] This presentation follows closely the insightful paper of Shorrocks (1995a). See also Spencer and Fisher (1992), Jenkins and Lambert (1993), and Shorrocks (1994).

terms of the poverty gap profile entails that the poverty level
is higher for all poverty measures satisfying continuity and
the basic axioms. The poverty gap profile is therefore a natural
way of representing this variable-measure poverty ordering.

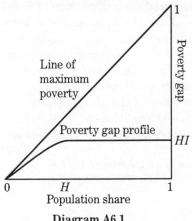

Diagram A6.1

Shorrocks (1995a) has also shown that several of the key
measures of poverty, including S^* and two P_α measures, can
be depicted with the aid of this profile. The headcount ratio
$P_1 = H$ is the population share at which the profile becomes
flat (given that there is no one with exactly the poverty line
income). The poverty gap $P_1 = HI$ is the maximum height of
the poverty profile.

Perhaps most interesting of all is Shorrocks' observation
that the S^* measure is simply the area under the poverty gap
profile expressed as a percentage of the area below the line of
maximum poverty.[120] Correspondingly, S^* can be written as
$\mu_g(1+G_g)$, where μ_g is the mean normalized poverty gap and G_g
the Gini coefficient of the distibution of normalized poverty
gaps. Just as the Gini coefficient G represents one particular
use of the Lorenz curve in terms of the *area* covered, and the
welfare standard $\mu(1 - G)$ corresponds well to the area below

---

[120] Alternatively, S^* is the area between the 45° line and the generalized
Lorenz curve of the 'censored–normalized' distribution as a percentage of the
area below the line of minimum poverty.

the generalized Lorenz curve, S^* also involves an area-centred use of the poverty gap profile. Thus, the measure S^* (i.e., the continuous version of the Sen poverty measure) has a close relation with the key unanimity quasi-ordering associated with a widely accepted class of poverty measures.[121]

This does not, of course, in general eliminate the necessity to scrutinize and compare the various admissible measures to decide which one to use in any particular exercises of poverty measurement. When congruence obtains, we are spared the necessity of further examination and can invoke the inter-section quasi-ordering of the different poverty measures. But when it does not, we have to look at the detailed characteristics of the rival measures in the context of the exercise at hand.

[121] We should also recall the relationship between the Pa measures and the stochastic dominance orderings underlying the various poverty orderings we have discussed.

A.7 Space, Capability, and Inequality

A.7.1 Inequality, welfarism, and justice

Much of this annexe has been concerned with inequality of incomes, but income is only one factor among many that influence the real opportunities people enjoy. For example, person A may be richer than person B in terms of income, and yet be more 'hard up' than B if a big part of her income has to go for medical attention she needs because of some chronic illness. The real opportunities that different persons enjoy are very substantially influenced by variations of individual circumstances (e.g., age, disability, proneness to illness, special talents, gender, maternity) and also by disparities in the natural and the social environment (e.g., epidemiological conditions, extent of pollution, prevalence of local crime). Under these circumstances, an exclusive concentration on inequalities in income distribution cannot be adequate for an understanding of economic inequality.

The importance of interpersonal variations in converting income into utility did receive some attention in *OEI-1973*. Indeed, this consideration was used in criticizing utilitarianism for its exclusive concentration on the *sum total* of utilities, ignoring the distribution of utilities (pp. 15–23, 43–6, 77–87). It was also the basis of the 'weak equity axiom' proposed there. But the interpersonal variations are important even if we do not try to judge equity or justice through the utility space (i.e., even if we do not adopt what is called a 'welfarist' approach). There is indeed an important general problem, central to the theory of justice, of interpersonal variations in converting incomes (and other external resources) into individual advantage—whether or not that advantage is judged by the level of utility of the person (on this see Sen 1980, 1992).

At the time *OEI-1973* was being written, some basic principles of the theory of justice were under active reconsideration, following the lead given by the pioneering work of John Rawls (1958, 1971).[122] One aspect of the Rawlsian move was extensively pursued in *OEI-1973*, to wit, the egalitarian arguments reflected in Rawls's 'maximin' criterion (and in the 'lexicographic' version of it, proposed in Sen 1970a and accepted by Rawls 1971).[123] The valuing of equality in the utility space led to systematic departures from the sum-ranking tradition of utilitarian welfare economics.[124] There was an attempt in *OEI-1973* to combine the consideration of efficiency issues with a concern for inequalities in the distribution of utilities.

However, the fuller structure of Rawls's theory of justice also involved:

(1) a foundational reasoning that invoked the idea of 'fairness', related to the procedure of the 'original position' used by Rawls;[125] and

(2) a denial of the unique status of utilities in judging individual advantage, which was a shared characteristic of utilitarian ethics and traditional welfare economics.

Even though Rawls himself did not put it this way, his argu-

---

[122] Aside from Rawls's works, there were strong influences from the writings on justice of a number of contemporary authors, in particular Harsanyi (1955), Hart (1961), Hare (1963), Suppes (1966), and Kolm (1969). Sen (1970a), which preceded *OEI-1973*, was also much concerned with the theory of justice.

[123] Different types of axiomatizations of 'lexicographic maximin' (sometimes called 'leximin') and alternative forms of the underlying 'equity preference' can be found in Hammond (1976, 1979), d'Aspremont and Gevers (1977), Arrow (1977), Sen (1977), Gevers (1979), Maskin (1979), Roberts (1980), Blackorby, Donaldson, and Weymark (1984), and d'Aspremont (1985).

[124] Phelps (1973) presented a valuable set of economists' responses to the Rawlsian theory of justice, concentrating particularly on the departure from sum ranking to maximin and its lexicographic version.

[125] The 'original position' is an imagined state in which people choose the basic structure of the society without knowing who they were going to be (thereby avoiding bias in favour of their own vested interests), and this primordial equality helps to make the chosen rules 'fair'.

ments amounted to a fundamental critique and rejection of welfarism (going much beyond the spurning of the utility *sum* as the basic criterion of decisions, as under utilitarianism, which is only one specific form of welfarism).[126]

Rawls's 'difference principle' entailed giving priority not necessarily to the least happy, but to the least advantaged, and in the Rawlsian way of reckoning, least advantage was identified with having the lowest index value of 'primary goods'.[127] Primary goods are general-purpose means that help anyone to promote their ends, and include 'rights, liberties and opportunities, income and wealth, and the social bases of self-respect' (Rawls 1971, pp. 60–5). The concentration on primary goods in the Rawlsian framework related to his view of individual advantage in terms of the opportunities the individuals enjoy to pursue their respective objectives. Rawls saw these objectives as the pursuit of individual 'conceptions of the good', which would vary from person to person. If, despite having the same basket of primary goods as another (or having a larger basket), a person ends up being less happy than the other person (e.g., because of having expensive tastes), then no injustice need be involved in this inequality in the utility space. A person, Rawls argued, has to take responsibility for her own preferences.[128]

The choice of 'space' in which to judge inequality has been

---

[126] The denial of welfarism was reflected both in Rawls's (1958, 1971) first principle of justice, which gave priority to liberty, and in his second principle, including the requirement that the maximin formula be applied not to individual utilities, but to individual holdings of 'primary goods'. In fact, the non-welfarist foundations of the Rawlsian system also differentiate it sharply from John Harsanyi's earlier derivation of utilitarianism from a thought experiment rather similar to the 'original position' (on this see Harsanyi 1955, 1976). See also Vickrey (1945).

[127] An alternative approach to assessing inter-individual inequality is to utilize the notion of 'envy' that one person may have reasons to feel *vis-à-vis* another, owing to the latter's more advantageous circumstances. On this basic approach and on the concept of 'envy free-ness', see Foley (1967), Varian (1975), Baumol (1986), and Young (1994), among other contributions.

[128] In a related line of argument, Dworkin (1981) has argued for 'equality of resources', broadening the Rawlsian coverage of primary goods to include insurance opportunities to guard against the vagaries of 'brute luck'.

a matter of some active discussion in recent years.[129] In a paper called 'Equality of What?' (Sen 1980), it has been argued that for many purposes, the appropriate space is neither that of utilities (as claimed by welfarists), nor that of primary goods (as demanded by Rawls). If the object is to concentrate on the individual's real opportunity to pursue her objectives, then account would have to be taken not only of the primary goods the person holds, but also of the relevant personal characteristics that govern the *conversion* of primary goods into the person's ability to promote her ends.[130] For example, a person who is disabled may hold a larger basket of primary goods and yet have less chance to pursue her objectives than an able-bodied person with a smaller basket of primary goods. Similarly, an older person or a person more prone to illness can be more disadvantaged in a generally accepted sense even with a larger bundle of primary goods.[131]

It is important to emphasize that focusing on the quality of life, rather than on income or wealth, or on psychological satisfaction, is not new in economics. Indeed, as argued in Sen (1987a, 1987b), the origin of the subject of economics was strongly motivated by the need to study the assessment of, and causal influences on, the conditions of living. The motivation is stated explicitly, with reasoned justification, by Aristotle (both in *Nicomachean Ethics* and in *Politics*), but it is also strongly reflected in the early writings on national accounts

[129] See Sen (1980, 1985a, 1992), Dworkin (1981, 1985), Rawls (1982, 1993), Roemer (1982, 1986, 1993, 1996), Streeten (1984, 1995), Griffin (1986), Erikson and Aberg (1987), Nussbaum (1988, 1993), Arneson (1989, 1990), Cohen (1989, 1990, 1995), Griffin and Knight (1990), Dasgupta (1993), Desai (1994), Crocker (1996), Walsh (1996), among other contributions.

[130] A person does have some opportunity of changing the 'conversion' relations, for example by cultivating special tastes, or by learning to use resources better. But nevertheless there are limits that constrain the extent to which such shifts can be brought about (e.g., in the case of disability or illness or old age).

[131] On the nature and pervasiveness of such variability, see Sen (1980, 1985b, 1992). The problem of different 'needs' considered in *OEI-1973* relates to this general issue. On the relevance of taking note of disparate needs in resource allocation, see also Ebert (1992, 1994), Balestrino (1994, 1996), Chiappero Martinetti (1994, 1996), Fleurbaey (1994, 1995a, 1995b), Granaglia (1994), Balestrino and Petretto (1995), Shorrocks (1995b), among other contributions.

and economic prosperity by William Petty, Gregory King, François Quesnay, Antoine Lavoisier, Joseph Louis Lagrange, and others. While the national accounts devised by these pioneers established the foundations of the modern concept of income, the focus of their attention was never confined to this one concept. Nor did they see importance of income to be intrinsic and uniform, rather than being instrumental and circumstantially contingent.[132]

A.7.2 Functionings and capabilities

The critique in Sen (1980) of welfarism and utilitarianism, on the one hand, and of the Rawlsian approach, on the other, was coupled with arguments for using an alternative informational perspective: the space of 'functionings', the various things a person may value doing (or being). The valued functionings may vary from such elementary ones as being adequately nourished and being free from avoidable disease, to very complex activities or personal states, such as being able to take part in the life of the community and having self-respect.[133]

The focus of this 'capability approach' could be either on the

---

[132] For example, the focus of attention of William Petty, who had experimented both with the income method and the expenditure method in estimating national income, included 'the Common Safety' and 'each Man's particular Happiness'. Petty's explicitly stated objective for undertaking his study related directly to the assessment of the condition of living of people, and combined scientific investigation with a motivating dose of seventeenth century politics ('to show' that 'the King's subjects are not in so bad a condition as discontented Men would make them'). That robust tradition has been systematically pursued in the contemporary economic literature on 'minimum needs', 'basic needs', and related concepts; see Pigou (1952), Adelman and Morris (1973), Sen (1973b), Herrera (1976), Grant (1978), Morris (1979), Streeten et al. (1981), Streeten (1984, 1994, 1995), Stewart (1985), UNICEF (1987), UNDP (1990, 1995), Desai, Sen, and Boltvinik (1992), Dasgupta (1993), Desai (1994), and Haq (1995), among others. UNDP's *Human Development Reports* in particular provide regular coverage of important aspects of 'human development' in many countries of the world.

[133] See also Sen (1984, 1985a, 1987a, 1992). This approach has clear linkages with Adam Smith's (1776) analysis of 'necessities' (on this see Sen 1981, pp. 17–18, 1984, pp. 332–8), and with Aristotle's discussions of well-being in *Nicomachean Ethics* and in *Politics* (on this see Nussbaum 1988, 1993). See also Mill (1859) and Marx (1875). The conceptual broadening has powerful implications on practical procedures for assessing advantage and deprivation; see also Crocker (1992), Nussbaum and Sen (1993), and Nussbaum and Glover (1995).

realized functionings (what a person is actually able to do) or on the *set* of alternatives she has (her real opportunities). A simple representation may be helpful. If the extent of each functioning enjoyed by a person can be represented by a real number, then a person's actual achievement is given by a *functioning vector* in an n-dimensional space of n functionings (presuming finiteness of distinct functionings).[134] The set of alternative functioning vectors available to her for choice is called her *capability set*. Diagram A7.1 illustrates a two-dimensional functioning space, with the capability set of a person being given by the shaded region **K**, and from this capability set, the person chooses one functioning vector **x** (though this need not necessarily be unique). It may be useful to think of choice in this space in terms of an indifference map of valued living, defined over the functioning vectors, and **x** can then be seen as belonging to the highest reachable indifference curve (as shown).[135]

The 'capability approach' can be used either with a focus on what *options* a person has—given by the *capability set*—or by the actual functioning combination she *chooses*—given by the *chosen functioning vector*. In the former procedure, what may be called the 'options application', the focus can be on the entire set **K**, whereas in the latter—the 'choice application'—the concentration is more narrowly on **x**. The *options application* is directly concerned with the freedom to choose over various

[134] When numerical representation of each functioning is not possible, the analysis has to be done in terms of the more general framework of seeing the functioning achievements as a 'functioning n-tuple', and the capability set as a set of such n-tuples in the appropriate space, which will not be a vector space.

[135] While the use of such an indifference map in explaining the valuation of functionings may be of considerable pedagogic value, especially in moving from the familiarity of the commodity space to the unaccustomed functioning space, it is important to recognize that the nature of the indifference map in the functioning space may not altogether mirror what we standardly presume in the case of commodity space. In particular, there may be considerable areas of incompleteness as well as fuzziness (on which see Sen 1985a). The recent literature on 'fuzzy set theory' can be helpful in analysing the valuation of functioning vectors and capability sets, on which see particularly Chiappero Martinetti (1994, 1996), and also Delbono (1989), Cerioli and Zani (1990), Balestrino (1994), Balestrino and Chiappero Martinetti (1994), Ok (1995), Casini and Bernetti (1996), among other contributions.

alternatives, whereas the choice application is involved with the results actually chosen. Both the versions of the capability approach have been used in the literature, and sometimes they have been combined.[136]

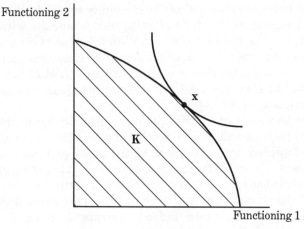

Functioning 2

K

x

Functioning 1

Diagram A7.1

How distant are the two applications? They do share a common 'space'—that of functionings—in contrast with, say, the utility space, or the space of Rawlsian 'primary goods'. But they can make quite different uses of this shared space. How significant is the contrast? Much would depend on the nature of the valuation procedure used, in the options application, to assess the value of the 'capability set'. A well-established tradition in economics suggests that the real value of a set of

[136] See Sen (1980, 1984, 1985a, 1985b), Hawthorn (1987), Kanbur (1987b), Williams (1987), Muellbauer (1987), Drèze and Sen (1989, 1995), Bourguignon and Fields (1990), Griffin and Knight (1990), Hossain (1990), Schokkaert and Van Ootegem (1990), UNDP (1990), Crocker (1992, 1996), Anand and Ravallion (1993), Pettini (1993), Nussbaum and Sen (1993), Balestrino (1994, 1996), Chiappero Martinetti (1994, 1996), Cornia (1995), Desai (1994), Granaglia (1994), Lenti (1994), Arrow (1995), Atkinson (1995), Balestrino and Petretto (1995), Fleurbaey (1995a, 1995b), Herrero (1995), Carter (1996), Qizilbash (1995, 1996), Casini and Bernetti (1996), Piacentino (1996), among other contributions.

options lies in the best use that can be made of them, and—given maximizing behaviour and the absence of uncertainty—the use that is *actually* made. The valuation of the opportunity, then, lies in the value of one element of it (to wit, the best option or the actually chosen option); this approach is called 'elementary evaluation' of the capability set.[137] In this case, the focusing on *chosen functioning vector* coincides with concentration on the *capability set*. With this type of elementary evaluation, the two uses of the capability approach share not only the identification of a relevant space (that of functionings), but also the 'focal variable' in that space (the chosen functioning vector).[138]

On the other hand, the options application can be used in other ways as well, since the value of a set need not invariably be identified with the value of the best—or the chosen—element of it. Importance can also be attached to having opportunities that are *not* taken up. This is a natural direction to go if the *process* through which outcomes are generated is of a significance of its own. Indeed, 'choosing' itself can be seen as a valuable functioning, and having an x when there is no alternative may be sensibly distinguished from choosing x when substantial alternatives exist.[139]

An alternative line of reasoning on the importance of opportunities suggests that the valuation be done not in terms of only one ('given') preference ordering (over functioning vectors), even if it is the one that the person opts for—possibly 'on balance'—to determine what is maximal in the available set. Rather, the valuation can be done by using a set of plausible preference orderings (preferences a person *could have* quite reasonably had), and this would give importance to having other opportunities even when the maximal alterna-

---

[137] On the nature and scope of elementary evaluation, see Sen (1985a).

[138] Cohen's (1989, 1990, 1995) arguments for concentrating on what he calls 'midfare' also lead to this particular focus; see also Arneson (1989, 1990).

[139] See Sen (1985a, 1985b). There remains the more difficult issue of determining how this process consideration should be incorporated. For various alternative proposals, and also axiomatized formulae, see Suzumura (1983), Wriglesworth (1985), Suppes (1987), Pattanaik and Xu (1990), Sen (1991a), Foster (1993), Herrero (1995), Arrow (1995), Puppe (1995), among others.

tive (according to the 'given' preference ordering), or the chosen option, is the same.[140]

There are different ways of seeing freedom and options, and little hope of an easy acceptance of a fully agreed 'indicator of freedom'. The importance of this type of discussion lies more in drawing attention to broader concerns than in offering a quick resolution of interpersonal comparison of freedoms (and thus of overall individual advantages that take note of the significance of freedom). While an analysis of economic inequality has to be sensitive to these issues, there exist rival claimants to ways of making interpersonal comparisons of advantage.[141]

A.7.3 On weights and valuations

Since functionings are robustly heterogeneous, the need to weigh them against one another arises under all approaches geared to functionings, whether the concentration is on realized functioning vectors x (as with the *choice application*), or on the capability sets K (as with the *options application*). The latter has the further task of comparing *sets* rather than *points* in this space, and involves the additional issue that the importance of freedom can stretch well beyond the value of the particular element that is chosen (except in the special case of elementary evaluation). But no matter whether we stop with valuing functioning vectors (as under the choice application), or go beyond it (as required by the options application), we have to value the functioning vectors *in the first place*. The

[140] This approach has been explored by Foster (1993) and Arrow (1995). It has analytical links to the instrumental value of 'flexibility' when one's own preferences are not fully known, for example because they may relate to the *future* (on which see Koopmans 1964 and Kreps 1979). The idea of considering plausible preferences even when the actual preference is known extends the scope of such reasoning very extensively.

[141] This leads to different views of inequality in any given social state, which in turn must influence the ranking of different social states in terms of inequality. Here too there is considerable opportunity of using 'less exacting' structures such as fuzzy sets and fuzzy rankings. On some suggestions for the use of fuzzy set reasoning in the evaluation of inequality, see Basu (1987b) and Ok (1995).

weighting of different functionings *vis-à-vis* each other is, thus, central to the capability approach.

This weighting requirement is often seen as a 'difficulty' with the capability approach. It is not, however, a special problem that arises *only* with this approach, since heterogeneity of factors that influence individual advantage is a pervasive feature of actual evaluation. While we can decide to close our eyes to this issue by simply *assuming* that there is something homogeneous called 'the income' in terms of which everyone's overall advantage can be judged and interpersonally compared (and that variations of needs, personal circumstances, prices, etc., can be, correspondingly, assumed away), this does not resolve the problem—only evades it. Real-income comparison involves aggregation over different commodities, and in judging comparative individual advantages, there is the further problem of interpersonal comparisons taking note of variations of individual conditions and circumstances.

In more fully worked-out theories, considerable heterogeneity is explicitly admitted. In Rawlsian analysis, primary goods are taken to be constitutively diverse (including 'rights, liberties, and opportunities, income and wealth, and the social bases of self-respect'), and Rawls (1971) proposes to deal with them through an overall 'index' of primary goods holdings.[142] Turning to utilities, while many utilitarians tend to assume that utility is homogeneous, the need to see it as having diverse contents—even for a given person—has been well discussed by Aristotle, John Stuart Mill, and many others.[143] It is only through arbitrary exclusion that the issue of hetero-

---

[142] Drawing on Arrow's (1951) impossibility theorem and its single-profile extensions, various 'impossibility theorems' have been presented about the existence of satisfactory overall indices of Rawlsian primary goods (see Plott 1978, Gibbard 1979, Blair 1988). As in the case of Arrow's Theorem and its variants, informational limitations play a crucial part in precipitating these impossibility results. The case against imposing such informational limitations is discussed in Sen (1991b).

[143] *Interpersonal comparison* of utilities raises other problems of diversity (viz. personal variations), which have been much discussed in the literature since Robbins's (1932, 1938) classic critiques (arguing that 'no common denominator of feelings is possible').

geneity can be avoided in the evaluation and comparison of individual advantages or welfares.

The problem is not, however, one of 'all or nothing'. When some functionings are selected as significant, an evaluative space is specified, and this itself leads to a 'partial ordering' over the alternative states of affairs. If an individual i has more of a significant functioning than person j, and at least as much of all such functionings, then person i clearly has a higher-valued functioning vector than j has. This partial ordering can be 'extended' by further specifying the possible weights. A unique set of weights will be *sufficient* to generate a *complete* order, but it is typically not necessary. With any given 'range' of weights (i.e., the weights being confined to a specified range), there will be a partial ordering, and this will get systematically extended as the range is made more and more narrow. Somewhere on the way—possibly well before the weights are unique—the ordering will become complete.[144] But even with an incomplete ordering many decision problems can be adequately resolved, and even those that are not fully resolved, can be substantially simplified (through the rejection of unambiguously lower-valued alternatives).

How are the weights to be selected? This is a judgemental exercise, and it can be resolved only through reasoned evaluation. In making personal judgements, the selection of the weights will be done by a person in the way she thinks is reasonable.[145] But in arriving at an 'agreed' range for *social*

[144] The formal relations between systematic narrowing of the range of weights, and monotonic extending of the generated orderings, have been explored in Sen (1970a, 1970b, 1982a), Blackorby (1975), Fine (1975), Basu (1980). The use of the 'intersection approach' in *OEI-1973* (pp. 72–5) relates directly to this procedure. See also the use of intersection quasi-orderings in the earlier sections of this annexe. The approach of intersection quasi-orderings can be combined together with 'fuzzy' representation of *valuation* as well as *measurement* of functionings, on which see Casini and Bernetti (1996) and also Chiappero Martinetti (1994, 1996).

[145] The central issue is the need to judge and evaluate—an exercise in *reasoning*, which is not the same thing as the *feelings* (such as pleasures and desires) on which classical utilitarianism concentrates. On the need for—and standards of—reasoning in evaluative exercises, see Rawls (1971, 1993), Scanlon (1982), Williams (1985), Nagel (1986), Nozick (1989), among other

evaluation (e.g., in social studies of poverty), there has to be some kind of a reasoned 'consensus' on weights (even if it is of an informal kind). While the possibility of arriving at a unique set of weights is rather unlikely, that uniqueness is not really necessary to make agreed judgements in many situations, and may not indeed be required even for arriving at a fully complete ordering.[146]

This way of looking at the problem raises two different types of issues. First, would the use of such weights—or *ranges* of weights—be necessarily arbitrary and baseless, in contrast with, say, utilizing already *available* weights in the form of market valuation, which can be reflected in real income comparisons? Second, can we really do any inequality analysis with *ordinal* comparisons only (if that is the form that capability comparisons take)?

The former issue is taken up first; the latter is postponed until section A.7.5. In the democratic context, values are given a foundation through their relation to informed judgements by the people involved. The discipline of such valuation has been extensively explored in the contemporary literature on social choice theory as well as public choice theory. While they differ somewhat in their approach, there is, as discussed in Sen (1995), much complementarity between them, and a more complete characterization of basing social judgements on public acceptance can be obtained by combining the two disciplines. It is not so much a question of holding a referendum on the values to be used, but the need to make sure that the weights—or ranges of weights—used remain open to criticism and chastisement, and nevertheless enjoy reasonable public acceptance. Openness to critical scrutiny, combined with—explicit or tacit—public consent, is a central requirement of non-arbitrariness of valuation in a democratic society.[147] The

contributions. In some modern versions of utilitarianism, the role of reasoning is stressed in the characterization of utility itself, thereby reducing the gap between the two perspectives; see Hare (1981) and Griffin (1986).

[146] See Chs. 7 and 7* in Sen (1970a).

[147] Some of the most insightful observations on this subject can be found in Frank Knight (1947).

SPACE, CAPABILITY, AND INEQUALITY   207

non-uniqueness of weights it may yield is part of the discipline of evaluation (as has been discussed already). The exercise is not basically different from what is needed for the setting of a 'poverty line', or the evaluation of an 'environmentally adjusted national income', or the use of an 'inequality index' in national statistics (like Atkinson's measure for a chosen α).

In this context, Robert Sugden has raised the important question as to whether the capability framework, which requires evaluative weights to be devised, is really 'operational' (Sugden 1993, p. 1953). T. N. Srinivasan (1994) has promptly answered the question in the negative, pointing out that the 'argument that varying importance of different capabilities in the capability framework is analogous to the varying value of different commodities in the real-income framework is not an adequate response' (p. 239). In defending this claim, Srinivasan quotes Sugden to the effect that 'the real-income framework includes an operational metric for weighting commodities—the metric of exchange value'.[148] How much of an argument is this for sticking to the commodity space and market valuation in making comparative judgements on personal advantages, rather than using information on functionings and other features of quality of life and individual advantage?

Certainly, market prices exist for commodities, and do not for functionings. But how can evaluatively significant weights—whether of commodities or of functionings—be simply 'read off' from some *other* exercise (in this case, of commodity exchange), without addressing the issue of values in *this* exercise (the comparison of individual advantages)? There are two distinct issues here of practical importance. The first, and perhaps less basic, is that the problems of externalities, inequalities, and other concerns may suggest that market prices be 'adjusted'. We have to decide whether such adjustments *should* be made, and if so, *how* this should be done, and in the process an evaluative exercise cannot really be avoided.

148 In fact, Sugden had gone on to say that it 'remains to be seen whether analogous metrics can be developed for the capability approach', taking a position rather less 'closed' than Srinivasan's.

For example, equating the millionaire's dollar to that of the pauper involves a procedure of comparison that is certainly open to evaluative questioning, even if that questioning is not encouraged.

The second—and the more fundamental—problem is that 'the metric of exchange value' (recommended by Srinivasan), though operational in its own context, was not devised to give us—and indeed cannot give us—*interpersonal comparisons* of welfare or advantage. Some confounding has occurred on this subject because of misreading the tradition—sensible within its context—of taking utility to be simply the numerical representation of a person's choice. That is a useful way of defining utility for the analysis of consumption behaviour of each person taken separately, but it does not, on its own, offer any procedure whatever for substantive interpersonal comparison. Samuelson's (1947) elementary point that 'it was not necessary to make interpersonal comparisons of utility in describing exchange' (p. 205) is the other side of the same coin: nothing about interpersonal comparison of utility is learnt from observing exchange or 'the metric of exchange value'.

To take the consumption of the same value of commodities by two persons as entailing the same utility for each involves a big jump in the reasoning. Sometimes the assumption is made that if two persons are observed to have the same demand function, then they must have the same level of interpersonally comparable utility for any given commodity bundle. But this too is a *non sequitur*.[149] If instead of *assuming* that each person gets the *same* utility as others do from the same commodity bundle, we had assumed that one gets exactly *half* the utility that another gets from each respective bundle, that too would be perfectly consistent with *all* the behavioural observations (including the shared demand function).

This is not merely a 'finicky' difficulty of theoretical interest; it can make a very big difference in practice as well. For

[149] Explanations on why this is an error have been repeated persistently; see Samuelson (1947), Graaff (1957, pp. 157–8), Gintis (1969), Fisher and Shell (1972, p. 3), Fisher (1987, 1990). Evidently, this has not prevented its recurrence.

example, *even if* a person who is disabled or ill or depressed happens to have the *same* demand function as another who is not disadvantaged in this way, it would be quite absurd to assume that she is having exactly the same utility or well-being from a given commodity bundle as the other can get from it.

At the practical level, perhaps the biggest difficulty in basing interpersonal comparisons of advantage on real-income comparisons lies in the diversity of human beings. Differences in age, gender, special talents, disability, proneness to illness, etc., can make two different persons have quite divergent substantive opportunities *even when* they have the very same commodity bundle. When we have to go beyond simply observing market choices, which tell us little about interpersonal comparisons, we have to use *additional* information, rather than simply the good old 'metric of exchange value'.

The evident fact that market-price-based evaluation of advantage or well-being or utility from commodity bundles gives the misleading impression—at least to some—that an already available 'operational metric' has been *pre-selected for evaluative use* is itself a limitation rather than an asset. For informed scrutiny by the public, the implicit values have to be made more explicit, rather than being shielded from scrutiny on the false ground that they are part of an 'already available' evaluative metric. There is a real need for openness to critical discussion of *evaluative* weights, and it is a need that applies to all procedures for devising such weights. It is not a special problem for assessing functionings or capabilities only.

A.7.4 Poverty as capability failure

Even though most poverty analysis is done in terms of lowness of income, the idea of going beyond that concept is not new. Rowntree (1901) noted one aspect of the problem when he talked about 'secondary poverty', in contrast with 'primary poverty' defined in terms of lowness of incomes. He was particularly concerned with influences that affect a family's consumption behaviour. He also considered the need for different poverty lines because of variations in the characteristics of persons, including differing levels of exertion in work.[150] These and other influences prevent a close correspondence between (1) poverty seen as lowness of income, and (2) poverty seen as the inability to meet some elementary and essential needs. Since we are ultimately concerned with the lives we can lead (and income is only instrumentally important in helping us to lead adequate lives), the case for taking the latter view of poverty is quite strong.[151]

If that view is taken, then seeing poverty as capability deprivation makes considerable sense. There is likely to be wide agreement that poverty exists when a person lacks the real opportunity of avoiding hunger or undernourishment or homelessness. These minimal capabilities and some elementary *social* abilities (such as the capability 'to appear in public without shame' and that 'to take part in the life of the community') were discussed in Sen (1983, 1985a).[152] This approach to poverty has received some attention in the recent

[150] Joseph Louis Lagrange had already discussed this issue in the late eighteenth century; on this and on the related literature and references, see Sen (1987a).

[151] Important contributions have been made to the understanding of poverty by the literature on 'basic needs' (see, for example, Streeten *et al.* 1981, Streeten 1984, Stewart 1985). The focus on particular deprivations rather than just on the lowness of income has enriched the study of poverty. (For some early thoughts on 'minimum needs', see also Pigou 1952, Part IV, pp. 758–67.) The 'basic needs' have, however, been typically characterized in terms of minimum amounts of commodities and specific facilities (such as food, housing, etc.), and as a result this approach needs supplementation by the consideration of interpersonal variations in converting commodities and resources into functional achievements. See also Fisher (1987).

[152] However, the focus on 'being sheltered' was less appropriate than avoiding *homelessness*, as O'Flaherty (1996) rightly points out (in his major study of homelessness in America). As O'Flaherty notes, 'the reasons that Sen gives for the superiority of the capability approach is peculiarly applicable to the study of homelessness' (p. 26): 'Being sheltered is a functioning that Sen cites several times, but being homeless implies deprivations that go beyond not being well sheltered. Homeless people are not secure, in their persons or in their possessions; they are subject to disease and premature death; without refrigerators or stoves they find it more difficult to be well nourished; saving money is nearly impossible; being neat and clean is hard, as is appearing in public without shame; receiving mail takes an effort; and participating in the life of the community is problematic. Homeless children have their educations disrupted, suffer the taunts of other children, and lack routine and predictability in their lives.'

literature. The claims have not included any denial that low income must be one of the strongest predisposing conditions for capability deprivation, but rather the following:

(1) poverty can be sensibly *defined* in terms of capability deprivation (the connection with lowness of income is only instrumental);

(2) there are influences on capability deprivation *other* than lowness of income; and

(3) the instrumental relation between low income and low capability is *parametrically variable* between different communities and even between different families and different individuals.[153]

Various reasons for parametric variations have been discussed. First, the relationship between income and capability would be strongly affected by the age of the person (e.g., by the specific needs of the old and the very young), by gender and social roles (e.g., through special responsibilities of maternity and also custom-determined family obligations), by location (e.g., by insecurity and violence in some inner-city living), by epidemiological atmosphere (e.g., through diseases endemic in a region), and by other variations over which a person may have no—or only limited—control.[154]

Second, there can be some 'coupling' of disadvantages between (1) income deprivation and (2) adversity in converting income into functionings.[155] Handicaps, such as age or

153 Poverty as 'capability deprivation' has been explored *inter alia* in Sen (1983, 1984, 1985a, 1992), Drèze and Sen (1989, 1995), Delbono (1989), Bourguignon and Fields (1990), Griffin and Knight (1990), Hossain (1990), Desai (1990, 1994), Schokkaert and Van Ootegem (1990), UNDP (1990), Balestrino (1994, 1996), Chiappero Martinetti (1994, 1996), Granaglia (1994), Van Parijs (1995), O'Flaherty (1996), among other contributions.

154 For example, hunger and undernutrition are related both to food intake and to the ability to make nutritive use of that intake. The latter is deeply affected by general health conditions, and that in turn depends much on communal health care and public health provisions; on this see Drèze and Sen (1989) and Osmani (1993). See also Bhargava (1992, 1994).

155 There is also the problem of 'coupling' in (1) undernutrition generated by income poverty, and (2) income poverty resulting from work deprivation due to undernutrition. On these connections, see Dasgupta and Ray (1986, 1987) and Dasgupta (1993).

disability or illness, reduce one's ability to earn an income.[156] But they also make it harder to convert income into capability, since an older, or more disabled, or more seriously ill person may need more income (for assistance, for prosthetics, for treatment) to achieve the same functionings (even when that achievement is at all possible).[157] This entails that 'real poverty' (in terms of capability deprivation) may be, in a significant sense, more intense than what appears in the income space.

Third, distribution within the family raises further complication with the income approach to poverty. If the family income is disproportionately used in the interest of some family members and not others (e.g., if there is a systematic 'boy preference' in the family allocation of resources), then the extent of the deprivation of the neglected members (girls in the example considered) may not be adequately reflected in terms of family income. This is a substantial issue in many contexts; sex bias does appear to be a major factor in the family allocation in many countries in Asia and north Africa. The deprivation of girls is more readily checked by looking at capability deprivation (in terms of greater mortality, morbidity, undernourishment, medical neglect, etc.) than can be found on the basis of income analysis.[158]

Fourth, *relative* deprivation in terms of *incomes* can yield *absolute* deprivation in terms of *capabilities*.[159] Being relatively poor in a rich country can be a great capability handicap,

[156] The large contribution of such handicaps to the prevalence of income poverty in UK was sharply brought out by Atkinson's (1970b) major empirical study. In his later works, especially Atkinson (1989), he has further pursued the connection between income handicap and deprivations of other kinds.

[157] On the nature of these functional handicaps, see Wedderburn (1961), Townsend (1979), Palmer, Smeeding, and Torrey (1988), among others.

[158] On this see Bardhan (1974, 1984), Chen, Huq, and D'Souza (1981), Kynch and Sen (1983), Sen (1984, 1985a, 1992a, 1992b), Drèze and Sen (1989, 1995), Harriss (1990), and other contributions. Detailed study of consumption composition and its relation to family composition can, however, provide indirect evidence of the relative deprivation of girls *vis-à-vis* boys; on this see Deaton and Muellbauer (1980, 1986) and Deaton, Ruiz-Castillo, and Thomas (1989).

[159] On this issue see Sen (1983, 1984), and the exchange between Townsend (1985) and Sen (1985c).

even when one's absolute income is high in world standards. In a generally opulent country, more income is needed to buy enough commodities to achieve the *same social functioning*. For example, as Adam Smith (1776) had noted (pp. 351–2), 'appearing in public without shame' may require more expensive clothing in a richer country than in a poorer one, given by the established standards. The same applies to the capability of 'taking part in the life of the community' to which many sociologists have paid serious attention (see for example Townsend 1979).[160]

If we wish to stick to the income space, these variations in the conversion of incomes into capabilities would require that the relevant concept of poverty be that of *inadequacy* (for generating minimally acceptable capabilities), rather than absolute *lowness* (independently of the circumstances that influence the conversion). The 'poverty-line' income can be, then, specific to a community, or a family, or even a person. This can deal reasonably well with some of the variations, such as the importance of *relative deprivation* in incomes. On the other hand, when the variations arise from handicaps that are not so easily compensated by higher personal income (such as living in an epidemiologically dangerous environment, or having an incurable and untreatable disease), this route of conversion into income space can be less satisfactory, and the need to look directly at the capabilities achieved (or not achieved) may be inescapable.

The discussion in this subsection has been entirely on the problem of *identification* of the poor, rather than on the derivation of an *aggregate* measure of poverty. There has so far been rather little direct work on the latter problem. While there is no difficulty in using the 'head-count measure' of

160 The need to take part in the life of a community may induce demands for modern equipment (televisions, videos, automobiles, etc.) in a country where such facilities are more or less universal, and this imposes a strain on a relatively poor person in a rich country even at a much higher level of income, compared with people in less opulent countries. Indeed, the paradoxical phenomenon of hunger in rich countries—even in the United States—has something to do with the competing demands of these expenses; on this see Sen (1992, Ch. 7).

poverty in this framework, 'distribution-adjusted poverty measures' are harder to define and use in this space, since they require a stricter 'metric' of poverty indicators and comparisons of 'intensities' of poverty. In the next section some ideas on ordering-based comparison of intensities will be explored.

A.7.5 Indirect assessment and ordinal intensity

Ordinal comparisons of capability achievements and deprivation help us to answer a set of questions on inequality and poverty, but they cannot serve as the informational basis of inequality measures and distribution-adjusted poverty measures of the kind studied in the earlier sections of this essay. Not only do inequality measures such as the coefficient of variation or the Gini index require stricter comparability, so does the use of Lorenz curves or of generalized Lorenz comparisons. As far as poverty measures are concerned, as was mentioned earlier, there is no difficulty in using the headcount measure, but with ordinal comparisons of advantage, there is no possibility of constructing indicators such as S, S^*, or P_α.

In so far as the relevance of the capability perspective is accepted, this raises the question as to where we might go from here. One possibility is to continue using more traditional measures of inequality and poverty defined on income spaces, but to supplement them by consideration of other types in a less formal way. For practical exercises much can be achieved through this route. The supplementation may focus either on ordinal comparisons of functionings themselves, or on instrumental variables other than income which are expected to influence the determination of capabilities. Such factors as the prevalence of unemployment (the effects of which extend far beyond the lowness of income it generates), availability and reach of health care, evidence of gender bias in family allocation, etc., can be used to add to the partial illumination provided by the traditional measures in the income space.[161]

---

[161] The recent work on different aspects of economic inequality in Italy, sponsored by the Bank of Italy (see Barca *et al.* 1996), is a good example of work of this kind.

Such extensions do not aim at a very precise 'bottom line', but rather enrich the overall understanding of the problems of inequality and poverty (by adding to what is seen in terms of measures of income inequality and income poverty) through explicitly considering other variables that influence the achievement of important capabilities by different sections of the population.[162]

The second line of approach is to begin with the classic space of incomes, and consider the other determinants of capabilities, to obtain 'adjusted incomes'. For example, the income level of a family may be adjusted downwards by illiteracy and upwards by high levels of education, and so on, to make them 'equivalent' in terms of capability achievement. This procedure has much promise of practical usefulness.[163] It relates both to the general literature on 'equivalence scales', and to particular exercises that have already been attempted in analysing family expenditure patterns for indirect assessment of not-directly-observed features (such as the presence or absence of sex bias within the family).[164]

This approach is, in principle, not altogether different from putting income and other considerations together to arrive at an overall assessment of individual advantages, but because of the use of the income space—albeit with adjusted values— more articulation and the use of stricter metrics are possible

[162] It is tempting to consider distribution measures in different spaces (such as distributions of incomes, longevities, literacies, etc.), and then to put them together. But this would be a misleading procedure, since much would depend on how these variables relate to each other in interpersonal patterns. For example, if people with low incomes also tend to have low literacy levels, then the two deprivations would be reinforced, whereas if they were orthogonal, this would not happen, and if they were oppositely related, then the deprivation in terms of one variable would be, at least to some extent, ameliorated by the other variable. By looking at the distribution indicators separately, without examining collinearity and covariance, we cannot decide which of the alternative possibilities hold.

[163] In a joint research project of Angus Deaton and Amartya Sen, supported by the MacArthur Foundation, this route is being explored, particularly by Deaton, Anne Case, and Christina Paxson.

[164] On this see Deaton (1995). Also Pollak and Wales (1979), Deaton and Muellbauer (1980, 1986), Deaton, Ruiz-Castillo, and Thomas (1989); see also the critical issues raised in Fisher (1987).

in this 'indirect' exercise. In some ways, this approach is similar to Atkinson's (1970a) choice of the income space to measure the effects of income inequality (in his calculation of 'equally distributed equivalent income'), rather than the utility space, as was originally proposed by Dalton (1920).

The third approach is to examine what can be said about inequality and poverty even on the basis of ordinal comparisons, possibly based on a partial ordering. While comparisons of 'intensity' are usually taken to require cardinal comparability, this is strictly speaking not true. Comparisons of intensity are, up to a point, possible even in terms of orderings only. The notion of 'ordinal intensity' can be defined in the following way.[165] Let (x,i) stand for the position of being person i in state x, and let P represent the strict ranking of advantage (in descending order), and take π to be a ranking of inequality of advantages (it will be a strict partial ordering). If we have, for $i = 1,2$:

$$(x,1)P(y,i), \text{ and } (y,i)P(x,2), \text{ then } x\pi y. \qquad (A7.1)$$

This is an unambiguous inequality ranking based on ordinal comparisons only.

Do such comparisons have much reach? They certainly can. To consider a practical example, we may examine the debate concerning the use of the DALY ('disability-adjusted life years') indicator in the World Bank's *World Development Report 1993*. DALY is gradually emerging as an important and widely used measure of the condition of ill health of a population and as a tool of policy making. Proposals have been made about making the minimization of DALYs a central criterion of resource allocation, and its use has been championed even outside the World Bank by a number of experts in the field.[166]

[165] On the characterization and different uses of 'ordinal intensity', see Sen (1976c, 1976d, 1978, 1980, 1982a). See also Blau (1975), Hammond (1976, 1979), d'Aspremont and Gevers (1977), Gevers (1979), Basu (1980), Roberts (1980a, 1980b), Suzumura (1983, 1996), d'Aspremont (1985). The basic idea of ordinal comparisons goes back at least to Luce and Raiffa (1957).

[166] Murray (1994) has argued powerfully in that direction. Anand and Hanson (1996) have analysed some of the limitations of this approach.

In the DALY approach, adjustments are made to the actual life years that people are expected to have (reflected in, say, life expectancy figures).[167] This is done through estimating the value of life years lost because of disability—using a scale from 0 (perfect health) to 1 (death). Aside from discriminating according to the 'burden of disease', there is also an age-related differentiation. The use of DALY raises two different types of problems. The first is the apparent arbitrariness of many of the corrections made,[168] but it is with the other problem with which we are concerned here.

The second problem, related to the issue at hand, is that the minimization of *aggregate* DALYs of a community would give less priority to saving the life years of people who are more disabled or impaired. Given the choice of saving the life of an able-bodied and a disabled person, the DALY criterion would recommend simply going for the former, since more disability-adjusted life years would be prevented that way. There is clearly a serious equity issue in using DALY in the proposed form of minimizing the disability-adjusted life years of a community. The policy of giving priority to saving the able-bodied would be to compound the disadvantage of the disabled: those who are already worse off because of disability would be made more worse off because of being discriminated against in the allocation of health care. It heaps a further handicap on a person who is already worse off.

All this is readily caught by the use of ordinal intensity. Indeed, if y represents the situation in which care was given indiscriminately to both able-bodied 1 and to disabled 2, and the allocation—of fixed resources—were to be shifted in the direction of minimizing DALYs (by favouring the able-bodied), we can go to a situation like x, with the following ranking of advantages:

$$(x,1)P(y,1), \ (y,1)P(y,2), \text{ and } (y,2)P(x,2). \qquad (A7.2)$$

This satisfies the antecedence of (A7.1), and allows us to draw

---

[167] The rationale of the basic idea of adjusting for quality of life is well discussed by A. Williams (1991). See also Culyer (1990).

[168] On this see Anand and Hanson (1996).

the conclusion, on the basis of ordinal intensity, that inequality is enhanced, in this case, by the pursuit of DALY: $x\pi y$.

Indeed, ordinal intensity can be used to argue also that a 'compensatory policy' of giving extra care to the disabled would have the opposite effect, and take us to a situation:

$$(y,1)P(z,1), \ (z,1)P(z,2), \ \text{and} \ (z,2)P(y,2). \quad\quad (A7.3)$$

The use of the reverse emphasis from that given by the pursuit of DALY minimization can, then, reduce inequality in advantages.

The inequality ranking $x\pi y$ and $y\pi z$, which draws only on ordinal comparison, does have some cutting power. The discussion here is, in fact, parallel to the example—with an able-bodied and disabled persons—considered in *OEI-1973* (pp. 16–18) to criticize the sum-ranking aggregativeness of utilitarianism, and also to motivate a rival principle: the 'weak equity axiom'. Indeed, that axiom itself does not need more than ordinal comparison for its articulation and imposition. This was done bearing in mind the possibility of ordinal comparability of utilities, but the same consideration would apply to the use of ordinal rankings of advantage based on the perspective of capabilities.[169]

How much further we can go in inequality analysis on the basis of ordinal comparisons alone remains to be seen.[170] But it is definitely one of the possible routes through which the consideration of the broader framework of advantages and capabilities can enrich the study of inequality and poverty. The other routes include, as already discussed, the use of supplementary indicators and the development of adjusted income measures, and they are also promising and potentially useful.

[169] Indeed, the Rawlsian difference principle is also based on ordinal comparisons only, as discussed in *OEI-1973*.

[170] On the limitations of ordinal information for aggregative purposes, see Gevers (1979), Basu (1980), Roberts (1980a), d'Aspremont (1985), among others.

A.7.6 A final remark

We may end this discussion on a pragmatic note. Many of the problems in the evaluation of inequality and poverty are much clearer than their solutions are. This makes the subject a good field for further analytical work. We hope we have been able to give some idea of where matters seem to stand at this time: what has been achieved, what is going on, and what more needs to be done.

While many of the problems considered in *OEI-1973* (and some not fully appreciated there) have been adequately addressed, new issues have come up which call for further attention. On balance, the subject looks as challenging today as it did—to one of the two authors of this annexe—a quarter of a century ago.

Bibliography

Aczel, J. (1966). *Lectures on Functional Equations and Their Applications*. Academic Press, London.

Adelman, I. and Morris, C. T. (1973). *Economic Growth and Social Equity in Developing Countries*. Stanford University Press, Stanford.

Aigner, D. J. and Heins, A. J. (1967). 'A Social Welfare View of the Measurement of Income Inequality', *Review of Income and Wealth*, Vol. 13.

Aitchison, J. and Brown, J. A. C. (1957). *The Lognormal Distribution*. Cambridge University Press, Cambridge.

Amiel, Y. and Cowell, F. A. (1992). 'Measurement of Income Inequality', *Journal of Public Economics*, Vol. 47.

Anand, S. (1977). 'Aspects of Poverty in Malaysia', *Review of Income and Wealth*, Vol. 23.

Anand, S. (1983). *Inequality and Poverty in Malaysia*. Oxford University Press, London.

Anand, S. (1993). 'Inequality between and within Nations', mimeographed, Center for Population and Development Studies, Harvard University.

Anand, S. and Hanson, K. (1996). 'Disability-Adjusted Life Years: A Critical Review', forthcoming in *Journal of Health Economics*.

Anand, S. and Ravallion, M. (1993). 'Human Development in Poor Countries: On the Role of Private Incomes and Public Services', *Journal of Economic Perspectives*, Vol. 7.

Anand, S. and Sen, A. (1996). 'Notes on the Measurement of Inequality in General Spaces', mimeographed, Harvard University.

Arneson, R. (1989). 'Equality and Equality of Opportunity for Welfare', *Philosophical Studies*, Vol. 56.

Arneson, R. (1990). 'Liberalism, Distributive Subjectivism, and Equal Opportunity for Welfare', *Philosophy and Public Affairs*, Vol. 19.

Arrow, K. J. (1951). *Social Choice and Individual Values*. Wiley, New York; second edition, 1963.

Arrow, K. J. (1963). 'Uncertainty and the Welfare Economics of Medical Care', *American Economic Review*, Vol. 53.

Arrow, K. J. (1965). *Aspects of the Theory of Risk-Bearing*. Yrjö Jahnssonin Säätiö, Helsinki.

Arrow, K. J. (1977). 'Extended Sympathy and the Possibility of Social Choice', *American Economic Review*, Vol. 67.

Arrow, K. J. (1995). 'A Note on Freedom and Flexibility', in Basu, Pattanaik, and Suzumura (1995).

Arrow, K. J. amd Hahn, F. H. (1971). *General Competitive Analysis*. Holden-Day, San Francisco, and Oliver & Boyd, Edinburgh.

Arrow, K. J. and Hurwicz, L. (1960). 'Decentralization and Computation in Resource Allocation', in R. W. Pfout (ed.), *Essays in Economics and Econometrics*. University of North Carolina Press, Chapel Hill, NC.

Atkinson, A. B. (1970a). 'On the Measurement of Inequality', *Journal of Economic Theory*, Vol. 2; reprinted in Atkinson (1983).

Atkinson, A. B. (1970b). *Poverty in Britain and the Reform of Social Security*. Cambridge University Press, Cambridge.

Atkinson, A. B. (1973). 'More on Measurement of Inequality', unpublished notes, mimeographed.

Atkinson, A. B. (1983). *Social Justice and Public Policy*. MIT Press, Cambridge, MA.

Atkinson, A. B. (1985). 'How should we measure poverty?' ESRC Programme on Taxation, Incentives and Distribution of Income Discussion Paper 82.

Atkinson, A. B. (1987). 'On the Measurement of Poverty', *Econometrica*, Vol. 55; reprinted in Atkinson (1989).

Atkinson, A. B. (1989). *Poverty and Social Security*. Wheatsheaf, New York.

Atkinson, A. B. (1995). 'Capabilities, Exclusion, and the Supply of Goods', in Basu, Pattanaik, and Suzumura (1995).

Atkinson, A. B. (1996). 'Promise and Performance: Why We Need an Official Poverty Report', in P. Barker (ed.), *Living as Equals*, Oxford University Press, Oxford.

Atkinson, A. B. and Bourguignon, F. (1982). 'The Comparison of Multi-dimensioned Distributions of Economic Status', *Review of Economic Studies*, Vol. 49.

Balestrino, A. (1994). 'Poverty and Functionings: Issues in Measurement and Public Action', *Giornale degli Economisti e Annali di Economia*, Vol. 53.

Balestrino, A. (1996). 'A Note on Functioning-Poverty in Affluent Societies', mimeographed, University of Pisa; presented at the Politeia meeting on 'Environment and Society in a Changing World: A Perspective from the Functioning Theory', 10 May 1996.

Balestrino, A. and Chiappero Martinetti, E. (1994). 'Poverty,

Differentiated Needs, and Information', mimeographed, University of Pisa and University of Pavia.

Balestrino, A. and Petretto, A. (1995). 'Optimal Taxation Rules for "Functioning"-Inputs', *Economic Notes*, Vol. 23.

Barca, F. *et al.* (1996). Forthcoming manuscript on 'Regional Differences, Inequality and Social Exclusion', Bank of Italy, Rome.

Bardhan, P. (1974). 'On Life and Death Questions', *Economic and Political Weekly*, Vol. 9 (Special Number).

Bardhan, P. (1984). *Land Labour and Rural Poverty: Essays in Development Economics*. Columbia University Press, New York.

Basmann, R. and Rhodes, G. (eds.) (1984). *Advances in Econometrics*, Vol. 3. JAI Press, Greenwich, CT.

Basu, K. (1981). *Revealed Preference of Government*. Cambridge University Press, Cambridge.

Basu, K. (1987a). 'Achievements, Capabilities and the Concept of Well-being', *Social Choice and Welfare*, Vol. 4.

Basu, K. (1987b). 'Axioms for Fuzzy Measures of Inequality', *Mathematical Social Sciences*, Vol. 14.

Basu K. and Foster, J. E. (1996). 'On measuring literacy', Working Paper No. 96-W02, Department of Economics, Vanderbilt University.

Basu, K., Pattanaik, P., and Suzumura, K. (eds.) (1995). *Choice, Welfare and Development*. Oxford University Press, Oxford.

Baumol, W. J. (1952). *Welfare Economics and the Theory of the State*. Harvard University Press, Cambridge, MA; second edition, 1966.

Baumol, W. J. (1960). 'On the Social Rate of Discount', *American Economic Review*, Vol. 58.

Baumol, W. J. (1975). Review of *On Economic Inequality*, *Economica*, Vol. 42.

Baumol, W. J. (1986). *Superfairness*. MIT Press, Cambridge, MA.

Bavetta, S. and Del Set, M. (1996). 'Rough Set Approximations and the Syntax of Freedom', mimeographed, Philosophy Department, London School of Economics.

Bawa, V. (1976). 'Optimal Rules for Ordering Uncertain Prospects', *Journal of Financial Economics*, Vol. 2.

Beach, C. M. and Davidson, R. (1983). 'Distribution Free Statistical Inference with Lorenz Curves and Income Shares', *Review of Economic Studies*, Vol. 50.

Beach, C. M. and Richmond, J. (1985). 'Joint Confidence Intervals for Income Shares and Lorenz Curves', *International Economic Review*, Vol. 26.

224   BIBLIOGRAPHY

Beckerman, W. (1979). 'The Impact of Income Maintenance on Poverty in Britain', *Economic Journal*, Vol. 89.

Bentham, J. (1789). *An Introduction to the Principles of Morals and Legislation*. Payne; also Clarendon Press, Oxford, 1907.

Bentzel, R. (1970). 'The Social Significance of Income Distribution Statistics', *Review of Income & Wealth*, Series 16, No. 3.

Berge, C. (1963). *Topological Spaces*. Oliver & Boyd, Edinburgh.

Bergson, A. (1938). 'A Reformulation of Certain Aspects of Welfare Economics', *Quarterly Journal of Economics*, Vol. 52.

Bergson, A. (1964). *The Economics of Soviet Planning*. Yale University Press, New Haven.

Bergson, A. (1966). *Essays in Normative Economics*. Harvard University Press, Cambridge, MA.

Béteille, A. (ed.) (1969). *Social Inequality*. Penguin, Harmondsworth.

Bhargava, A. (1992). 'Malnutrition and the Role of Individual Variation with Evidence from India and the Philippines', *Journal of the Royal Statistical Society*, Part A, Vol. 155.

Bhargava, A. (1994). 'Modelling the Health of Filipino Children', *Journal of the Royal Statistical Society*, Part A, Vol. 157.

Bhattacharya, N. and Mahalanobis, B. (1969). 'Regional Disparities in Household Consumption in India', *Journal of the American Statistical Association*, Vol. 62.

Blackorby, C. (1975). 'Degrees of Cardinality and Aggregate Partial Ordering', *Econometrica*, Vol. 43.

Blackorby, C., Bossert, W., and Donaldson, D. (1995). 'Income Inequality Measurement: The Normative Approach', Discussion Paper 95.23, Department of Economics, University of British Columbia.

Blackorby, C. and Donaldson, D. (1977). 'Utility versus Equity: Some Plausible Quasi-Orderings', *Journal of Public Economics*, Vol. 7.

Blackorby, C. and Donaldson, D. (1978). 'Measures of Relative Equality and their Meaning in Terms of Social Welfare', *Journal of Economic Theory*, Vol. 18.

Blackorby, C. and Donaldson, D. (1980a). 'A Theoretical Treatment of Indices of Absolute Inequality', *International Economic Review*, Vol. 21.

Blackorby, C. and Donaldson, D. (1980b). 'Ethical Indices for the Measurement of Poverty', *Econometrica*, Vol. 48.

Blackorby, C. and Donaldson, D. (1984). 'Ethically Significant Ordinal Indexes of Relative Inequality', in Basmann and Rhodes (1984).

Blackorby, C., Donaldson, D., and Auersperg, M. (1981). 'A New Procedure for the Measurement of Inequality within and among Population Subgroups', *Canadian Journal of Economics*, Vol. 14.

Blackorby, C., Donaldson, D., and Weymark, J. (1984). 'Social Choice with Interpersonal Utility Comparisons: A Diagrammatic Introduction', *International Economic Review*, Vol. 25.

Blackorby, C., Primont, D., and Russell, R. (1978). *Duality, Separability and Functional Structure: Theory and Economic Applications*. North-Holland, Amsterdam.

Blair, D. H. (1988). 'The Primary-Goods Indexation Problem in Rawls' *Theory of Justice*', *Theory and Decision*, Vol. 24.

Blau, J. H. (1975). 'Liberal Values and Independence', *Review of Economic Studies*, Vol. 42.

Bös, D., Rose, M., and Seidl, C. (eds.) (1988). *Welfare and Efficiency in Public Economics*. Springer-Verlag, Berlin.

Bourguignon, F. (1979). 'Decomposable Income Inequality Measures', *Econometrica*, Vol. 47.

Bourguignon, F. and Fields, G. (1990). 'Poverty Measures and Anti-Poverty Policy', *Recherches Economiques de Louvain*, Vol. 56.

Bowles, S. (1972). 'Unequal Education and the Reproduction of the Social Division of Labor', in M. Carney (ed.), *Schooling in a Corporate Society*. David McKay.

Brandt, R. B. (1979). *A Theory of the Good and the Right*. Oxford University Press, Oxford.

Breit, W. and Culbertson, W. P., Jr. (1970). 'Distributional Equality and Aggregate Utility: Comment', *American Economic Review*, Vol. 60.

Broome, J. (1987). 'What's the Good of Equality?', in J. Hey (ed.), *Current Issues in Microeconomics*. Macmillan, London.

Carter, I. (1996). 'The Concept of Freedom in the Work of Amartya Sen: An Alternative Consistent with Freedom's Independent Value', mimeographed.

Casini, L. and Bernetti, I. (1996). 'Environment, Sustainability, and Sen's Theory', mimeographed, University of Naples and University of Florence; presented at the Politeia meeting on 'Environment and Society in a Changing World: A Perspective from the Functioning Theory', 10 May 1996.

Cerioli, A. and Zani, S. (1990). 'A Fuzzy Approach to the Measurement of Poverty', in Dagum and Zenga (1990).

Chakravarty, S. R. (1983a). 'Ethically Flexible Measures of Poverty', *Canadian Journal of Economics*, Vol. 16.

Chakravarty, S. R. (1983b). 'A New Index of Poverty', *Mathematical Social Sciences*, Vol. 6.

Chakravarty, S. R. (1983c). 'Measures of Poverty Based on the Representative Income Gap, Sankhyā', *The Indian Journal of Statistics*, Series B, Vol. 45.

Chakravarty, S. R. (1988). 'Extended Gini Indexes of Inequality', *International Economic Review*, Vol. 29.

Chakravarty, S. R. (1990). *Ethical Social Index Numbers*. Springer-Verlag, Berlin.

Champernowne, D. (1952). 'The Graduation of Income Distribution', *Econometrica*, Vol. 20.

Champernowne, D. (1953). 'A Model of Income Distribution', *Economic Journal*, Vol. 63.

Chen, L. C., Huq, E., and D'Souza, D. (1981). 'Sex Bias in the Family Allocation of Food and Health Care in Rural Bangladesh', *Population and Development Review*, Vol. 7.

Chiappero Martinetti, E. (1994). 'A New Approach to Evaluation of Well-being and Poverty by Fuzzy Set Theory', *Giornale degli Economisti*, Vol. 53.

Chiappero Martinetti, E. (1996). 'Standard of Living Evaluation Based on Sen's Approach: Some Methodological Suggestions', mimeographed, University of Pavia; presented at the Politeia meeting on 'Environment and Society in a Changing World: A Perspective from the Functioning Theory', 10 May 1996.

Clark, J. B. (1902). *Distribution of Wealth*. Macmillan.

Clark, S., Hemming, R., and Ulph, D. (1981). 'On Indices for the Measurement of Poverty', *Economic Journal*, Vol. 91.

Cohen, G. A. (1989). 'On the Currency of Egalitarian Justice', *Ethics*, Vol. 99.

Cohen, G. A. (1990). 'Equality of What? On Welfare, Goods and Capabilities', *Recherches Economiques de Louvain*, Vol. 56.

Cohen, G. A. (1995). *Self-ownership, Freedom, and Equality*. Cambridge University Press, Cambridge.

Cornia, G. A. (1995). 'Poverty in Latin America in the 1980s: Extent, Causes and Possible Remedies', *Giornale degli Economisti*, Vol. 53.

Cowell, F. A. (1977). *Measuring Inequality*. Phillip Allan, Oxford; see also Cowell (1995).

Cowell, F. A. (1980). 'On the Structure of Additive Inequality Measures', *Review of Economic Studies*, Vol. 47.

Cowell, F. A. (1984). 'The Structure of American Income Inequality', *Journal of Income and Wealth*, Vol. 30.

Cowell, F. A. (1985). '"A Fair Suck of the Sauce Bottle" or, What Do You Mean by Inequality?', *Economic Record*, Vol. 61.

Cowell, F. A. (1988a). 'Inequality Decomposition: Three Bad Measures', *Bulletin of Economic Research*, Vol. 40.

Cowell, F. A. (1988b). 'Poverty Measures, Inequality and Decomposability', in Bös, Rose, and Seidl (1988).

Cowell, F. A. (1995). *Measuring Inequality*, second edition. Prentice-Hall/Harvester, London.

Cowell, F. A. and Kuga, K. (1981a). 'Inequality Measurement: An Axiomatic Approach', *European Economic Review*, Vol. 15.

Cowell, F. A. and Kuga, K. (1981b). 'Additivity and the Entropy Concept: An Axiomatic Approach to Inequality Measurement', *Journal of Economic Theory*, Vol. 25.

Creedy, J. (1977). 'The Principle of Transfers and the Variance of Logarithms', *Oxford Bulletin of Economics and Statistics*, Vol. 39.

Crocker, D. (1992). 'Functioning and Capability: The Foundations of Sen's and Nussbaum's Development Ethic', *Political Theory*, Vol. 20.

Crocker, D. (1996). 'Consumption, Well-being and Capability', mimeographed, Institute of Philosophy and Public Policy, University of Maryland.

Culyer, A. J. (1990). 'Commodities, Characteristics of Commodities, Characteristics of People, Utilities, and the Quality of Life', in S. Baldwin, C. Godfrey, and C. Propper (eds.), *Quality of Life: Perspectives and Policies*. Routledge, London.

Dagum, C. and Zenga, M. (eds.) (1990). *Income and Wealth Distribution, Inequality and Poverty*. Springer-Verlag, Berlin.

Dahrendorf, R. (1968). *Essays in the Theory of Society*. Stanford University Press, Stanford.

Dalton, H. (1920). 'The Measurement of the Inequality of Incomes', *Economic Journal*, Vol. 30.

Dalton, H. (1925). *Inequality of Incomes*. London.

Dardanoni, V. (1992). 'On Multidimensional Inequality Measurement', mimeo.

Dasgupta, P. (1993). *An Inquiry into Well-being and Destitution*. Clarendon Press, Oxford.

Dasgupta, P. and Ray, D. (1986). 'Inequality as a Determinant of Malnutrition and Unemployment: Theory', *Economic Journal*, Vol. 96.

Dasgupta, P. and Ray, D. (1987). 'Inequality as a Determinant of Malnutrition and Unemployment: Policy', *Economic Journal*, Vol. 97.

Dasgupta, P., Sen, A. K., and Starrett, D. (1973). 'Notes on the Measurement of Inequality', *Journal of Economic Theory*, Vol. 6.

d'Aspremont, C. (1965). 'Axioms for Social Welfare Ordering', in L. Hurwicz, D. Schmeidler, and H. Sonnenschein (eds.), *Social Goals and Social Organization*. Cambridge University Press, Cambridge.

d'Aspremont, C. (1985). 'Axioms for Social Welfare Ordering', in L. Hurwicz, D. Schmeidler, and H. Sonnenschein (eds.), *Social Goals and Social Organization*. Cambridge University Press, Cambridge.

d'Aspremont, C. and Gevers, L. (1977). 'Equity and the Informational Basis of Collective Choice', *Review of Economic Studies*, Vol. 46.

Davies, J. and Hoy, M. (1995). 'Making Inequality Comparisons when Lorenz Curves Cross', *American Economic review*, Vol. 85.

Deaton, A. S. (1995). *Microeconometric Analysis for Development Policy: An Approach from Household Surveys*. Johns Hopkins University Press for the World Bank, Baltimore, MD.

Deaton, A. S. and Muellbauer, J. (1980). *Economics and Consumer Behaviour*. Cambridge University Press, Cambridge.

Deaton, A. S. and Muellbauer, J. (1986). 'On Measuring Child Costs: With Applications to Poor Countries', *Journal of Political Economy*, Vol. 94.

Deaton, A. S., Ruiz-Castillo, J., and Thomas, D. (1989). 'The Influence of Household Composition on Household Expenditure Patterns: Theory and Spanish Evidence', *Journal of Political Economy*, Vol. 97.

Debreu, G. (1959). *The Theory of Value*. Wiley, New York.

Debreu, G. (1960). 'Topological Methods in Cardinal Utility', in K. J. Arrow, S. Karlin, and P. Suppes (eds.), *Mathematical Methods in the Social Sciences*. Stanford University Press, Stanford.

Delbono, F. (1989). 'Poverta come incapacita: Premesse teoriche, identificazione e misurazione', *Rivista Internazionale di Scienze Sociali*, Vol. 97.

Desai, M. J. (1990). 'Poverty and Capability: Towards an Empirically Implementable Measure', mimeographed, London School of Economics.

Desai, M. (1991). 'Human Development: Concepts and Measurement', *European Economic Review*, Vol. 35.

Desai, M. (1994). *Poverty, Famine and Economic Development*. Elgar, Aldershot.

Desai, M., Sen, A., and Boltvinik, J. (1992). *Social Progress Index: A Proposal*. UNDP, Bogota.

Diamond, P. (1967). 'Cardinal Welfare, Individualistic Ethics, and Interpersonal Comparisons of Utility: A Comment', *Journal of Political Economy*, Vol. 75.

Dobb, M. H. (1933). 'Economic Theory and the Problems of a Socialist Economy', *Economic Journal*, Vol. 43; reprinted in *On Economic Theory and Socialism*, Routledge, London.

Dobb, M. H. (1937). *Political Economy and Capitalism*. Routledge, London.

Dobb, M. H. (1951). *Soviet Economic Development since 1917*. Routledge, London.

Dobb, M. H. (1969). *Welfare Economics and the Economics of Socialism*. Cambridge University Press, Cambridge.

Domar, E. (1966). 'The Soviet Collective Farm as a Producer Cooperative', *American Economic Review*, Vol. 56.

Donaldson, D. and Weymark, J. A. (1980). 'A Single-Parameter Generalisation of the Gini Indices of Inequality', *Journal of Economic Theory*, Vol. 22.

Donaldson, D. and Weymark, J. A. (1986). 'Properties of Fixed Population Poverty Indices', *International Economic Review*, Vol. 27.

Dorfman, R., Samuelson, P. A., and Solow, R. M. (1958). *Linear Programming and Economic Analysis*. McGraw-Hill, New York.

Drèze, J. and Sen, A. K. (1989). *Hunger and Public Action*. Clarendon Press, Oxford.

Drèze, J. and Sen, A. (eds.) (1990). *The Political Economy of Hunger*, 3 vols. Clarendon Press, Oxford.

Drèze, J. and Sen, A. (1995). *India: Economic Development and Social Opportunity*. Oxford University Press, Delhi and Oxford.

Dutta, B. and Ray, D. (1989). 'A Concept of Egalitarianism under Participation Constraints', *Econometrica*, Vol. 57.

Dworkin, R. (1981). 'What is Equality? Part 1: Equality of Welfare', and 'What is Equality? Part 2: Equality of Resources', *Philosophy and Public Affairs*, Vol. 10.

Dworkin, R. (1985). *A Matter of Principle*. Harvard University Press, Cambridge, MA.

Easterlin, R. A. (1995). 'Will Raising the Incomes of All Increase the Happiness of All?', *Journal of Economic Behavior and Organization*, Vol. 27.

Ebert, U. (1988). 'On the Decomposition of Inequality: Partitions into Non-overlapping Subgroups', in Eichhorn (1988).

Ebert, U. (1992). 'On Comparisons of Income Distributions When

230   BIBLIOGRAPHY

Household Types Are Different', Economics Discussion Paper V-86-92, University of Oldenberg.

Ebert, U. (1994). 'Social Welfare When Needs Differ: An Axiomatic Approach', Department of Economics, University of Oldenberg.

Eichhorn, W. (1978). *Functional Equations in Economics*. Addison-Wesley, London.

Eichhorn, W. (ed.) (1988). *Measurement in Economics*. Physica-Verlag, New York.

Eichhorn, W. and Gehrig, W. (1982). 'Measurement of Inequality in Economics', in B. Korte (ed.), *Modern Applied Mathematics*. North-Holland, Amsterdam.

Ellman, M. (1966). 'Individual Preferences and the Market', *Economics of Planning*, No. 3.

Ellman, M. (1971). *Soviet Planning Today*. Cambridge University Press, Cambridge.

Elster, J. and Hylland, A. (eds.) (1986). *Foundations of Social Choice Theory*. Cambridge University Press, Cambridge.

Elster, J. and Roemer, J. (eds.) (1991). *Interpersonal Comparisons of Well-being*. Cambridge University Press, Cambridge.

Éltetö, O. and Frigyes, E. (1968). 'New Income Inequality Measures as Efficient Tools for Causal Analysis and Planning', *Econometrica*, Vol. 36.

Erikson, R. and Aberg, R. (1987). *Welfare in Transition: A Survey of Living Conditions in Sweden (1968–81)*. Clarendon Press, Oxford.

Esteban, J.-M. and Ray, D. (1994). 'On the Measurement of Polarization', *Econometrica*, Vol. 62.

Fields, G. S. (1980). *Poverty, Inequality and Development*. Cambridge University Press, Cambridge.

Fields, G. S. (1993). 'Inequality in Dual Economy Models', *Economic Journal*, Vol. 103.

Fields, G. S. and Fei, J. C. S. (1978). 'On Inequality Comparisons', *Econometrica*, Vol. 46.

Fine, B. J. (1975). 'A Note on Interpersonal Aggregation and Partial Comparability', *Econometrica*, Vol. 43.

Fine, B. J. (1985). 'A Note on the Measurement of Inequality and Interpersonal Comparability', *Social Choice and Welfare*, Vol. 1.

Fine, B. J. and Fine, K. (1974). 'Social Choice and Individual Ranking, II', *Review of Economic Studies*, Vol. 41.

Fishburn, P. C. (1970). *Utility Theory and Decision Making*. Wiley, New York.

Fishburn, P. C. and Willig, R. D. (1984). 'Transfer Principles in Income Distribution', *Journal of Public Economics*, Vol. 25.

Fisher, F. M. (1956). 'Income Distribution, Value Judgements and Welfare', *Quarterly Journal of Economics*, Vol. 70.

Fisher, F. M. (1987). 'Household Equivalence Scales and Interpersonal Comparisons', *Review of Economic Studies*, Vol. 54.

Fisher, F. M. (1990). 'Household Equivalence Scales: Reply', *Review of Economic Studies*, Vol. 57.

Fisher, F. M. and Rothenberg, J. (1961). 'How Income Ought to be Distributed: Paradox Lost', *Journal of Political Economy*, Vol. 69.

Fisher, F. M. and Rothenberg, J. (1962). 'How Income Ought to be Distributed: Paradox Enow', *Journal of Political Economy*, Vol. 70.

Fisher, F. M. and Shell, K. (1972). *The Economic Theory of Price Indices*, Academic Press, New York.

Fleming, M. (1952). 'A Cardinal Concept of Welfare', *Quarterly Journal of Economics*, Vol. 66.

Fleurbaey, M. (1994). 'On Fair Compensation', *Theory and Decision*, Vol. 36.

Fleurbaey, M. (1995a). 'Three Solutions for the Compensation Problem', *Journal of Economic Theory*, Vol. 65.

Fleurbaey, M. (1995b). 'Equality and Responsibility', *European Economic Review*, Vol. 39.

Folbre, N. (1994). *Who Pays for the Kids? Gender and the Structures of Constraint*. Routledge, New York.

Foley, D. (1967). 'Resource Allocation in the Public Sector', *Yale Economic Essays*, Vol. 7.

Foster, J. E. (1983). 'An Axiomatic Characterisation of the Theil Measure of Income Inequality', *Journal of Economic Theory*, Vol. 31.

Foster, J. E. (1984). 'On Economic Poverty: A Survey of Aggregate Measures', in Basmann and Rhodes (1984).

Foster, J. E. (1985). 'Inequality Measurement', in H. P. Young (ed.), *Fair Allocation*. American Mathematical Society, Providence, RI.

Foster, J. E. (1993). 'Notes on Effective Freedom', mimeographed; presented at the Stanford Workshop on Economic Theories of Inequality, sponsored by the MacArthur Foundation.

Foster, J. E. (1994a). 'Normative Measurement: Is Theory Relevant?', *The American Economic Review*, Vol. 84.

Foster, J. E. (1994b). 'Inequality and Poverty', notes prepared for this annexe, mimeographed, Department of Economics, Vanderbilt University.

Foster, J. E. and Jin, Y. (1996). 'Poverty Orderings for the Dalton Utility-Gap Measures', in S. Jenkins, A. Kapteyn, and B. Van Praag (eds.), *The Distribution of Welfare and Household* Production. Cambridge University Press, Cambridge (forthcoming).

Foster, J. E. and Ok, E. A. (1996). 'Lorenz Dominance and The Variance of Logarithms', mimeographed, Department of Economics, Vanderbilt University.

Foster, J. E. and Shneyerov, A. A. (1996a). 'Path Independent Inequality Measures', mimeographed, Department of Economics, Vanderbilt University.

Foster, J. E. and Shneyerov, A. A. (1996b). 'An Elementary Characterization of Generalized Entropy Inequality Measures', mimeographed, Department of Economics, Vanderbilt University.

Foster, J. E. and Shorrocks, A. F. (1988a). 'Poverty Orderings', *Econometrica*, Vol. 56.

Foster, J. E. and Shorrocks, A. F. (1988b). 'Poverty Orderings and Welfare Dominance', *Social Choice and Welfare*, Vol. 5.

Foster, J. E. and Shorrocks, A. F. (1988c). 'Inequality and Poverty Orderings', *European Economic Review*, Vol. 32.

Foster, J. E. and Shorrocks, A. F. (1991). 'Subgroup Consistent Poverty Indices', *Econometrica*, Vol. 59.

Foster, J. E., Greer, J., and Thorbecke, E. (1984). 'A Class of Decomposable Poverty Measures', *Econometrica*, Vol. 52.

Foster, J. E., Majumdar, M., and Mitra, T. (1990). 'Inequality and Welfare in Market Economies', *Journal of Public Economics*, Vol. 41.

Friedman, M. (1947). 'Lerner on the Economics of Control', *Journal of Political Economy*, Vol. 55; reprinted in *Essays in Positive Economics*, University of Chicago Press, 1964.

Fuchs, V. (1965). 'Toward a Theory of Poverty', *Task Force on Economic Growth and Opportunity, The Concept of Poverty*. Chamber of Commerce of the United States of America, Washington, D.C.

Fuchs, V. (1976). 'Redefining Poverty and Redistributing Income', *The Public Interest*, Vol. 8.

Fuchs, V. (1988). *Women's Quest for Economic Equality*. Harvard University Press, Cambridge, MA.

Gärdenfors, P. (1973). 'Positionalist Voting Functions', *Theory and Decision*, Vol. 4.

Gastwirth, J. L. (1971). 'A General Definition of the Lorenz Curve', *Econometrica*, Vol. 39.

Gevers, L. (1979). 'On Interpersonal Comparability and Social Welfare Orderings.' *Econometrica*, Vol. 47.

Gibbard, A. (1979). 'Disparate Goods and Rawls's Difference Principle: A Social Choice Theoretic Treatment', *Theory and Decision*, Vol. 11.

Gini, C. (1912). *Variabilità e mutabilità*. Bologna.

Gini, C. (1936). 'On the Measure of Concentration with Especial Reference to Income and Wealth', Cowles Commission.

Gintis, H. (1969). 'Alienation and Power: Toward a Radical Welfare Economics', Ph.D. dissertation, Harvard University.

Glewwe, P. (1991). 'Household Equivalent Scales and the Measurement of Inequality: Transfers from the Poor to the Rich Could Decrease Inequality', *Journal of Public Economics*, Vol. 44.

Gorman, W. M. (1968a). 'The Structure of Utility Functions', *Review of Economic Studies*, Vol. 35.

Gorman, W. M. (1968b). 'Conditions for Additive Separability', *Econometrica*, Vol. 36.

Graaff, J. de v. (1957). *Theoretical Welfare Economics*. Cambridge University Press, Cambridge.

Graaff, J. de v. (1977). 'Equity and Efficiency as Components of General Welfare', *South African Journal of Economics*, Vol. 45.

Graaff, J. de v. (1985). 'Normative Measurement Theory', mimeographed, All Souls College, Oxford.

Granaglia, E. (1994). 'Più o meno eguaglianza di risorse? Un falso problema per le politiche sociali', *Giornale degli Economisti e Annali di Economia*, Vol. 53. [Abstract in English: 'More or less equality? A misleading question for social policy'.]

Grant, J. P. (1978). *Disparity Reduction Rates in Social Indicators*. Overseas Development Council, Washington, D.C.

Greer, J. and Thorbecke, E. (1986). 'Pattern of Food Consumption and Poverty in Kenya and Effects of Food Prices', *Journal of Development Economics*, Vol. 24.

Griffin, J. (1981). 'Equality: On Sen's Weak Equity Axiom', *Mind*, Vol. 90.

Griffin, J. (1986). *Well-being*. Clarendon Press, Oxford.

Griffin, K. and Knight, J. (eds.) (1990). *Human Development and the International Development Strategies for the 1990s*. Macmillan, London.

Hadar, J. and Russell, W. (1969). 'Rules for Ordering Uncertain Prospects', *American Economic Review*, Vol. 59.

Haddad, L. and Kanbur, R. (1990). 'How Serious Is the Neglect of Intra-household Inequality?', *Economic Journal*, Vol. 100.

Hagenaars, A. (1986). *Perception of Poverty*. North-Holland, Amsterdam.

Hagenaars, A. (1987). 'A Class of Poverty Indices', *International Economic Review*, Vol. 28.

Hamada, K. (1973). 'A Simple Majority Rule on the Distribution of Income', *Journal of Economic Theory*, Vol. 6.

Hamada, K. and Takayama, N. (1977). 'Censored Income Distributions and the Measurement of Poverty', *Bulletin of the International Statistical Institute*, Book I, Vol. 47.

Hammond, P. J. (1971). 'Utility Differences and Additively Separable Preferences', mimeographed, University of Essex.

Hammond, P. J. (1976a). 'Equity, Arrow's Conditions and Rawls' Difference Principle', *Econometrica*, Vol. 44.

Hammond, P. J. (1976b). 'Why Ethical Measures of Inequality Need Interpersonal Comparisons', *Theory and Decision*, Vol. 7.

Hammond, P. J. (1977). 'Dual Interpersonal Comparisons of Utility and the Welfare of Income Distribution', *Journal of Public Economics*, Vol. 6.

Hammond, P. J. (1978). 'Economic Welfare with Rank Order Price Weighting', *Review of Economic Studies*, Vol. 45.

Hammond, P. J. (1979). 'Equity in Two Person Situations: Some Consequences', *Econometrica*, Vol. 47.

Hammond, P. J. (1985). 'Welfare Economics', in G. Feiwel (ed.), *Issues in Contemporary Microeconomics and Welfare*. SUNY Press, Albany, NY.

Hansson, B. (1977). 'The Measurement of Social Inequality', in R. Butts and J. Hintikka (eds.), *Logic, Methodology, and Philosophy of Science*. Reidel, Dordrecht.

Haq, Mahbub ul (1995). *Reflections on Human Development*. Oxford University Press, New York.

Hardy, G., Littlewood, J., and Polya, G. (1934). *Inequalities*. Cambridge University Press, London.

Hare, R. M. (1952). *The Language of Morals*. Clarendon Press, Oxford.

Hare, R. M. (1963). *Freedom and Reason*. Clarendon Press, Oxford.

Hare, R. M. (1981). *Moral Thinking: Its Levels, Methods and Point*. Clarendon Press, Oxford.

Harriss, B. (1990). 'The Intrafamily Distribution of Hunger in South Asia', in Drèze and Sen (1990).

Harsanyi, J. C. (1955). 'Cardinal Welfare, Individualistic Ethics and Interpersonal Comparisons of Utility', *Journal of Political Economy*, Vol. 63.

Harsanyi, J. C. (1976). *Essays in Ethics, Social Behavior and Scientific Explanation*. Reidel, Dordrecht.

Hart, H. L. A. (1961). *The Concept of Law*. Clarendon Press, Oxford.

Hawthorn, G. (1987). 'Introduction', in Sen *et al.* (1987a).

Herrero, Carmen (1995). 'Capabilities and Utilities', mimeographed, University of Alicante & IVIE, Spain.

Hirschberg, J. G., Maasoumi, E., and Slottje, D. J. (1991). 'Cluster Analysis for Measuring Welfare and Quality of Life across Countries', *Journal of Econometrics*, Vol. 50.

Hoffman, C. (1964). 'Work Incentive Policy in Communist China', *The China Quarterly*.

Hoffman, C. (1967). *Work Incentive Practices and Policies in the People's Republic of China, 1953–1965*. Albany, NY.

Hossain, I. (1990). *Poverty as Capability Failure*. Swedish School of Economics, Helsinki.

Iyengar, N. S. (1968). 'On a Measure of Income Inequality', *Journal of Osmania University*, Golden Jubilee Volume.

Jenkins, S. (1989). 'The Measurement of Economic Inequality', in L. Osberg (ed.), *Readings on Economic Inequality*. Sharpe, New York.

Jenkins, S. and Lambert, P. (1993a). 'Ranking Income Distributions When Needs Differ', *Review of Income and Wealth*, Vol. 39.

Jenkins, S. and Lambert, P. (1993b). 'Poverty Orderings, Poverty Gaps, and Poverty Lines', Discussion Paper 93-07, Department of Economics, University College of Swansea.

Jorgenson, D. W., Lau, L. J., and Stoker, T. M. (1980). 'Welfare Comparison under Exact Aggregation', *American Economic Review*, Vol. 70.

Jorgenson, D. W. and Slesnick, D. T. (1984). 'Inequality in the Distribution of Individual Welfare', *Advances in Econometrics*, Vol. 3.

Kakwani, N. C. (1980a). *Income Inequality and Poverty*. Oxford University Press, New York.

Kakwani, N. C. (1980b). 'On a Class of Poverty Measures', *Econometrica*, Vol. 48.

Kakwani, N. C. (1981). 'Welfare Measures: An International Comparison', *Journal of Development Economics*, Vol. 8.

Kakwani, N. C. (1984a). 'Issues in Measuring Poverty', *Advances in Econometrics*, Vol. 3.

Kakwani, N. C. (1984b). 'Welfare Rankings of Income Distribution', in Basmann and Rhodes (1984).

Kakwani, N. C. (1986). *Analysing Redistribution Policies*. Cambridge University Press, Cambridge.

Kakwani, N. C. (1995). 'Inequality, Welfare and Poverty: Three Interrelated Phenomena', mimeographed, University of New South Wales.

Kakwani, N. C. and Podder, N. (1983). 'On the Estimation of the Lorenz Curve from Grouped Observations', *International Economic Review*, Vol. 14.

Kanbur, S. M. R. (1984). 'The Measurement and Decomposition of Inequality and Poverty', in F. van der Ploeg (ed.), *Mathematical Methods in Economics*. Wiley, New York.

Kanbur, S. M. R. (1987a). 'Transfers, Targeting and Poverty', *Economic Policy*, Vol. 4.

Kanbur, S. M. R. (1987b). 'The Standard of Living: Uncertainty, Inequality and Opportunity', in Sen (1987a).

Kant, I. (1785). *Grundlegung zur Metaphysik der Sitten*; English translation by T. K. Abbott, *Fundamental Principles of the Metaphysics of Ethics*. Longmans, London, 1970.

Kenen, P. B. and Fisher, F. M. (1957). 'Income Distribution, Value Judgments and Welfare', *Quarterly Journal of Economics*, Vol. 71.

Khinchin, A. (1957). *Mathematical Formulations of Information Theory*. Dover, New York.

Klappholz, K. (1972). 'Equality of Opportunity, Fairness and Efficiency', in M. H. Peston an B. A. Corry (eds.), *Essays in Honour of Lord Robbins*. Weidenfeld and Nicolson, London.

Knight, F. (1947). *Freedom and Reform: Essays in Economic and Social Philosophy*. Harper, New York; republished, Liberty Press, Indianapolis, 1982.

Kolm, S. C. (1969). 'The Optimal Production of Social Justice', in J. Margolis and H. Guitton (eds.), *Public Economics*. Macmillan, London.

Kolm, S. C. (1976a). 'Unequal Inequalities I', *Journal of Economic Theory*, Vol. 12.

Kolm, S. C. (1976b). 'Unequal Inequalities II', *Journal of Economic Theory*, Vol. 13.

Kolm, S. C. (1979). 'Multidimensional Egalitarianisms', *Quarterly Journal of Economics*, Vol. 91.

Koopmans, T. C. (1957). *Three Essays on the State of Economic Science*. McGraw-Hill, New York.

Koopmans, T. C. (1964). 'On Flexibility of Future Preference', in M. W. Shelley and G. L. Bryan (eds.), *Human Judgements and Optimality*. Wiley, New York.

Krelle, W. and Shorrocks, A. F. (eds.) (1978). *Personal Income Distribution*. North-Holland, Amsterdam.

Kreps, D. (1979). 'A Representation Theorem for Preference for Flexibility', *Econometrica*, Vol. 47.

Kundu, A. (1981). 'Measurement of Poverty—Some Conceptual Issues', *Anvesak*, Vol. 11.

Kundu, A. and Smith, T. E. (1983). 'An Impossibility Theorem for Poverty Indices', *International Economic Review*, Vol. 24.

Kynch, J. and Sen, A. K. (1983). 'Indian Women: Well-Being and Survival', *Cambridge Journal of Economics*, Vol. 7.

Lambert, P. J. (1989). *The Distribution and Redistribution of Income: A Mathematical Analysis*. Basil Blackwell, Oxford.

Lambert, P. J. and Aronson, J. R. (1993). 'Inequality Decomposition Analysis and the Gini Coefficient Revisited', *Economic Journal*, Vol. 103.

Lange, O. (1936–7). 'On the Economic Theory of Socialism', *Review of Economic Studies*, Vol. 4; reprinted in O. Lange and F. M. Taylor, *On the Economic Theory of Socialism*, University of Minnesota Press, 1952.

Lange, O. (1938). 'The Foundations of Welfare Economics', *Econometrica*, Vol. 10; reprinted in K. J. Arrow and T. Scitovsky (eds.), *Readings in Welfare Economics*. Irwin, Homewood, IL.

Le Grand, J. (1991). *Equity and Choice*. HarperCollins, London.

Lenti, R. T. (1994). 'Sul contributo alla cultura dei grandi economisti: Liberta, diseguaglianza e poverta ne pensiore di Amartya K. Sen', *Rivista Milanese di Economia*, Vol. 53.

Leonard, D. (1990). 'Household Equivalence Scales: Comment', *Review of Economic Studies*, Vol. 57.

Lerner, A. P. (1944). *The Economics of Control*. Macmillan, London.

Lewis, G. W. and Ulph, D. (1988). 'Poverty, Inequality and Welfare', *Economic Journal*, Vol. 98.

Lipton, M. (1985). 'A Problem in Poverty Measurement', *Mathematical Social Sciences*, Vol. 10.

Little, I. M. D. (1950). *A Critique of Welfare Economics*. Clarendon Press, Oxford.

Lorenz, M. O. (1905). 'Methods for Measuring Concentration of Wealth', *Journal of the American Statistical Association*, Vol. 9.

Love, R. and Wolfson, M. C. (1976). 'Income Inequality: Statistical

Methodology and Canadian Illustrations', *Statistics Canada*, Ottawa.

Luce, R. D. and Raiffa, H. (1957). *Games and Decisions*. Wiley, New York.

Lydall, H. F. (1966). *The Structure of Earnings*. Clarendon Press, Oxford.

Maasoumi, E. (1986). 'The Measurement and Decomposition of Multi-Dimensional Inequality', *Econometrica*, Vol. 54.

Maasoumi, E. (1989). 'Continuously Distributed Attributes and Measures of Multivariate Inequality', *Journal of Econometrics*, Vol. 42.

Maasoumi, E. (1995). 'Empirical Analysis of Inequality and Welfare', in M. H. Pesaran and M. R. Wickens (eds.), *Handbook of Applied Econometrics*. Blackwell, Oxford.

Maasoumi, E. and Nickelsburg, G. (1988). 'Multivariate Measures of Well-Being and an Analysis in the Michigan Data', *Journal of Business and Economics Statistics*, Vol. 6.

Maasoumi, E. and Zandvakili, S. (1986). 'A Class of Generalized Measures of Mobility with Applications', *Economic Letters*, Vol. 22.

Majumdar, T. (1983). *Investment in Education and Social Choice*. Cambridge University Press, Cambridge.

Malinvaud, E. (1967). 'Decentralized Procedures for Planning', in E. Malinvaud and M. O. L. Bacharach, *Activity Analysis in the Theory of Growth and Planning*. Macmillan, London.

Mandel, E. (1968). *Marxist Economic Theory*. Merlin Press, London.

Marglin, S. A. (1963). 'The Social Rate of Discount and the Optimal Rate of Investment', *Quarterly Journal of Economy*, Vol. 77.

Marglin, S. A. (1966). 'Industrial Development in the Labor-Surplus Economy', mimeographed.

Marshall, A. (1890). *Principles of Economics*. Macmillan, London.

Marshall, A. W. and Olkin, I. (1979). *Inequalities: Theory of Majorization and Its Applications*. Academic Press, New York.

Marx, K. (1875). *Critique of the Gotha Program*, English translation in K. Marx and F. Engels, *Selected Works*, Vol. II. Foreign Language Publishing House, Moscow; International Publishers, New York, 1938.

Marx, K. (1887). *Capital: A Critical Analysis of Capitalist Production*, Vol. I. Sonnenschein, London; republished by Allen and Unwin, 1938.

Maskin, E. (1979). 'Decision-making under Ignorance with Implications for Social Choice', *Theory and Decision*, Vol. 11.

May, K. O. (1952). 'A Set of Independent, Necessary and Sufficient Conditions for Simple Majority Decision', *Econometrica*, Vol. 20.

Meade, J. E. (1965). *Efficiency, Equity and the Ownership of Property*. Harvard University Press, Cambridge, MA.

Meade, J. E. (1976). *The Just Economy*. Allen & Unwin, London.

Mehran, F. (1976). 'Linear Measures of Income Inequality', *Econometrica*, Vol. 44.

Mill, J. S. (1859). *On Liberty*; republished, Penguin, Harmondsworth, 1974.

Mincer, J. (1958). 'Investment in Human Capital and Personal Income Distribution', *Journal of Political Economy*, Vol. 66.

Mincer, J. (1970). 'The Distribution of Labor Incomes: A Survey with Special Reference to the Human Capital Approach', *Journal of Economic Literature*, Vol. 8.

Mirrlees, J. A. (1971). 'An Exploration in the Theory of Optimum Income Taxation', *Review of Economic Studies*, Vol. 38.

Mookherjee, D. and Shorrocks, A. F. (1982). 'A Decomposition Analysis of the Trend in U.K. Income Inequality', *Economic Journal*, Vol. 92.

Moothathu, T. S. K. (1990–1). 'Lorenz Curve and Gini Index', *Calcutta Statistical Association Bulletin*, Vol. 40.

Morris, M. D. (1979). *Measuring the Conditions of the World's Poor. The Physical Quality of Life Index*. Pergamon Press, Oxford.

Moulin, H. (1988). *Axioms of Cooperative Decision Making*. Cambridge University Press, Cambridge.

Muellbauer, J. (1974). 'Inequality Measures, Prices and Household Composition', *Review of Economic Studies*, Vol. 41.

Muellbauer, J. (1987). 'Professor Sen on the Standard of Living', in Sen (1987a).

Murray, C. J. L. (1994). 'Quantifying the Burden of Disease: The Technical Basis for Disability Adjusted Life Years', *Bulletin of the World Health Organization*, Vol. 72.

Nagel, T. (1986). *The View From Nowhere*. Clarendon Press, Oxford.

Newbery, D. M. G. (1970). 'A Theorem on the Measurement of Inequality', *Journal of Economic Theory*, Vol. 2.

Nove, A. (1961). *The Soviet Economy*. New York.

Nozick, R. (1974). *Anarchy, State and Utopia*. Basic Books, New York.

Nozick, R. (1989). *The Examined Life*. Simon & Schuster, New York.

Nurske, R. (1953). *Problems of Capital Formation in Underdeveloped Countries*. Blackwell, Oxford.

Nussbaum, M. C. (1988). 'Nature, Function, and Capability: Aristotle on Political Distribution', *Oxford Studies in Ancient Philosophy*, Supplementary Volume.

Nussbaum, M. C. (1993). 'Non-relative Virtues: An Aristotelian Approach', in Nussbaum and Sen (1993).

Nussbaum, M. C. and Glover, J. (eds.) (1995). *Women, Culture, and Development*. Clarendon Press, Oxford.

Nussbaum, M. C. and Sen, A. K. (eds.) (1993). *The Quality of Life*. Clarendon Press, Oxford.

Nygård, F. and Sandström, A. (1982). *Measuring Income Inequality*. Almqvist and Wicksell International, Stockholm.

OECD (1971). *Education and Distibution of Income*. Paris.

O'Flaherty, B. (1996). *Making Room: The Economics of Homelessness*, Harvard University Press, Cambridge, MA.

Ok, E. (1995). 'Fuzzy Measurement of Income Inequality: A Class of Fuzzy Inequality Measures', *Social Choice and Welfare*, Vol. 12.

Orshansky, M. (1965). 'Counting the Poor: Another Look at the Poverty Profile', *Social Security Bulletin*, Vol. 28.

Osmani, S. R. (1982). *Economic Inequality and Group Welfare: A Theory of Comparison with Application to Bangladesh*. Clarendon Press, Oxford.

Osmani, S. R. (ed.) (1993). *Nutrition and Poverty*. Clarendon Press, Oxford.

Palmer, J., Smeeding, T., and Torrey, B. (eds.) (1988). *The Vulnerable*. The Urban Institute, Washington, D.C.

Pareto, V. (1897). *Cours d'Économie Politique*. Rouge, Lausanne.

Pareto, V. (1897). *Manuale di economia politica*. Societa Editrice Libraria, Milan.

Parfit, D. (1984). *Reasons and Persons*. Clarendon Press, Oxford.

Pattanaik, P. (1971). *Voting and Collective Choice*. Cambridge University Pres, Cambridge.

Pattanaik, P. and Xu, Y. (1990). 'On Ranking Opportunity Sets in Terms of Freedom of Choice', *Recherches Économiques de Louvain*, Vol. 56.

Pettini, A. (1993). *Bennesse ed Equità: Il Contributo di Amartya Sen*. Leo S. Olschki Editore, Florence, Italy.

Phelps, E. S. (ed.) (1973). *Economic Justice*. Penguin, Harmondsworth.

Phelps, E. S. (1977). 'Recent Developments in Welfare Economics', in M. Intriligator (ed.), *Frontiers of Quantitative Economics*, Vol. II. North-Holland, Amsterdam.

Piacentino, D. (1996). 'Functioning and Social Equity', mimeographed, University of Urbino; presented at the Politeia meeting on 'Environment and Society in a Changing World: A Perspective from the Functioning Theory', 10 May 1996.

Pigou, A. C. (1912). *Wealth and Welfare*. Macmillan, London.

Pigou, A. C. (1920). *The Economics of Welfare*. Macmillan, London.

Pigou, A. C. (1952). *The Economics of Welfare*, fourth edition. Macmillan, London.

Plott, C. (1978). 'Rawls' Theory of Justice: An Impossibility Result', in H. W. Gottinger and W. Leinfellner (eds.), *Decision Theory and Social Ethics*. Reidel, Dordrecht.

Pollak, R. A. and Wales, T. J. (1979). 'Welfare Comparisons and Equivalent Scales', *American Economic Review*, Vol. 69.

Pratt, J. W. (1964). 'Risk Aversion in the Small and Large', *Econometrica*, Vol. 32.

Puppe, C. (1995). Article on measuring freedom, in *Social Choice and Welfare*, Vol. 12.

Puppe, C. (1996). 'An Axiomatic Approach to "Preference for Freedom or Choice"', *Journal of Economic Theory*, Vol. 68.

Pyatt, G. (1976). 'On the Interpretation and Disaggregation of Gini Coefficients', *Economic Journal*, Vol. 86.

Pyatt, G. (1987). 'Measuring Welfare, Poverty and Inequality', *Economic Journal*, Vol. 97.

Pyatt, G. (1990). 'Social Evaluation Criteria', in Dagum and Zenga (1990).

Qizilbash, M. (1995). 'Capability, Well-being and Human Development', Discussion Paper 9515 in Economics and Econometrics, University of Southampton.

Qizilbash, M. (1996). 'The Concept of Well-being', Discussion Paper 9634 in Economics and Econometrics, University of Southampton.

Rae, D. (1981). *Equalities*. Harvard University Press, Cambridge, MA.

Ramsey, F. P. (1928). 'A Mathematical Theory of Savings', *Economic Journal*, Vol. 38.

Ravallion, M. (1994). *Poverty Comparisons*. Harwood Academic Publishers, Chur, Switzerland.

Rawls, J. (1958). 'Justice as Fairness', *Philosophical Review*, Vol. 67.

Rawls, J. (1971). *A Theory of Justice*. Harvard University Press, Cambridge, MA.

Rawls, J. (1982). 'Social Unity and Primary Goods', in Sen and Williams 1982.

Rawls, J. (1993). *Political Liberalism*. Columbia University Press, New York.

Ricci, U. (1916). *L'indice di variabilita e la curve dei redditi*. Rome.

Riley, J. (1987). *Liberal Utilitarianism*. Cambridge University Press, Cambridge.

Riskin, C. (1971). 'Homo Economicus vs. Homo Sinicus: A Discussion of Work Motivation in China', Conference on New Perspectives for the Study of Contemporary China, mimeographed, Montreal.

Robbins, L. (1932). *An Essay on the Nature and Significance of Economic Science*. Allen and Unwin, London.

Robbins, L. (1938). 'Interpersonal Comparisons of Utility: A Comment', *Economic Journal*, Vol. 48.

Roberts, K. W. S. (1980a). 'Possibility Theorems with Interpersonally Comparable Welfare Levels', *Review of Economic Studies*, Vol. 47.

Roberts, K. W. S. (1980b). 'Interpersonal Comparability and Social Choice Theory', *Review of Economic Studies*, Vol. 47.

Roberts, K. W. S. (1980c). 'Price Independent Welfare Prescriptions', *Journal of Public Economics*, Vol. 13.

Robertson, D. H. (1952). *Utility and All That*. Allen & Unwin, London.

Robinson, J. (1933). *Economics of Imperfect Competition*. Macmillan, London.

Robinson, J. (1956). *The Accumulation of Capital*. Macmillan, London.

Robinson, J. (1960). *Collected Economic Papers—II*. Blackwell, Oxford.

Robinson, J. (1969). *The Cultural Revolution in China*. Penguin, Harmondsworth.

Roemer, J. E. (1982). *A General Theory of Exploitation and Class*. Harvard University Press, Cambridge, MA.

Roemer, J. E. (1985). 'Equality of Talent', *Economics and Philosophy*, Vol. 1.

Roemer, J. E. (1986). 'An Historical Materialist Alternative to Welfarism', in J. Elster and A. Hylland (eds.), *Foundations of Social Choice Theory*. Cambridge University Press, Cambridge.

Roemer, J. E. (1993). 'A Pragmatic Theory of Responsibility for the Egalitarian Planner', *Philosophy & Public Affairs*, Vol. 22.

Roemer, J. E. (1996). *Theories of Distributive Justice*. Harvard University Press, Cambridge, MA.

Rothschild, M. and Stiglitz, J. E. (1970). 'Increasing Risk I: A Definition', *Journal of Economic Theory*, Vol. 2.

Rothschild, M. and Stiglitz, J. E. (1973). 'Some Further Results on the Measurement of Inequality', *Journal of Economic Theory*, Vol. 6.

Rowntree, B. S. (1901). *Poverty: A Study of Town Life*. Longmans, London.

Runciman, W. G. (1966). *Relative Deprivation and Social Justice.* Routledge, London.

Runciman, W. G. and Sen, A. K. (1965). 'Games, Justice and the General Will', *Mind*, Vol. 74.

Russell, R. R. (1985). 'Decomposable Inequality Measures', *Review of Economic Studies*, Vol. 52.

Samuelson, P. A. (1947). *Foundations of Economic Analysis*. Harvard University Press, Cambridge, MA.

Samuelson, P. A. (1950a). 'Economic Theory and Wages', in J. E. Stiglitz (ed.), *The Collected Scientific Papers of Paul A. Samuelson*. MIT Press, Cambridge, MA, 1966.

Samuelson, P. A. (1950b). 'Evaluation of Real National Income', *Oxford Economic Papers*, New Series, Vol. 2.

Samuelson, P. A. (1964). 'A. P. Lerner at Sixty', *Review of Economic Studies*, Vol. 31.

Saposnik, R. (1981). 'Rank Dominance in Income Distributions', *Public Choice*, Vol. 36.

Saposnik, R. (1983). 'On Evaluating Income Distributions: Rank Dominance, the Suppes-Sen Grading Principle of Justice and Pareto Optimality', *Public Choice*, Vol. 40.

Satchell, S. E. (1987). 'Source and Subgroup Decomposition Inequalities for the Lorenz Curve', *International Economic Review*, Vol. 28.

Scanlon, T. M. (1975). 'Preference and Urgency', *Journal of Philosophy*, Vol. 72.

Scanlon, T. (1982). 'Contractualism and Utilitarianism', in Sen and Williams (1982).

Schokkaert, E. and Van Ootegem, L. (1990). 'Sen's Concept of the Living Standard Applied to the Belgian Unemployed', *Recherches Économiques de Louvain*, Vol. 56.

Schutz, R. R. (1951). 'On the Measurement of Income Inequality', *American Economic Review*, Vol. 41.

Schwartz, J. and Winship, C. (1980). 'The Welfare Approach to Measuring Inequality', in K. F. Schuessler (ed.), *Sociological Methods*. Jossey-Bass, San Francisco.

Seidl, C. (1988). 'Poverty Measurement: A Survey', in Bös, Rose, and Seidl (1988).

Sen, A. K. (1961). 'On Optimizing the Rate of Saving', *Economic Jounal*, Vol. 71.

Sen, A. K. (1964). 'Working Capital in the Indian Economy: A Conceptual Framework and Some Estimates', in P. N. Rosenstein-Rodan (ed.), *Pricing and Fiscal Policies*. MIT Press, Cambridge, MA.

Sen, A. K. (1966). 'Labour Allocation in a Cooperative Enterprise', *Review of Economic Studies*, Vol. 33.

Sen , A. K. (1967a). 'Isolation, Assurance and the Social Rate of Discount', *Quarterly Journal of Economics*, Vol. 81.

Sen, A. K. (1967b). 'The Nature and Classes of Prescriptive Judgments', *Philosophical Review*, Vol. 17.

Sen, A. K. (1969a). 'A Game-Theoretic Analysis of Theories of Collectivism in Allocation', in T. Majumdar (ed.), *Growth and Choice*. Oxford University Press, London.

Sen, A. K. (1969b). 'Planners' Preferences: Optimality, Distribution and Social Welfare', in J. Margolis and H. Guitton (eds.), *Public Economics*. Macmillan, London.

Sen, A. K. (1970a). *Collective Choice and Social Welfare*. Holden-Day, San Francisco; republished North-Holland, Amsterdam, 1979.

Sen, A. K. (1970b). 'Interpersonal Aggregation and Partial Comparability', *Econometrica*, Vol. 38; reprinted in Sen (1982a).

Sen, A. K. (1970c). 'The Impossibility of a Paretian Liberal', *Journal of Political Economy*, Vol. 78; reprinted in Sen (1982a).

Sen, A. K. (1972). 'Choice, Orderings and Morality', Bristol Conference on Practical Reason; published in S. Körner (ed.), *Practical Reason* (Oxford: Blackwell, 1974); reprinted in Sen (1982a).

Sen, A. K. (1973a). *On Economic Inequality*. Clarendon Press, Oxford; first edition of *this* book.

Sen, A. K. (1973b). 'On the Development of Basic Income Indicators to Supplement GNP Measures', *United Nations Economic Bulletin for Asia and the Far East*, Vol. 24.

Sen, A. K. (1973c). 'Poverty, Inequality and Unemployment: Some Conceptual Issues in Measurement', *Economic and Political Weekly*, Vol. 8.

Sen, A. K. (1974). 'Informational Basis of Alternative Welfare Approaches: Aggregation and Income Distribution', *Journal of Public Economics*, Vol. 3.

Sen, A. K. (1976a). 'Real National Income', *Review of Economic Studies*, Vol. 43; reprinted in Sen (1982a).

BIBLIOGRAPHY 245

Sen, A. K. (1976b). 'Poverty: An Ordinal Approach to Measurement', *Econometrica*, Vol. 44; reprinted in Sen (1982a).

Sen, A. K. (1976c). 'Welfare Inequalities and Rawlsian Axiomatics', *Theory and Decision*, Vol. 7.

Sen, A. K. (1976d). 'Liberty, Unanimity and Rights', *Economica*, Vol. 43; reprinted in Sen (1982a).

Sen, A. K. (1977). 'On Weights and Measures: Informational Constraints in Social Welfare Analysis', *Econometrica*, Vol. 45; reprinted in Sen (1982a).

Sen, A. K. (1978). 'Ethical Measurement of Inequality: Some Difficulties', in Krelle and Shorrocks (1978); reprinted in Sen (1982a).

Sen, A. K. (1979a). 'Personal Utilities and Public Judgements: Or What's Wrong with Welfare Economics?', *Economic Journal*, Vol. 89; reprinted in Sen (1982a).

Sen, A. K. (1979b). 'Interpersonal Comparisons of Welfare', in M. Boskin (ed.), *Economics and Human Welfare: Essays in Honor of Tibor Scitovsky*. Academic Press, New York; reprinted in Sen (1982a).

Sen, A. K. (1979c). 'The Welfare Basis of Real Income Comparisons: A Survey', *Journal of Economic Literature*, Vol. 17; reprinted in Sen (1984).

Sen, A. K. (1979d). 'Issues in the Measurement of Poverty', *Scandinavian Journal of Economics*, Vol. 81.

Sen, A. K. (1980). 'Equality of What?', in S. McMurrin (ed.), *Tanner Lectures on Human Values*. Cambridge University Press, Cambridge; reprinted in Sen (1982a).

Sen, A. K. (1981). *Poverty and Famines: An Essay on Entitlement and Deprivation*. Clarendon Press, Oxford.

Sen, A. K. (1982a). *Choice, Welfare and Measurement*. Blackwell, Oxford, and MIT Press, Cambridge, MA.

Sen, A. K. (1982b). 'Rights and Agency', *Philosophy and Public Affairs*, Vol. 11.

Sen, A. K. (1983). 'Poor, Relatively Speaking', *Oxford Economic Papers*, Vol. 35; reprinted in Sen (1984).

Sen, A. K. (1984). *Resources, Values and Development*. Blackwell, Oxford, and Harvard University Press, Cambridge, MA.

Sen, A. K. (1985a). *Commodities and Capabilities*. North-Holland, Amsterdam.

Sen, A. K. (1985b). 'Well-being, Agency and Freedom: The Dewey Lectures 1984', *Journal of Philosophy*, Vol. 82.

246 BIBLIOGRAPHY

Sen, A. K. (1985c). 'A Sociological Approach to the Measurement of Poverty: A Reply to Professor Peter Townsend', *Oxford Economic Papers*, Vol. 37.

Sen, A. K. (1987a). *The Standard of Living*, ed. by G. Hawthorn, and with comments from K. Hart, R. Kanbur, J. Muellbauer, and B. Williams.

Sen, A. K. (1987b). *On Ethics and Economics*. Blackwell, Oxford.

Sen, A. K. (1990a). 'Justice: Means versus Freedoms', *Philosophy and Public Affairs*, Vol. 19.

Sen, A. K. (1990b). 'Welfare, Freedom and Social Choice: A Reply', *Recherches Économiques de Louvain*, Vol. 56.

Sen, A. K. (1991a). 'Welfare, Preference and Freedom', *Journal of Econometrics*, Vol. 50.

Sen, A. K. (1991b). 'On Indexing Primary Goods and Capabilities', mimeographed, Harvard University.

Sen, A. K. (1992a). *Inequality Reexamined*, Oxford University Press, Oxford, and Harvard University Press, Cambridge, MA.

Sen, A. K. (1992b). 'Missing Women', *British Medical Journal*, Vol. 304.

Sen, A. K. (1994). 'Well-being, Capability and Public Policy', *Giornale degli Economisti e Annali di Economia*, Vol. 53.

Sen, A. K. (1995). 'Rationality and Social Choice', *American Economic Review*, Vol. 85.

Sen, A. K. and Williams, B. (eds.) (1982). *Utilitarianism and Beyond*. Cambridge University Press, Cambridge.

Sheshinski, E. (1972). 'Relation between a Social Welfare Function and the Gini Index of Inequality', *Journal of Economic Theory*, Vol. 4.

Shorrocks, A. F. (1980). 'The Class of Additively Decomposable Inequality Measures', *Econometrica*, Vol. 48.

Shorrocks, A. F. (1982). 'Inequality Decomposition by Factor Components', *Econometrica*, Vol. 50.

Shorrocks, A. F. (1983). 'Ranking Income Distributions', *Economica*, Vol. 50.

Shorrocks, A. F. (1984). 'Inequality Decomposition by Population Subgroups', *Econometrica*, Vol. 52.

Shorrocks, A. F. (1988). 'Aggregation Issues in Inequality Mesurement', in Eichhorn (1988).

Shorrocks, A. F. (1995a). 'Revisiting the Sen Poverty Index', *Econometrica*, Vol. 63.

Shorrocks, A. F. (1995b). 'Inequality and Welfare Comparisons for

Heterogeneous Populations', mimeographed, Department of Economics, University of Essex.

Shorrocks, A. F. and Foster, J. E. (1987). 'Transfer Sensitive Inequality Measures', *Review of Economic Studies*, Vol. 54.

Shorrocks, A. F. and Slottje, D. J. (1995). 'Approximating Unanimity Orderings: An Application to Lorenz Dominance', Discussion Paper, University of Essex.

Sidgwick, H. (1874). *The Methods of Ethics*. Macmillan, London.

Silber, J. (1989). 'Factor Components, Population Subgroups and the Computation of the Gini Index of Inequality', *Review of Economics and Statistics*, Vol. 71.

Silber, J. (ed.) (1996). *Income Inequality Measurement: From Theory to Practice*, mimeographed, to be published.

Smeeding, T., Torrey, B., and Rein, M. (1988). 'Patterns of Income and Poverty: The Economic Status of Children and the Elderly in Eight Countries', in Palmer, Smeeding, and Torrey (1988).

Smith, A. (1776). *An Inquiry into the Nature and Causes of the Wealth of Nations*; republished, eds. R. H. Campbell and A. S. Skinner, Clarendon Press, Oxford, 1976.

Spencer, B. D. and Fisher, S. (1992). 'On Comparing Distributions of Poverty Gaps', *Sankhya: The Indian Journal of Statistics*, Series B, Vol. 54.

Srinivasan, T. N. (1994). 'Human Development: A New Paradigm or Reinvention of the Wheel?', *American Economic Review*, Papers and Proceedings, Vol. 84.

Stark, T. (1972). *The Distribution of Personal Income in the United Kingdom 1949–1963*. Cambridge University Press, Cambridge.

Stewart, F. (1985). *Planning to Meet Basic Needs*. Macmillan, London.

Streeten, P. (1984). 'Basic Needs: Some Unsettled Questions', *World Development*, Vol. 12.

Streeten, P. (1994). 'Human Development: Means and Ends', *American Economic Review*, Papers and Proceedings, Vol. 84.

Streeten, P. (1995). *Thinking about Development*. Cambridge University Press, Cambridge.

Streeten, P. *et al.* (1981). *First Things First*. Oxford University Press, New York.

Strotz, R. H. (1958). 'How Income Ought to be Distributed: A Paradox in Distributive Ethics', *Journal of Political Economy*, Vol. 66.

Strotz, R. H. (1961). 'How Income Ought to be Distributed: Paradox Regained', *Journal of Political Economy*, Vol. 69.

Subramanian, S. (1995). 'Two Notes on the Measurement of Inequality and Poverty', Working Papers 132 and 133, Madras Institute of Development Studies.

Sugden, R. (1993). 'Welfare, Resources and Capabilities: A Review of *Inequality Reexamined* by Amartya Sen', *Journal of Economic Literature*, Vol. 31.

Suppes, P. (1966). 'Some Formal Models of Grading Principles', *Synthese*, Vol. 6.

Suppes, P. (1977). 'The Distributive Justice of Income Inequality', *Erkenntnis*, Vol. 11.

Suppes, P. (1987). 'Maximizing Freedom of Decision: An Axiomatic Analysis', in G. R. Feiwel (ed.), *Arrow and the Foundations of Economic Policy*. Macmillan, London.

Suzumura, K. (1983). *Rational Choice, Collective Decisions and Social Welfare*. Cambridge University Press, Cambridge.

Suzumura, K. (1996). 'Interpersonal Comparisons and Justice', in K. J. Arrow, A. K. Sen, and K. Suzumura (eds.), *Social Choice Reexamined*. Macmillan, London.

Takayama, N. (1979). 'Poverty, Income Inequality and Their Measures: Professor Sen's Axiomatic Approach Reconsidered', *Econometrica*, Vol. 47.

Tawney, R. H. (1931). *Equality*. Allen & Unwin, London.

Temkin, L. S. (1986). 'Inequality', *Philosophy and Public Affairs*, Vol. 15.

Temkin, L. S. (1993). *Inequality*. Oxford University Press, New York.

Testfatsion, L. (1976). 'Stochastic Dominance and the Maximisation of Expected Utility', *Review of Economic Studies*, Vol. 43.

Theil, H. (1967). *Economics and Information Theory*. North-Holland, Amsterdam.

Thistle, P. D. (1989). 'Ranking Distributions with Generalised Lorenz Curves', *Southern Economic Journal*, Vol. 56.

Thomson, W. (1996). 'On the Axiomatic Method', mimeographed, University of Rochester.

Thon, D. (1979). 'On Measuring Poverty', *Review of Income and Wealth*, Vol. 25.

Thon, D. (1982). 'An Axiomatization of the Gini Coefficient', *Mathematical Social Sciences*, Vol. 2.

Thorbecke, E. and Berrian, D. (1992). 'Budgetary Rules to Minimize Societal Poverty in a General Equilibrium Context', *Journal of Development Economics*, Vol. 39.

Tinbergen, T. (1970). 'A Positive and Normative Theory of Income Distribution', *Review of Income and Wealth*, Series 16, No. 3.

Townsend, P. (1962). 'The Meaning of Poverty', *British Journal of Sociology*, Vol. 8.

Townsend, P. (1979). *Poverty in the United Kingdom*. Penguin, London.

Townsend, P. (1985). 'A Sociological Approach to the Measurement of Poverty: A Rejoinder to Professor Amartya Sen', *Oxford Economic Papers*, Vol. 37.

Tsui, K.-Y. (1995). 'Multidimensional Generalizations of the Relative and Absolute Inequality Indices: The Atkison-Kolm-Sen Approach', *Journal of Economic Theory*, Vol. 67.

Tungodden, B. (1994). 'Essays on Poverty and Normative Economics', Doctoral Dissertation, Norwegian School of Economics and Business Administration, University of Bergen.

Tuomala, M. (1992). *Optimal Income Taxation and Redistribution*. Clarendon Press, Oxford.

UNDP (1990). *Human Development Report 1990*. Oxford University Press, New York.

UNDP (1995). *Human Development Report 1995*. Oxford University Press, New York.

UNICEF (1987). *The State of the World's Children*. Oxford University Press, Oxford.

Van Parijs, P. (1990). 'Equal Endowment as Undominated Diversity', *Recherches Économiques de Louvain*, Vol. 56.

Van Parijs, P. (1995). *Real Freedom for All: What (If Anything) Can Justify Capitalism*. Clarendon Press, Oxford.

Varian, H. (1975). 'Distributive Justice, Welfare Economics and the Theory of Fairness', *Philosophy and Public Affairs*, Vol. 4.

Vickrey, W. (1945). 'Measuring Marginal Utility by Reactions to Risk', *Econometrica*, Vol. 13.

Vickrey, W. (1960). 'Utility, Strategy and Social Decision Rules', *Quarterly Journal of Economics*, Vol. 74.

Walsh, V. (1996). 'Amartya Sen on Inequality, Capability and Needs', *Science and Society*, Vol. 59.

Ward, B. (1958). 'The Firm in Illyria: Market Syndicalism', *American Economic Review*, Vol. 48.

Watts, H. W. (1968). 'An Economic Definition of Poverty', in D. P. Moynihan (ed.), *On Understanding Poverty*. Basic Books, New York.

Wedderburn, D. (1962). 'Poverty in Britain Today: The Evidence', *Sociological Review*, Vol. 10.

Wedgwood, J. (1939). *The Economics of Inheritance*. Penguin, Harmondsworth.

Weymark, J. A. (1981). 'Generalized Gini Inequality Indices', *Mathematical Social Sciences*, Vol. 1.

Weymark, J. A. (1984). 'Arrow's Theorem with Social Quasi-Orderings', *Public Choice*, Vol. 42.

Wiles, P. J. (1962). *The Political Economy of Communism*. Oxford.

Williams, A. (1991). 'What is Wealth and Who Creates it?', in J. Hutton, S. Hutton, T. Pinch, and A. Shiell (eds.), *Dependency to Enterprise*. Routledge, London.

Williams, B. (1962). 'The Idea of Equality', in P. Laslett and W. G. Runciman (eds.), *Philosophy, Politics and Society*, Second Series. Blackwell, Oxford.

Williams, B. (1973). 'A Critique of Utilitarianism', in J. J. C. Smart and B. Williams (eds.), *Utilitarianism: For and Against*. Cambridge University Press, Cambridge.

Williams, B. (1985). *Ethics and the Limits of Philosophy*. Fontana, London, and Harvard University Press, Cambridge, MA.

Williams, B. (1987). 'The Standard of Living: Interests and Capabilities', in Sen (1987a).

World Bank (1993). *World Development Report 1993*. Oxford University Press, New York.

Wriglesworth, J. (1985). *Libertarian Conflicts in Social Choice*. Cambridge University Press, Cambridge.

Yaari, M. E. (1987). 'The Dual Theory of Choice under Risk: Risk Aversion without Diminishing Marginal Utility', *Econometrica*, Vol. 55.

Yaari, M. E. (1988). 'A Controversial Proposal Concerning Inequality Measurement', *Journal of Economic Theory*, Vol. 44.

Yaari, M. E. and Bar-Hillel, M. (1984). 'On Dividing Justly', *Social Choice and Welfare*, Vol. 1.

Yitzhaki, S. (1979). 'Relative Deprivation and the Gini Coefficient', *Quarterly Journal of Economics*, Vol. 93.

Yitzhaki, S. (1983). 'On an Extension of the Gini Inequality Index', *International Economic Review*, Vol. 24.

Yntema, D. B. (1933). 'Measures of the Inequality in the Personal Distribution of Wealth and Income', *Journal of the American Statistical Association*, Vol. 28.

Young, H. P. (1994). *Equity in Theory and Practice*. Princeton University Press, Princeton, NJ.

Zheng, B. (1996). 'A Survey on Aggregate Poverty Measures', *Journal of Economic Surveys*, forthcoming.

Index of Names

254 INDEX OF NAMES

Deaton, A. S. 212n., 215n.
Debreu, G. 5n., 6n., 40n., 102n.
Delbono, F. 200n., 211n.
Desai, M. 198n., 199n., 201n., 211n.
Diamond, P. 40n., 45n.
Dobb, M. H. 90, 91n., 95n.
Domar, E. 98n.
Donaldson, D. 115n., 117n., 128, 129, 130–1, 134n., 135n., 137n., 142n., 151n., 154–5, 173, 174, 175n., 196n.
Dorfman, R. 102n.
DrËze, J. 166n., 201n., 211n., 212n.
D'Souza, D. 212n.
Dworkin, R. 197n., 198n.

Easterlin, R. A. 184n.
Ebert, U. 198n.
Edgeworth, F. Y. 122
Eichhorn, W. 110n., 153n.
Ellman, M. 95n., 97n.
Elster, J. 115n.
Erikson, R. 198n.

Fei, J. C. S. 144n.
Fields, G. S. 119n., 144n., 169n., 201n., 211n.,
Fine, B. J. 171n., 205n.
Fine, K. 115n., 171n.
Fishburn, P. C. 5n., 14n., 40n.
Fisher, F. M. 40n., 66n., 130n., 190n., 192n., 208n., 210n., 215n.
Fleming, M. 14n.
Fleurbaey, M. 120n., 198n., 201n.
Foley, D. 114n., 197n.
Friedman, M. 83n., 85,
Fuchs, V. 165n.

Gärdenfors, P. 171n.
Gastwirth, J. L. 139n.
Gehrig, W. 110n.
Gevers, L. 115n., 196n., 216n., 218n.
Gibbard, A. 204n.
Gini, C. 29–34
Gintis, H. 208n.
Glover, J. 199n.
Gorman, W. M. 40n.

Graaff, J. de v. 130n., 208n.
Granaglia, E. 198n., 201n., 211n.
Grant, J. P. 199n.
Greer, J. 178, 179, 181n.
Griffin, J. 120n., 198n., 206n.
Griffin, K. 198n., 201n., 211n.

Hahn, F. H. 6n., 102n.
Hamada, K. 40–1, 149, 176n.
Hammond, P. J. 40n., 115n., 130n., 171n., 173n., 196n., 216n.
Hanson, K. 216n., 217n.
Hansson, B. 119n.,
Haq, Mahbub ul 199n.
Hardy, G. 54, 56n.
Hare, R. M. 14n., 196n., 206n.
Harriss, B. 212n.
Harsanyi, J. C. 14n., 40n., 45n., 196n., 197n.
Hart, H. L. A. 196n.
Hawthorn, G. 201n.
Heins, A. J. 2n., 16
Hemming, R. 173n., 178, 179n., 182n., 189n.
Herrero, C. 201n., 202n.
Hoffman, C. 95n.
Hossain, I. 201n., 211n.
Hoy, M. 147n.
Huq, E. 212n.
Hurwicz, L. 102n.

Jenkins, S. 110n., 190n., 192n.
Jevons, W. S. 81
Jin, Y. 189n.
Jorgenson, D. W. 114n., 116n., 130n.

Kakwani, N. C. 110n., 130n., 136n., 142n., 164, 171n., 173n., 175n., 179n.
Kanbur, S. M. R. 149n., 181n., 201n.
Kant, I. 14n.
Kenen, P. B. 66n.
Khinchin, A. 152n.
King, G. 199
Klappholz, K. 103n.
Knight, F. 206n.
Knight, J. 198n., 201n., 211n.
Kolm, S. C. 54n., 80n., 114n., 115, 125n., 131n., 138n., 196n.

Subject Index